⫚ **W9-BGJ-391**

RECLAIMING DESIRE

4 Keys to Finding Your Lost Libido

ANDREW GOLDSTEIN, M.D.,
AND MARIANNE BRANDON, PH.D.

RODALE

Notice

This book is intended as a reference volume only, not as a medical manual. The information presented here is intended to help you make informed decisions about your sexual health. It is not a substitute for any treatment that may have been prescribed by your doctor. If you suspect that you have a medical problem, we urge you to seek competent medical help.

Mention of specific companies, organizations, or authorities in this book does not imply endorsement by the publisher, nor does mention of specific companies, organizations, or authorities imply that they endorse this book.

Any Internet addresses and telephone numbers were accurate at the time the book went to press.

Printed in the United States of America
Rodale Inc. makes every effort to use acid-free (∞), recycled paper (♲).

Book design by Joanna Williams
Interior chapter opener photographs © Taxi/Getty Images

Library of Congress Cataloging-in-Publication Data

Goldstein, Andrew, M.D.
    Reclaiming desire : 4 keys to finding your lost libido / Andrew Goldstein and Marianne Brandon.
        p.   cm.
    Includes bibliographical references and index.
    ISBN 1–57954–683–8 hardcover
    1. Sex instruction for women.   2. Women—Sexual behavior.   3. Sexual desire disorders.   I. Brandon, Marianne.   II. Title.
HQ46.G65   2004
306.7'082—dc22   2004000294

Distributed to the book trade by St. Martin's Press

2   4   6   8   10   9   7   5   3   1   hardcover

RODALE

WE **INSPIRE** AND **ENABLE** PEOPLE TO IMPROVE
THEIR LIVES AND THE WORLD AROUND THEM

FOR MORE OF OUR PRODUCTS
WWW.RODALESTORE.COM
(800) 848-4735

To my patients: Every day you continue to teach and inspire me. Your willingness to discuss and share the most intimate parts of your lives is the foundation of this book.

—Andrew

To the teachers I have lost, Sheldon and Fred, and to the one I hope will be with me forever, Steve.

—Marianne

CONTENTS

ACKNOWLEDGMENTS

My journey toward authorship would not have been possible without the constant encouragement of patients, friends, and family.

In particular, I want to thank David Atwood and Victoria Skurnick, who started Marianne and me down the right road to publishing this book; Beth Wright, Ahuva Munzer, Reine Goldstein, and Virginia Heffernan, who read early drafts of the manuscript and offered their candid suggestions; our agent, Jane Dystel, whose steady hand expertly guided us through the publishing process; our editor, Susan Berg, whose great enthusiasm and caring for this project greatly enriched it; and Holly Moores, our trusted office manager at the Sexual Wellness Center, who provided the organization necessary to keep my flights of fancy on course.

My entire family has been extraordinary in their support of this project. Special thanks go to my parents, Elaine and Albert; my brothers, Mark and Peter; my in-laws, Hanna and Jeff; and my daughters, Lena and Mimi, who lovingly climbed on me as I wrote this book on my laptop. Although they didn't help me finish any faster, the joy that they bring to my life inspires me every day.

I cannot say thank you enough to my coauthor, Marianne Brandon. She truly is a gifted psychologist whose commitment to helping women is inspirational. Her humor, her vision, and her hard work have made the Sexual Wellness Center, and this book, possible.

Of course, I extend my deepest gratitude and appreciation to my wife, Gail, whose extraordinary and unconditional support is the driving force behind all my projects, including this one. She has worn many hats: editor, cheerleader, publicist, and postmaster. She even tolerates the gentle ribbing of her friends, who have taken to calling me a "sexpert." But mostly, she has shown me boundless love, without which I could not have attempted to write this book.

—Andrew Goldstein, M.D.

I would like to express my heartfelt gratitude to Susan Berg, our tireless editor at Rodale. Without her help, this book probably still would be a confusing mass of information.

I also am indebted to our agent, Jane Dystel. Thank you, Jane, for believing in us and guiding us through the initial stages of the publishing process. Thanks, too, to Steve Chandler for his willingness to offer feedback on much of the manuscript.

To Andrew Goldstein, my colleague and friend, thank you for inviting me to join you in this tremendous idea, which has changed my life. And to my parents, thank you for giving me life and for loving and encouraging me from the moment I joined this world.

Finally, words cannot adequately express my gratitude for my husband, Steve. Your belief in me and my work has given me strength to stretch and grow in ways I never could have imagined.

—Marianne Brandon, Ph.D.

INTRODUCTION

Writing this book has been a mission for us and the fulfillment of a promise to our clients—many of whom are
among the estimated 40 million American women who struggle
with diminished sex drives. Even before we decided to go into practice together, we recognized low libido as a widespread, though
often unspoken, problem among women (as well as men). Regardless of why these women came to us in the first place, a lack of
sexual desire often surfaced as an ancillary issue.

Between the two of us, we have treated and counseled hundreds of women with one unifying complaint: They have lost their
libidos. We've learned that we're much more successful in helping
these women when we combine our expertise in medicine and psychology. We've come to understand that a number of factors influence a woman's sex drive—not just her physical or emotional state,
as the conventional wisdom would suggest. By the same token, a decline in sex drive seldom results from one single cause. Any treatment that targets just one aspect of low libido—a pill or a cream,
for example—likely will fail.

This isn't to suggest that medications aren't useful. They are.
But in our experience, they're even more effective when they're
combined with self-exploration, stress reduction, and couples
therapy.

Our clients have helped to change our perspective on libido.
We now understand it as a product of a woman's physical, emotional, intellectual, and spiritual health. All four of these compo-

nents are necessary for a robust sex drive and a satisfying sex life. As long as they remain in balance, a woman will feel sexually vital and alive.

Fundamentally, then, reclaiming desire is about maintaining balance among the physical, emotional, intellectual, and spiritual aspects of your being. Just what is balance? It's allowing yourself to be all that you are meant to be. It's understanding and accepting who you really are.

Those of us raised in Western cultures seem best able to grasp the concept of balance when we think in terms of physiology. We don't question the necessity of certain hormones, like testosterone and dopamine, being present in just the right proportions in order to experience desire. The same rule applies to our emotions, our thoughts, and our spiritual beliefs. The fact that we can't measure them with a blood test makes them no less important.

This book is the first to address low libido in a holistic manner. In our experience, women inherently know that they can't have strong sex drives and fulfilling sex lives unless they are physically, emotionally, intellectually, and spiritually well. Our goal is to help women with libido trouble identify which of these four components may be lacking. We've even developed an exclusive self-test especially for this purpose (see page 24). Once we pinpoint where the problem lies, we draw on a variety of disciplines—including conventional medicine, hormone replacement, naturopathy, body-work, and individual and couples therapy—to facilitate a return to balance and a healthy sex drive.

What causes imbalance in the first place? As we'll explain in the following pages, the hectic, high-stress lifestyle that has become the norm in our society certainly is a factor. Simply put, most women feel that they don't have the time or the energy to attend to their own needs. In the grand scheme of their lives, sex becomes a low priority. Major transitions—marriage, childbirth, menopause, divorce—complicate the picture even more. (We explore the sexual implications of these life-changing events in part VI.) Yet even in the absence of significant upheaval, a woman's body and psyche can accumulate wounds that manifest as low libido over time.

In writing this book, we made certain editorial decisions that we feel deserve acknowledgment and explanation. For example, as you'll see, we consistently use masculine pronouns (*he, him, his*) when referring to a woman's partner. This is not meant to imply that the information and advice applies only to heterosexual couples. On the contrary, the same issues can arise in same-sex relationships. Unfortunately, accommodating this in the text made for a very confusing read. So we chose to conform to conventional writing style.

Furthermore, though the personal stories throughout the book tend to involve women with partners, our message is equally applicable to women not currently in established long-term relationships. Contrary to popular perception, low libido is just as common among those who are unattached. In fact, many of our clients come to us for help in rekindling their sexual desire before pursuing an intimate connection with someone.

Incidentally, the personal stories are composites; they do not reflect the life or experience of any one person. We have the utmost respect for our clients and their struggles. We honor their privacy by handling their cases with absolute confidentiality. We're deeply grateful to them for opening up to us and for providing the insights that have shaped our understanding of low libido. They have enriched our lives by including us in their personal journeys to explore and embrace their sexuality.

We believe that sexual desire is the birthright of all women. Losing that desire can undermine a woman's perception of herself, her relationship with her body, and the raw physical pleasure that once was available to her. In the absence of sexual passion, she may relinquish other personal passions as well. As a result, she feels incomplete. Her relationship with her partner may suffer, too, as the strain of her low libido drives a wedge between them. Even in marriage, they may feel isolated and alone.

Although satisfying sex does not guarantee the success of a relationship, it clearly helps to reinforce the bond between partners. After all, their sex life is completely unique to their couplehood; it's the one place for them to go alone together. So if anything erodes this intimate connection, it ultimately can tear the very fabric of the relationship. Both partners feel it, and both get scared.

Is this outcome inevitable? We don't think so. That's why we've written this book: to show women why they lose, and how they can recover, their libidos. Though we don't offer a quick fix, it is, we feel, an effective one.

The fact is, restoring a healthy sex drive requires time and effort. It also presents an opportunity to achieve a greater understanding of yourself, your relationships, and your sexuality. This is the essence of reclaiming desire: attending to the whole woman—body, mind, and spirit.

PART I

WHY DESIRE FADES—AND HOW YOU CAN BRING IT BACK

CHAPTER 1

RETHINKING LOW LIBIDO

W e are a culture fascinated by sex. In fact, sex may be the hottest commodity driving our economy. We use it to sell everything from chewing gum to cars.

Sex can be traded for power, attention, money, and control on both a societal and personal level. It can add excitement, drama, mystery, danger, and intrigue to our existence.

For most of us, sex represents much more than procreation or even physical pleasure. Particularly for women, feeling sexually attractive is an integral part of self-esteem. How a woman feels about her body and her sexuality helps determine how she views herself in general.

This is why a decline in sexual desire results in significant distress for many women. It not only can extinguish positive sexual experiences, it also can undermine a marital or romantic relationship by negatively affecting the level of physical and emotional intimacy between a woman and her partner. In a more general sense, it can prevent a woman from getting all that she wants from her life.

Low libido shows no regard for age, ethnicity, or lifestyle. It affects women who have children as well as those who do not; women who consider themselves to be attractive as well as those who are unhappy with or critical of their appearance. Low libido is common even among women who clearly love their partners. It affects singles, newlyweds, and those who have been married for decades.

Among the goals of this book is to dispel the myth that low libido is rare and relegated to just one type of woman. The simple truth is this: Most women report a decline in their sexual desire at some point in their lives. So if you don't want sex as much as you used to, you are not alone.

In fact, some health professionals believe that diminished sexual desire has become a new epidemic in our society. Researchers are just beginning to investigate this phenomenon statistically. According to recent estimates, more than one-third of women in the United States have problems with their sex drives. Even this statistic may be low, as people may be embarrassed to respond to such personal interview questions honestly.

Myths and Misunderstandings

In cases of low libido, most health professionals try to identify a single, specific physical or psychological cause. And they tend to attribute the apparent increase in sexual "dysfunction" among women to the fast-paced, stressful lifestyle that is the modern norm.

We disagree, at least partially. In our opinion, a decline in sexual desire is neither a diagnosable nor a pathological condition. What's more, though the stress and demands inherent in our lifestyles never help a woman's libido, we believe that the reasons behind a loss of interest in sex are much more complex than that.

We propose that a decline in sexual desire is a normal and perhaps even an appropriate response to the complicated challenges inherent in life and intimate relationships. Rather than something to be ashamed of, it is a sign of a fundamental imbalance in our lives.

This imbalance can have any number of causes—for example, the multiple responsibilities at home and in the workplace that leave little time for pleasure; a simmering anger at our partners for ignoring our needs; or old belief patterns, such as "Mature women aren't sexual and don't really enjoy making love." Chances are, if your excitement for sex is diminished, your excitement for life in general is compromised.

Many women recall feeling so sexual and turned on by their partners early in their relationships that they just can't grasp feeling differently now. Our society perpetuates a myth that sexual desire should remain consistently strong in a loving couple. So when women don't want sex, they tend to assume that they are somehow "abnormal." Further complicating matters, they are often too ashamed and embarrassed to talk about it or to seek help. Their reluctance to open up only creates a sense of self-consciousness and isolation.

It doesn't help that we're surrounded by people who appear to have satisfying sex lives. Neighbors, coworkers, and friends—even complete strangers who walk hand in hand—all seem to enjoy healthy sexual relationships. Popular movies feature exciting sex scenes in which women are overcome with passion for their partners. Song lyrics describe people turned on by each other, flirting with each other, lusting after each other. Ads in magazines and on TV show sexy models passionately embracing their partners in what appears to be a prelude to sex. One popular commercial even hints that a woman will have an orgasm just by using a certain brand of shampoo.

Everywhere we look, we are presented with images of passionate people wanting each other and wanting sex. It's no wonder that women with low libido are reluctant to talk about their plight. Despite the frequent jokes about the demise of sex after marriage, few women feel comfortable openly admitting that they don't want to make love to their partners. Often they're reluctant to tell even their closest friends that they've lost interest in sex. As with any issue, when we remain silent about our pain, we prevent ourselves from healing.

Body, Mind—And More

As a gynecologist and a clinical psychologist who see female clients on a daily basis, we realize that many women want and expect more for themselves sexually. We opened our Sexual Wellness Center in 1999 to respond to women's concerns about a variety of sexual issues, including low libido.

What do we mean by *sexual wellness*? We interpret it as a holistic concept, with four primary dimensions: physical, emotional, intellectual, and spiritual. All four must be present and in balance for a person to feel "well" sexually.

We believe that applying this holistic approach is essential to fully and accurately evaluating women who are having problems with their libidos. When a patient tells us that her interest in sex is waning, our first step is to explore the following:

- Her physical health, including underlying medical problems, hormone levels, medications, and lifestyle factors such as nutrition and exercise
- Her emotional well-being—whether she is depressed, stressed, or anxious, and whether she is satisfied with her life, her marriage, and herself
- Her intellectual fulfillment, both in her private life and in the life she shares with her partner and family
- Her spiritual beliefs and needs, and their impact on her sexuality

By identifying and treating problems in each of these core areas, we help make sex more gratifying for each woman. Once this is achieved, sexual desire often takes care of itself.

The majority of our patients come to us because of low libido. Many of them have attempted to get help elsewhere but saw no significant improvement in their sex drives. We suspect that most conventional treatments fail because their focus is exclusively physical (adjusting a woman's hormone levels, for example) or psychological (examining a woman's sexual history or current emotional state). They don't take into account the interplay of these and other factors that collectively shape a woman's sexual desire.

From our clinical experience, we've come to understand libido as a function of all that defines a woman—including her body, her relationships, and her lifestyle. This is why so many cases of low libido have such complex, and surprising, causes. The good news is that most of these causes are completely treatable.

It Isn't Just "Sparks"

More often than not, the women who come to our Sexual Wellness Center are longing for what might best be described as spontaneous desire. That is, they want to find themselves suddenly and without reason experiencing the sort of intense sensations that indicate they want to have sex. These sensations may take many forms—warmth or tingling in the genitals, frequent positive thoughts about sex, or perhaps some undefined physical or emotional need.

Unfortunately, *spontaneous desire* is a misnomer. What our clients remember as spontaneous was anything but. Rather, their feelings of desire kicked in with some sort of stimulus—perhaps an attractive man walking by, a romantic scene in a movie, hot water cascading down their bodies as they showered, or a partner's loving caress. Whatever it was, they were receptive to it at that moment, and they responded by wanting to make love. For most women in mature relationships, this is the nature of desire: Rather than occurring spontaneously, it is a reaction to a stimulus.

Sometimes our clients find this reality disappointing. They would rather experience sexual desire as effortless and dependable, like hunger. In fact, it can be effortless—if they allow themselves to be open to sexual stimuli, which are all around them.

For most of our clients, the goal of treatment is not to experience spontaneous desire. Rather, it is to relearn how to be open and responsive to a sexual stimulus—that is, their partners—long enough for their desire to build. Admittedly, this takes commitment and effort. For a multitude of reasons, which we explore in the following pages, women sometimes shut down sexually. They must work to want sex again.

Your Journey Begins Here

You cannot simply will yourself to experience a desire for sex. Like joy or peace, it is a feeling generated from deep within you. The goal of our Sexual Wellness Center, and this book, is to help women who have had very fulfilling sex lives recapture the balance that is necessary for their passion to return.

We attend to the whole woman—body, mind, and spirit—using a combination of conventional medical interventions, naturopathy, and individual and couples psychotherapy. We have found this holistic approach to be essential to helping a woman find her lost libido.

We've written this book to provide a path for women like you, who wish to embark on a more meaningful and fulfilling journey to reclaim sexual desire. Along the way, we'll explore how the physical, emotional, intellectual, and spiritual aspects of your self combine to influence your sexuality. We'll explain how these dimensions can slip out of balance, and how restoring this balance will not only reinvigorate your sex drive but also lay the foundation for a more stimulating, satisfying life.

In working with our clients, we've found it helpful to conceptualize sexual desire by using the analogy of an onion. There are many layers to an onion. Those near the outside may be larger and more visible, but those underneath are just as important to the onion's integrity. We must break through the thin, sometimes damaged outer layers to get to the more substantive inner ones.

Although the purpose of the onion's skin is to protect its contents, we must remove the skin to get to the more vulnerable bulb inside. Eating the onion with its skin on would dramatically alter our experience of it.

Like the onion, a woman's sexuality consists of multiple layers, some more apparent than others. The outer layers serve as defenses, protecting from uncomfortable emotions like shame, guilt, and fear. The inner layers consist of the thoughts, feelings, and perceptions that shape a woman's desire for sex. We must examine the more obvious layers before we can delve into the inner, more mysterious ones.

All aspects of your sexuality are important and influential in your ability to receive and give sexual pleasure. You can access the inner, more potent layers of your sexual desire only if you first remove the protective shell placed around it.

For some women, removing this protective shell—if only momentarily—can be the most difficult step toward reclaiming their sexual desire. It may involve a level of vulnerability with themselves and their partners that they would prefer to avoid. Self-examination can be a challenging, even frightening process. However, the understanding that comes from self-examination offers extraordinary rewards. Give yourself the gift of exploring and taking responsibility for *your* sexual desire.

CHAPTER 2

GETTING TO KNOW YOUR SEX DRIVE

Over the years, experts in sexual health have struggled to define sexual desire. Often they resort to primarily physiological indices, such as vaginal lubrication or genital swelling caused by increased blood flow; psychological indices, such as the perception of wanting to make love; or a combination of the two.

Rather than attempting to generalize something so unique and personal as sexual desire, we encourage you to define this state for yourself. By creating your own measures, you can determine whether or not you are personally satisfied with your sex drive.

When we look at women who have reached sexual maturity since the sexual revolution of the 1970s, we find that as a group, they have embraced a less restrictive view of their sexuality. This freedom has allowed them to experience great sex and great sex lives. They have known lust; they are comfortable with a strong libido. They know their bodies and have confidence in their ability to satisfy themselves.

At the same time, women in this age group—between 20 and 50—inevitably encounter countless physical and emotional hurdles (marriage, career, and childbirth, to name a few). They may notice a decline in their passion and sexual desire during these transitions. Though it is unfortunate, it is common—almost universal.

Some women who lose libido don't particularly miss it. They seem to live without sex quite contentedly. For the vast majority, however, a decline in sex drive takes a tremendous physical and emotional toll. These women speak of feeling deficient, ashamed, sad, angry, anxious, or unfulfilled. Or they may oscillate between all of these emotions.

After years of enjoying an exciting and fulfilling sex life, a woman may mourn the loss of what was an integral part of herself and her relationship with her partner. Sometimes this loss leaves her feeling confused and overwhelmed. At other times, she is so detached and distant from her sexual self that she becomes convinced she no longer cares about her lack of desire. But, clearly, she does.

The Many Faces of Sexual Dysfunction

Margaret sat in her dark kitchen, crying into the phone. Her closest friend, Linda, listened silently on the other end, unable to help. "When Frank and I were first together, I was turned on just by looking at him," Margaret recalled. "His smile and sincerity were so sexy to me. I enjoyed just being around him, and I loved turning him on. It made me feel so good when he wanted to make love to me.

"But when I look at him now, after being married for 8 years, I never think of making love to him. I miss the closeness and the connection we used to share, but I just can't seem to muster the will to want him. I know it sounds terrible, but I'd rather be left alone. I don't want to have sex, but Linda, I'm so afraid that Frank is going to have an affair!"

A decline in sexual desire is just one type of sexual disorder that affects women. Until recently, such problems went largely ignored in medical and research circles. They devoted the lion's share

11

of their attention to sexual dysfunction in men, developing and refining treatment protocols for common male conditions like premature ejaculation and erectile dysfunction.

We are happy to report that this double standard is finally
changing, as physicians and scientists have begun investigating female sexual dysfunction. We applaud this change, which is bringing
to light the prevalence and severity of female sexual concerns.

Female sexual dysfunction can manifest itself in a variety of
ways. The most common problems, as identified by the *Diagnostic and
Statistical Manual of Mental Disorders*, fourth edition, text revision (or
DSM-IV-TR), generally fall into one of four major categories: sexual
pain disorders, orgasmic disorders, sexual arousal disorders, and
sexual desire disorders. All significantly affect not only women's sexuality but also their relationships and overall life satisfaction.

Although we will review the four categories of sexual dysfunction below, the rest of the book will focus exclusively on low libido.
We want to note, too, that other types of sexual problems—such as
substance-induced sexual dysfunction and sexual dysfunction caused
by a medical condition—can occur in women. But these conditions
are much less common than the ones highlighted here.

Sexual pain disorders. Until recently, sexual pain disorders
were largely unstudied and misunderstood. Yet they affect approximately 7 percent of women, according to an extensive study of the
prevalence of sexual dysfunction in the United States, published in
the *Journal of the American Medical Association* (*JAMA*) in 1999.
They've been linked to a variety of causes, both physical (such as
vaginal infections and hormonal imbalances) and psychological (relationship problems).

Dyspareunia, or pain during intercourse, can result from poor
lubrication—perhaps because of lack of foreplay or diminished blood
flow to the vagina. Poor lubrication also can stem from a deficiency
of estrogen, which causes a condition known as atrophic vaginitis.

Certain factors can raise a woman's risk of atrophic vaginitis, such as surgical removal of the ovaries (oophorectomy); use of contraceptives, including Depo-Provera and birth control pills; and the decline in estrogen associated with perimenopause and menopause.

Some women may experience pain during intercourse because of an underlying condition that causes tearing or scarring of the vulva or vagina. Examples of these include lichen sclerosus and erosive lichen planus.

Another sexual pain disorder, vulvar vestibulitis, affects the vestibule—that is, the entrance of the vagina. In some women, the vestibule has such a proliferation of pain nerve endings that any kind of pressure—whether from a penis, a tampon, or even clothing—triggers severe pain.

Vaginismus, which involves involuntary spasms of the muscles in the outer third of the vagina, sometimes occurs in conjunction with other sexual pain disorders. Or it may result from a psychological trauma such as sexual abuse. In our opinion, doctors too often attribute pain during intercourse to vaginismus, rather than pinpointing the true physiological cause.

A thorough discussion of sexual pain disorders is beyond the scope of this book. If you experience pain during intercourse, we encourage you to consult a physician who specializes in sexual pain disorders for an accurate diagnosis. To find one in your area, start by checking the resources on page 312.

Orgasmic disorders. This type of sexual dysfunction affects approximately 25 percent of the female population in the United States at some point in their lives. These women either have never experienced an orgasm (primary anorgasmia) or seem to have lost their ability to do so (secondary anorgasmia). Unfortunately, they may be too ashamed to talk with their partners about their inability to climax, choosing to fake orgasms. This can lead to more-complicated problems over time, as secrets create distance between partners.

Like most sexual dysfunction in women, orgasmic disorders can have both physical and psychological causes. For example, certain classes of medications can impair a woman's ability to climax. On the other hand, some women become so uncomfortable at the prospect of losing control during sex that they can't achieve an orgasm.

Sexual arousal disorders. The term *sexual arousal disorder* may be confusing, as it seems to encompass low libido. In fact, it refers to an impaired physical response when making love.

A woman who has a sexual arousal disorder cannot attain or maintain sufficient genital lubrication for comfortable sexual intercourse. Her vagina remains dry despite receiving adequate genital stimulation. Sexual arousal disorders can result in painful intercourse, particularly if a couple chooses not to use additional lubrication such as K-Y jelly.

According to the *JAMA* article cited above, sexual arousal disorders affect approximately 14 percent of women in the United States. The disorders may be more common among women at or past menopause, because the decline in hormones—especially estrogen—can compromise vaginal lubrication. Psychological problems, such as depression and anxiety, also can cause sexual arousal disorders.

Sexual desire disorders. This category of sexual dysfunction includes sexual aversion disorder and hypoactive sexual desire disorder. In sexual aversion disorder, a woman is so repulsed by sex that she avoids all sexual contact. Just the prospect of sex may trigger a response ranging from moderate anxiety to intense psychological distress. Many experts attribute sexual aversion disorder to some sort of psychological trauma, such as past sexual abuse.

Hypoactive sexual desire disorder (HSDD) is an elaborate name for low libido. The *DSM*-IV-TR defines HSDD as "persistently or recurrently deficient (or absent) sexual fantasies and desire for sexual activity." A woman who has HSDD exhibits little motivation to seek sexual stimuli and little frustration at thwarted opportunities for sexual interaction.

HSDD is the most common sexual disorder in women, affecting an estimated 22 to 43 percent of the female population in this country. To receive a diagnosis of HSDD, a woman must experience significant distress or interpersonal difficulty because of her low libido. This is an important point, because if a woman doesn't want sex but isn't bothered by it, she is not considered diagnosable.

When deciding on treatment for a case of HSDD, most experts consider three core characteristics of the disorder. The first relates to onset—whether a woman has had low libido all her adult life or whether she has lost interest in sex over time. The second asks about occurrence—whether the woman experiences low libido all the time (generalized) or only in certain circumstances, such as when she's with a particular partner (situational). The third involves cause—whether the disorder results from psychological factors alone or from a combination of physiological and psychological factors.

Note that virtually all cases of HSDD have a psychological component. Even when libido declines because of a physiological problem, such as a hormonal imbalance, it is likely to produce secondary psychological symptoms such as anxiety or impaired self-esteem.

As you might imagine, HSDD often occurs with other types of female sexual dysfunction. For example, if a woman experiences pain during intercourse, she may lose interest in making love. Or if she repeatedly tries and fails to have an orgasm, she might feel bad about herself and eventually avoid sex altogether.

Lack of Balance May Be to Blame

When women come to our Sexual Wellness Center seeking help for low libido, they invariably ask the same question: "What's wrong with me?" In our experience, a decline in sexual desire seldom has a single cause. The collection of factors that influences a woman's sex drive is as unique as the woman herself.

This is why we believe so strongly in a holistic approach to treating low libido. If we were to focus on just the physiological or psychological components of sex drive, we likely would overlook other underlying issues that might prevent a woman from fully recovering her sexual desire.

As we explained in chapter 1, our approach involves creating a profile of a woman's libido by assessing what we've identified as the four primary dimensions of sexual wellness—physical, emotional, intellectual, and spiritual. All of these dimensions contribute to a healthy libido and an active sex life.

For example, to desire sex, a woman must be in good physical health. Her hormones of desire (estrogen, testosterone, and dopamine) must be in balance. The skin and nerves of her vagina, clitoris, and nipples must be sensitive to arousal. She must know her body and her erogenous zones. She must be able to have sex without pain.

Beyond physical health, a woman must possess the emotional hardiness to acknowledge and experience the full range of feelings that come into play in an intimate relationship. They may be sexual or nonsexual, pleasurable and positive, or uncomfortable and negative. An emotionally healthy woman easily moves through her full range of feelings without fixating on one or avoiding another. She can be passionate, empowered, desired, vulnerable, open, and loved.

Intellectual health, our third dimension of sexual wellness, is not measured by level of education or IQ. It is much more complex than that. A woman who is intellectually healthy feels stimulated and useful in her life. She perceives herself as competent and appropriately challenged. This filters into all aspects of her life, including her sexuality. Her thoughts about sex, and her sexual expression, are positive and reaffirming.

A woman's spiritual beliefs and needs play a powerfully influential role in her libido. In its broadest sense, spiritual health refers
to a woman's ability to find meaning and worth in herself and her
life. Of course, this means something different to everyone. It is
personal and specific to a woman's unique psychology and belief
system. It may or may not revolve around a relationship with God
or a higher power.

Bringing spirituality into an intimate relationship enhances
desire and the overall sexual experience. It allows for a sense of transcendence, as well as a deeper and more meaningful connection between a couple. The act of making love becomes richer and more
desirable when physical pleasure is not the only component of what
a woman gets for herself and shares with her partner.

Through the rest of the book, we will further explore each of
these four dimensions and their respective effects on libido. In general, when they are optimized and in balance, a woman will find happiness and fulfillment in her life and in her intimate relationships. But
if something disrupts this equilibrium, a woman's sex drive will suffer.

How Relationships Influence Libido

*Dawn knew she couldn't say no again that night. It had been weeks—no,
months—since she and her husband, Eric, had made love. She was all too
familiar with the routine; they had fallen into it maybe 15 years before.
First, Eric would go down on her for 3 minutes or so. Did he really enjoy
that, or was he just doing it to get her wet? She had no idea. Then he
would climb on top of her and thrust for about 2 minutes. Eric would come,
and then Dawn could sleep.*

*Should she take a risk and suggest they try something different for
a change? She briefly recalled how exciting sex was in the first years of
their marriage. "Oh, who really cares," she thought. "I'll just plan what
I need to pick up from the grocery store tomorrow."*

Just as internal issues rooted in the four dimensions of sexual wellness—things like hormonal imbalance, repressed anger, and poor self-esteem—can undermine libido, so can external factors. Chief among these is the relationship dynamics between a woman and her partner.

Through our interaction with clients at the Sexual Wellness Center, we've seen firsthand how a decline in sexual desire can be a direct and natural consequence of the challenges inherent in an intimate relationship. Because a woman's libido is so incredibly sensitive, it responds to a wide range of these challenges—some obvious, others quite subtle. As long as they are ignored or unresolved, libido is a likely casualty.

When a woman loses interest in sex, she may begin to doubt the "rightness" of her romantic partnership or marriage. It is not unusual for women to wonder whether they still love their partners, especially if their experience of making love has deteriorated over time. They may feel that sex is not worth the effort or is just plain bad.

Indeed, women with low libido often describe their sex lives as monotonous, uninteresting, or unstimulating. Worse, they feel bored, angry, and alienated from their partners because of bad sex. At the same time, they feel they can't do anything about it. They worry that opening up about their dissatisfaction will hurt their partners, or they're convinced that their partners wouldn't want to try to change anyway.

Most couples consider sex to be an important part of relating—though this isn't true for everyone. We know partners who dismiss sex as an unimportant or unnecessary aspect of their bond with one another. They are comfortable with making love very rarely, or even not at all. They prefer a certain amount of space in their relationships. If they love each other, they find less personal, nonphysical ways to share intimacy and feel connected.

These couples are the exception rather than the rule. Most of us believe that in a reasonably solid relationship, wanting to make love is a natural and expected outgrowth of our connection with our partners. And if we don't get that urge to have sex, we are left feeling demoralized, distressed, and somehow defective. Our lack of desire becomes an albatross around our necks. It is a dark secret that slowly and insidiously taints our perception of ourselves and weakens our relationships with our partners.

For women, the insecurities that arise from not wanting sex with a partner become worse with the experience of feeling turned on by other men. Fantasizing about someone other than a partner can lead a woman to wonder whether her body is telling her that she is no longer in love, or that she and her partner have lost their ability to connect meaningfully. Though this may be true, more than likely her low libido means something altogether different. In fact, her body could be telling her that she and her partner share a tremendous capacity for intimacy that they haven't fully explored— perhaps because they fear being so close to another person, as much as they desire it.

It is easy to blame your partner if you are not enjoying sex. You may even be able to identify why your partner turns you off, or at least why your partner no longer sparks your sex drive. The truth is, it is more fruitful to look within yourself to understand your lack of desire. This is because any change in your self-understanding and behavior will have an impact on your partner, ultimately influencing the dynamic between the two of you. Besides, giving someone else the responsibility for your satisfaction is never a good idea.

This doesn't mean that your criticisms of your partner are not valid. They very likely get to the heart of the relationship issues that the two of you need to address. However, if you put your goals in someone else's hands, you probably will never reach them. Nowhere is this more apparent than in the bedroom.

While we're on the subject of relationship dynamics and

libido, we want to mention that one partner's struggle with sexual dysfunction can weaken the other's sex drive. For example, if a man struggles with premature ejaculation or erectile dysfunction, sex can become more emotionally stressful and less physically pleasurable for both partners. As a result, the woman may lose interest in making love.

Making Love Worth Wanting

All this talk about sexual desire begs the question: What makes sex desirable? In other words, exactly what *is* good sex? Although every woman must answer this for herself, we can identify certain elements that seem to be essential for a pleasurable sexual experience. But first, let's look at what *isn't* good sex.

Unfortunately, our society promotes the misguided view that good sex is primarily dependent on superficial variables such as a woman's body type and weight. Of course, this "cultural wisdom" couldn't be further from the truth. Whether or not a woman experiences good sex has little to do with the size of her waist. But like any message we are repeatedly exposed to, we come to believe it over time. In this way, it inhibits a healthy libido—and good sex! It is so destructive because it encourages women to feel ashamed when their bodies aren't perfect (whose is?), and it allows the truth about good sex to remain ignored and unexplored.

Our society also buys into the notion that good sex always involves intercourse and orgasm by both partners, preferably at the same time. This approach to sexuality is restrictive and unrealistic. The most-rewarding sexual experiences are much more rich, diverse, and creative. They grow from powerful connections of hearts and minds. Unfortunately, few of us seize the opportunity to explore the sexual possibilities. It's no wonder so many Western women lose interest in sex.

Truly good sex, however, begins with a willingness to be open and vulnerable, to give pleasure freely and receive it fully. It also depends on both partners' commitment to shared intimacy, both physical and emotional. Relying on just one form of intimacy without the other is like trying to enjoy a movie without popcorn. It's pleasant enough, but it isn't quite as satisfying.

Brigitte and her husband, Adam, continue to enjoy good sex after 8 years of marriage. Here she describes one of their sexual encounters.

"I was exhausted after a long day at work. As I drove home, all I could think about was grabbing some leftovers from the fridge and crashing on the couch. But Adam was so sweet. He had made dinner for the two of us.

"After we finished eating, I just wanted to go upstairs and collapse into bed. But Adam followed me to our bedroom. When he embraced me and kissed me, I responded in spite of myself. His insistent, demanding touch changed my whole frame of mind. I wanted him, and I gave in to him. After he brought me to orgasm, I returned the favor. He knows my body and my turn-ons so well. And when he holds me after sex, I feel so safe and loved."

If you're like most people, you may be wondering whether to believe Brigitte's story. After all, she and Adam have been together for nearly a decade; how can they still share such passion for each other? Perhaps a story of boring sex would be more believable. Why is Brigitte so responsive to her husband's sexual advances?

Brigitte obviously enjoys making love to Adam. On this particular evening, she allowed herself to yield to his power over the situation, and his control over her body. It created the illusion of risk, which heightened the sense of passion for both of them. But Brigitte knew that she was safe and that Adam would never hurt her.

Brigitte doesn't always submit to Adam. Sometimes they reverse roles, and he becomes more open and vulnerable to her wishes and desires. This adds an unpredictable quality to their lovemaking, and richness and depth to their erotic experience.

Just as an illusion of risk contributes to good sex, so, too, does an element of mystery. When partners uncover or reveal something "secret" while making love, it intensifies their sensations of stimulation and arousal. Brigitte and Adam achieve this by allowing themselves to feel physically and emotionally exposed during their intimate encounters. For example, Brigitte may keep her eyes open while she climaxes, so Adam can make loving eye contact with her at the height of passion. Or Adam might disclose a sexual fantasy that he was keeping to himself. Their options for sharing themselves on a most personal, intimate level are almost endless.

Because of the positive dynamics in their relationship, Brigitte and Adam are able to bring a sense of spirituality to their lovemaking. That is, their physical interaction creates a strong spiritual connection that sustains them as individuals and as a couple. They know they are loved, nurtured, and cared for on a deep, powerful, personal level.

Good sex, then, is a complex concoction of openness and secrecy, risk and control, personal satisfaction and mutual fulfillment. With too little of any one ingredient, sex is boring and not worth the effort. Too much of one, and sex turns threatening—prompting discomfort, anxiety, and shame. Above all, sustaining a healthy, balanced sex life requires mindful attention to the physical, emotional, intellectual, and spiritual dimensions of our selves, as well as our relationships with our partners. We may be entitled to good sex, but we must earn it through effort and commitment.

Rediscover Your Desire—And Yourself

Most of us have experienced the pleasure of sexual desire. The fact is, many women with diminished sex drive simply have lost touch with what feels like good sex to them. Sex went from easy and enjoyable to a tangled mass of anxiety, frustration, and disappointment.

So many of our clients at the Sexual Wellness Center say that they want to get their libidos back. But when they describe the sex they've been having, we're not surprised that they lost their libidos in the first place. Most healthy, mature women are not going to want mediocre or bad sex. Why would they?

Somehow, we come to believe that we should want sex with our partners, regardless of the quality of the lovemaking experience. This is an interesting notion, but it doesn't necessarily translate well into other aspects of our lives. For example, would we expect to desire a massage with a mediocre masseuse? Would we expect to desire a dress made from fabric that irritates our skin? These examples seem absurd initially, but their point is clear: We want only what feels good.

Of course, what feels sexually enticing and exciting to one person can be completely unappealing to the next. A loving, committed relationship provides a safe and trusting environment where both partners can explore and express their sexual needs and preferences.

The goal of our practice, and this book, is to help regain what women know is inherently natural for them: a healthy sex drive. At the same time, they can use the challenge of low libido to foster a deeper understanding of themselves, their relationships, and their sexuality.

We encourage you to take advantage of your dissatisfaction with your libido, seizing a rare opportunity for self-growth and greater self-knowledge. Now is the time to identify and heal whatever is interfering with your ability to get what you want from your life, your relationships, and yourself. In this way, you can help revive your libido—and create a more satisfying sex life to boot.

CHAPTER 3

THE SEXUAL DESIRE SELF-TEST

At the Sexual Wellness Center, we've helped hundreds of women to successfully rediscover and reinvigorate their sexual desire. Every case has been unique, driven by a host of internal and external forces that shape not only a woman's sexuality but also her life as a whole.

This is why we believe so strongly in a holistic approach to treating low libido. If we assumed a more narrow view, defining low libido as a purely physical or psychological problem, we probably would overlook the real reason—or reasons—for declining sex drive. As a result, our clients might not see real improvement in their sexual interest and response.

We've developed the following self-test to assist in our diagnostic process. As you'll see, it evaluates the state of your libido based on what we've determined to be the four core components of sexual wellness: physical health, emotional resilience, intellectual fulfillment, and spiritual contentment. As we mentioned in chapters 1 and 2, if even one of these components tips out of balance, the rest will follow suit. This explains why your sex drive may not be as potent as it once was.

To take this self-test, simply answer each question based on the following scale.

Not at all true		**Sometimes true**		**Always true**
0	1	2	3	4

Please be honest with yourself, and take time to really think about each response. Remember, the purpose of the self-test is to identify the component or components that may be undermining your sexual desire. Your responses will serve as guideposts for your journey toward a stronger sense of your sexual self and a more satisfying sex life.

PHYSICAL HEALTH

____1. I don't eat a particularly healthy diet.

____2. I am not all that physically active.

____3. I drink and/or smoke more than I should.

____4. I always feel tired.

____5. My genitals feel numb when stimulated.

____6. For me, sex can be uncomfortable or even painful.

____7. I can't focus on pleasurable physical sensations when making love.

____8. I never take time to pamper my body with things like hot baths and massages.

____9. I can't remember the last time I felt sensual.

____10. I don't like when my partner sees me naked.

____ **TOTAL**

TESTOSTERONE

____1. I fantasize or dream about sex less often than I used to.

____2. I masturbate less often than I used to.

____3. During sex, I climax more slowly, and my orgasms feel less intense.

____4. My nipples feel less sensitive.

____5. My pubic hair is thinning.

____6. I have difficulty analyzing problems and thinking clearly.

____7. I seem to be losing muscle mass.

____8. Overall, my energy is low.

____9. One or both of my ovaries have been removed.

____10. I use hormone replacement therapy or birth control pills.

____**TOTAL**

DOPAMINE

____1. I always feel tired.

____2. I sleep more than usual.

____3. I'm less physically active than I used to be.

____4. I seem to lack motivation.

____5. My self-confidence has declined.

____6. I seldom spend time with friends or make plans for activities that I once enjoyed.

____7. Generally, I'm not all that happy.

____8. I am not engaged in life.

____9. I have given birth or breastfed within the past year.

____10. I am taking medication for depression or anxiety.

____**TOTAL**

EMOTIONAL RESILIENCE

____1. I feel sad much of the time.

____2. Often I am too irritable or "on edge" to make love.

____3. I get angry with my partner over the most minor things.

____4. I struggle just to manage my daily routine.

____5. I don't enjoy life as much as I used to.

____6. I feel very uncomfortable with my physical appearance.

____7. I am unable to relax during sex because I am so self-conscious.

____8. I avoid telling my partner how I really feel.

____9. I am not empowered in my relationship with my partner.

____10. I have experienced some form of sexual trauma.

____**TOTAL**

INTELLECTUAL FULFILLMENT

____1. I avoid opportunities to learn new things.

____2. My partner and I rarely just talk anymore.

____3. From a young age, I learned that sex is wrong or dirty.

____4. I was raised to believe that "proper" women don't masturbate or talk during sex.

____5. After a certain age, women shouldn't be interested in sex anyway.

____6. When my partner and I make love, I tend to focus on what feels uncomfortable or unpleasant.

____7. I'm not as open to experimenting during sexual encounters as I used to be.

____8. I don't have sexual fantasies.

____9. I don't tell my partner about my sexual preferences; he should know what I like.

____10. I know very little about my partner's sexual preferences.

____**TOTAL**

SPIRITUAL CONTENTMENT

____ 1. My life lacks purpose or meaning.

____ 2. I feel unfulfilled, as though I'm not getting what I want from life.

____ 3. I don't engage in hobbies that would nurture my soul.

____ 4. I am so busy that I tend to neglect my spiritual self.

____ 5. Outside of sex, my partner and I seldom spend "quality time" together.

____ 6. My partner and I don't connect on a spiritual level.

____ 7. My partner and I share no common life goals.

____ 8. Sometimes I feel that my partner doesn't really know me.

____ 9. I don't experience any particular warmth or passion for my partner when making love.

____ 10. Sex between my partner and me is boring.

____ **TOTAL**

Interpreting Your Scores

Once you've added up your score for each component, you can compare them to determine where you're doing well and where you may need improvement. We suggest focusing on the component with the highest score first. The higher any one score, the greater the likelihood of an imbalance that could be affecting your libido.

PHYSICAL HEALTH

Your physical health is the foundation of your sexuality. Although specific medical conditions can diminish sexual desire, improper self-care—poor eating habits, inadequate exercise, excessive alcohol consumption—just as easily may be to blame. We've noticed, too, that many women who experience declines in their sex drives simply have lost touch with their physical selves. If you tallied your highest score in the physical health component, we suggest beginning your exploration of your low libido in part II.

A high score in the testosterone or dopamine section points to a potential deficiency in one of these hormones. Many women notice a dramatic improvement in their sex drives when they take steps to raise their testosterone and/or dopamine to normal levels. To learn about the role of testosterone in a healthy libido, see chapter 7; for more on dopamine, see chapter 8.

EMOTIONAL RESILIENCE

According to conventional medical wisdom, if a doctor can't pinpoint a physical cause for a woman's declining sexual desire, then it must have a psychological cause. We rarely, if ever, see a case that's so cut-and-dried. Your emotions do, however, play a crucial role in your sexual interest and response. If you are dealing with stress or depression, for example, you probably won't experience a return of your sex drive until you address the underlying emotional upheaval. A poor body image also can take a toll on your libido, as can past sexual trauma. If you scored high on emotional resilience, you'll want to turn to part III first.

Keep in mind, too, that emotional struggles between partners often play out in the sexual arena. Do you feel anger, frustration, or disappointment in your relationship? Until you and your partner work through these feelings, you may continue to resist physical intimacy. For more information about the issues that commonly entangle relationships and could undermine your sex drive, see part VI.

INTELLECTUAL FULFILLMENT

A high score in this component suggests that you aren't getting enough intellectual stimulation and satisfaction from your life.

As a result, you may not be all that interested in sex. The same can happen if you and your partner aren't connecting on an intellectual level. Boredom with the nonsexual aspects of your relationship often translates to boredom in the bedroom.

The intellectual component of sexual wellness also encompasses your thoughts, beliefs, and attitudes about sex and sexuality. If you're like most women, you've accumulated this information over a lifetime—from your parents, from your religion, and from society at large. Reclaiming your desire may mean shedding some of these myths and misconceptions.

If you need to work on intellectual fulfillment, turn to part IV.

SPIRITUAL CONTENTMENT

Many of our clients express surprise when we ask questions about their spiritual contentment. In fact, spirituality has a direct impact on sexuality. If you don't make an effort to nurture your spiritual self, you will feel some sense of emptiness in your sex life. Fostering a spiritual bond with your partner is important, too. It adds a depth to your sexual encounters that you can't experience otherwise.

If you have a high score in the spiritual component of sexual wellness, your primary task is to clarify and seek purpose and meaning in your life and in your relationship with your partner. For help, see part V.

PART II

THE FIRST KEY:
PHYSICAL HEALTH

CHAPTER 4

START WITH YOUR BODY

- Good physical health lays the foundation for a strong, sensitive libido.
- Certain medical conditions can interfere with your sex drive, as can certain medications.
- Being overweight can undermine sexual desire not only by depleting energy levels and restricting movement, but also by feeding a woman's self-consciousness.
- Basic self-care—eating a balanced diet, engaging in regular exercise, and getting adequate rest—can restore optimum health and reinvigorate libido.

When women first notice a decline in their sex drives, they often attribute it to a physical problem of one sort or another. As we tell our clients at the Sexual Wellness Center, that usually isn't the case. Though physical factors may contribute to their low libidos, other factors—emotional, intellectual, and spiritual— probably are in the mix as well.

Maintaining good physical health is, however, essential to realizing your sexual potential. Your libido can thrive when your body is well. That's because your body is able to channel more of its energy to your sex drive so that you experience it fully.

In addition, when you're physically healthy, you have multiple options in the sexual positions you use and in the intensity you are comfortable with while making love. The more varied your sexual encounters are, the more interesting and fun they can be, and the more desirable sex becomes.

Common Sex-Drive Offenders

By the same token, disease can limit sexual desire and pleasure for some women. If your body is in physical distress, your energy will be diverted toward attempting to cope with and correct the under-lying problem. In such circumstances, sex becomes a low priority in comparison with your general physical health.

Women who suffer from arthritis or back pain, for example, may experience discomfort when using certain sexual positions. What's more, they may be reluctant to "let go" during intercourse, for fear of doing more harm. For women who have diabetes, the nerve damage that often occurs with the disease can interfere with sexual response. Cancer can take a huge physical and emotional toll, robbing women of their energy for and interest in sex.

An in-depth discussion of all the medical conditions that can af-fect libido is beyond the scope of this book. Our point is that they shouldn't dampen your sex life if you don't want them to. Other re-sources offer a wealth of tips and tools to make sex more comfortable and pleasurable. Let's suppose you have a health problem that results in chronic pain. With the strategic placement of a few specially de-signed pillows or slings, you can enjoy a pain-free lovemaking expe-rience. To learn more about such devices, we suggest checking out the resources listed on page 312.

If you're taking any kind of medication, be aware that certain classes of pharmaceuticals can inhibit your sex drive. Among the more common culprits are antidepressants, antihistamines, steroids and other anticholinergics, and medications for incontinence. Anti-hypertensives, which are prescribed for high blood pressure and other cardiovascular problems, also can have a negative effect on libido. Drugs in this class include beta blockers, calcium channel blockers, and diuretics.

The good news is that sexual side effects of medications are fixable. You just need to let your doctor know about them. She may be able to adjust your dosage or, if necessary, switch you to another medicine. It may take a little time, but your libido should bounce back.

Weighing Down Desire

Your weight plays a major role in your physical health. Unfortunately, a majority of American women—55 percent, by one estimate—weigh more than they should. They may not realize it, but their extra pounds contribute to poor exercise tolerance, low energy, restricted movement, and a weakened cardiovascular system. Any one of these can sabotage a healthy libido.

Then, too, many overweight women feel self-conscious about their physical size. In their view, their stature negatively affects their sexual encounters.

More than likely, these women realize that they would benefit from slimming down. But taking off, and keeping off, extra weight can be a struggle. For starters, eating healthfully and exercising regularly—the cornerstones of any effective weight-loss program—take time, a commodity that is in short supply these days. Good intentions to take a walk over lunch or to prepare a healthy dinner at home routinely give way to the demands and responsibilities of daily living.

To be sure, adding a few ingredients to a prepackaged entrée that can be on the table in 5 minutes is much easier than cooking from scratch. But the nutritional content of such "fast foods" hardly compares with the nutritional content of fresh, whole ingredients.

When our bodies don't get the vitamins and minerals they need, they just keep sending out hunger signals, begging for sustenance. So we eat more of the same unhealthy fare—and we gain weight rather than losing.

Of course, sometimes we eat for emotional reasons rather than physical ones. Most of us subconsciously equate food with nurturance. It began when we were infants and our meals came with our mothers' undivided love and attention. As we grew up, food took on new roles—as a reward when we earned good grades, or as treats when we were sick. Not surprisingly, we continue to associate food with satisfaction and solace as adults.

Unfortunately, when we eat to soothe ourselves, we tend to choose foods that aren't particularly nutritious. We may feel better in the short term, but our waistlines will suffer over time. This can set up a vicious cycle, as our dissatisfaction with our appearance makes us crave certain comfort foods even more.

If you are an emotional eater, you can benefit from learning other techniques to achieve a state of calm and contentment—without food. We suggest trying the exercises described in chapter 11.

For weight loss in general, plans and programs abound. We don't recommend one as better than all the others, because we know that what works for one person might be ineffective for someone else. Finding the best approach for you may require some trial and error. Just remember to choose one that combines a sensible, balanced eating plan with regular, moderate physical activity. And be sure that it complements your lifestyle. Otherwise, you may not stick with it.

Self-Care Essentials

Not so coincidentally, good nutrition and regular exercise are essential to optimum physical health. So is adequate rest. If you neglect this most basic self-care, your body won't function efficiently and will be more susceptible to illness. Your sex drive will suffer as a result.

Taking care of your physical health should be a top priority. But if you're like most women, it probably has slipped to the bottom of your to-do list. Family and work responsibilities all too easily supersede your own needs. Just remember: When you give precedence to yourself and your health, you inevitably have more energy for everyone and everything else in your life. On the other hand, ignoring your body's most basic needs deprives others as well, because you have less to give to them.

At the Sexual Wellness Center, we routinely see women who eat more processed foods than fresh foods, who seldom exercise, who get just 5 to 6 hours of sleep a night, or who regularly rely on alcohol to unwind after a stressful day. Invariably, these women know that their lifestyles bear some blame for their diminished sex drive. Yet they're dismayed to learn that the first step in our treatment program is basic self-care. As we explain, they can't expect their libidos to return if their physical health isn't up to par.

Your libido is incredibly sensitive; it knows when your body isn't receiving adequate nutrition, exercise, or sleep. If you're like most women, you're falling short in at least one of these core components of physical health. Your willingness and commitment to work at correcting any underlying deficiency likely will have a direct, positive impact on your sex drive. With this in mind, let's explore each core component in turn.

CHOOSE YOUR FOODS WISELY

"Does what I eat *really* matter, as far as whether or not I want sex?" At the Sexual Wellness Center, we hear some variation on this question almost every time we bring up the topic of nutrition to one of our clients. And we understand their skepticism. After all, they—like the rest of us—have been getting mixed messages about what they should and should not eat. Should they limit fats? What about carbohydrates? Can they get enough of the essential nutrients from foods alone, or should they take supplements, too? Staying on top of the latest nutrition recommendations is tough even for us health professionals. For our clients, the ever-changing and often conflicting information can be overwhelming.

Even our recommendations tend to vary from one woman to the next, depending on individual health status and lifestyle. But we do have some general nutritional guidelines that we follow. They're driven by the latest nutrition research as well as time-tested knowledge of the female body's basic nutrition needs.

The disturbing fact is that even though we Americans are more attuned to our eating habits than ever before, we also are suffering from more chronic degenerative diseases than ever before. The national rates of heart disease, cancer, and diabetes are at all-time highs. Even more disconcerting, obesity has reached epidemic proportions. None of these trends is going to change its uphill climb anytime soon.

Nutrition experts now attribute these troubling numbers to the "new" American diet that combines substantial reductions in fat with substantial increases in refined carbohydrates. Take a moment to mentally browse through your kitchen cupboards. Do you see white flour, white bread, bagels, crackers, popcorn, and pastas? All of these are refined carbohydrates, which in large quantities are responsible for a number of adverse effects in the body.

When you eat any kind of carb, it breaks down into blood sugar, or glucose. Your body responds by directing your pancreas to release insulin. This hormone helps remove the glucose from your bloodstream by escorting it into cells, which use it for energy.

The trouble with refined carbohydrates is that they break

down quickly. Your pancreas must churn out more and more insulin to sweep glucose from your bloodstream. This sets in motion a chain of events that eventually leads to a fundamental disruption of the metabolic process. And that, in turn, can diminish your libido.

To understand how, you need to know a little bit about metabolism. We tend to associate it with calorie burning and weight loss. In a more general sense, it's the continual rebuilding and breaking down of bodily tissues. The rebuilding phase depends on the so-called anabolic hormones—sex hormones, growth hormones, and insulin. During the breakdown phase, the catabolic hormones—thyroid hormones and corticosteroids—come into play.

By following a diet that covers all your nutritional bases, you keep the anabolic and catabolic hormones in balance. This allows your metabolism to function at peak efficiency. But if you eat too many carbohydrates, it shakes up your hormonal equilibrium by triggering the release of excess insulin. To restore balance, your body cuts back production of the remaining anabolic hormones or boosts levels of the catabolic hormones. Either course of action sets the stage for potential health problems.

Of course, if your body chooses the first option, you're going to run low on sex hormones—the very hormones that drive your libido. So you can see how a high intake of refined carbohydrates can lower your desire for sex in the long run. By the same token, restricting carbohydrate consumption may help revive a flagging sex drive.

And you don't need to worry about losing out on essential nutrients. The fact is, the refining process strips carbohydrates of much of their nutritional value. The irony is that your body needs certain vitamins and minerals to help break down refined carbs on their journey through the digestive system. In the absence of these nutrients in the foods themselves, your body has to raid its own stores. This can worsen any developing or existing nutritional deficiency.

The lack of nutrients in refined carbohydrates becomes even more significant when you consider some additional facts. With farmland becoming scarce, much of the soil for growing grains and other crops has been overused and depleted of key minerals. So the grains that eventually pass through the refining process don't contain a lot of nutrients to begin with. What's more, many commercial farming operations continue to rely on pesticides to protect their crops, even though these chemicals are suspected of serious adverse effects on human health. Their risks and benefits have stirred much controversy and debate.

With refined carbohydrates, the new nutritional wisdom is that we're eating too many. The opposite is true for dietary fat: We may not be getting enough.

Think back to the early to mid-1990s, the height of the low-fat craze. We were told that the less fat we ate, the better off we would be. Fat became public enemy number one, with cholesterol a close second. Yet the fact is, both substances are essential for health and for life.

In particular, your body uses certain fats—the beneficial fats found in olive oil, canola oil, and flaxseed oil—as building blocks for estrogen, testosterone, and a multitude of other hormones. So if you restrict your fat intake too much, it could be detrimental to your libido.

You should still be wary of harmful fats known as trans fatty acids. They're a by-product of hydrogenation, a process that turns liquid vegetable oil to solid fat through extreme temperatures and pressure. Manufacturers use hydrogenation to produce margarine and solid vegetable shortening, among other staples. These products may have a long shelf life, but it comes at a price. Studies have linked the trans fats in these items to heart disease, cancer, diabetes, immune dysfunction, and obesity. These harmful fats also may block the complex metabolic pathways that convert cholesterol into sex hormones.

Like dietary fat, cholesterol has gotten a bad reputation for its suspected role in the formation of arterial blockages that lead to heart attacks and strokes. The latest research suggests that other, lesser-known substances may, in fact, be doing the damage. Cholesterol has benefits all its own. Besides serving as a precursor to estrogen, progesterone, and testosterone, it supports the manufacture of vitamin D and bile salts. And it's vital to the structure and integrity of the body's membranes.

The point is, your body needs just the right mix of an assortment of nutrients—good fats, cholesterol, vitamins, minerals, and amino acids—to function at its best, generally and sexually. Too much or too little of any single substance can throw your entire system out of whack. To nourish your body properly, Steven Saltzman, M.D., the nutritional consultant for the Sexual Wellness Center, offers these guidelines.

- Steer clear of refined carbohydrates—namely, anything made with white flour or white sugar.
- Avoid foods that contain trans fats.
- Build your meals around high-quality proteins such as lean meats, seafood, milk, and eggs.
- Choose fresh foods over packaged ones, which have little if any nutritional value.
- Buy organic when you can.

GET UP AND *MOVE!*

So many of our clients cringe when we mention exercise. Frankly, we don't blame them. Many of us don't have time to work out. And the rest of us just don't like it.

Still, exercise is one of the essentials of optimum physical health. It's great for your libido, too.

Consider physical activity from an evolutionary perspective. We humans have never been as sedentary as we are today. Many of us move very little in the course of our daily routines. Women who work outside the home spend much of their time sitting on the job. Those who choose to stay home to raise their kids may have more opportunities to be active, but even in their case, modern conveniences limit their energy expenditures.

Western cultures would never forgo their washing machines, automobiles, dishwashers, garage door openers, and the luxury of purchasing butter rather than churning it. But these advances have significantly reduced our activity levels. Interestingly, this "benefit" has evolved only in the last 100 years, even though we humans have inhabited Earth for centuries longer.

The effects of inactivity are emotional as well as physical. In one of the more revolutionary theories to date, some experts propose that depression—which has been on the rise in recent years—may be the body's natural response to a sedentary lifestyle. Research will determine whether this theory stands up over time. Scientists already have convincing proof that exercise is a tremendously effective mood regulator.

Apparently, it's good for the libido, too. In studies, women report that they feel more sexually receptive after exercise. What's more, those who work out regularly tend to be more comfortable with their bodies, which means they probably are more confident and at ease when making love.

To reap the most benefits from exercise, we recommend aiming for at least 30 minutes of physical activity most days of the week. The good news is that you don't need to go for lung-burning runs or bench-press your body weight to notice improvement in your health and your libido. Actually, we discourage our clients from limiting their view of physical activity to gyms and exercise videos. Instead, be creative. Sign up for a dance class with your partner or a friend. Walk your dog. Take horseback riding lessons with your kids. Choose something that you truly enjoy. It will stir your life energy and increase your commitment to regular exercise and optimum health.

MAKE TIME FOR SLEEP

You spend about one-third of your life in a state of sleep. Contrary to popular perception, this isn't wasted time. Your body depends on the respite for rejuvenation and self-healing.

Like good nutrition and regular exercise, adequate rest is essential to optimum health. "Adequate," for most adults, is at least 7 hours a night. Your body will determine how much it needs. If it doesn't get enough, you'll know. You'll feel tired and lack energy; you may not be able to concentrate. And you almost certainly won't want sex.

If you have trouble sleeping, the following strategies may help improve your odds of experiencing deep, restful slumber.

- Limit your consumption of coffee and other caffeinated beverages, particularly after the morning hours.
- Try to eat dinner no less than 4 hours before bedtime.
- If you exercise in the evening, conclude your workouts at least 3 hours before bedtime.
- Establish a nightly routine to alert your body that sleep is imminent.
- Use deep breathing, guided imagery, or another technique to promote relaxation. (For instructions, see chapter 11.)

- Avoid watching TV, reading, and doing paperwork in bed. You want your body to associate your bed with sleep—and, of course, with sex!

- Keep paper and a pen by your bed, so you can write down worries rather than ruminate over them.

If you continue to toss and turn through the night, or if you feel exhausted during the day, see your doctor. You may have an underlying medical condition such as sleep apnea, which can disrupt your sleep habits.

BE PRUDENT ABOUT ALCOHOL

Alcohol consumption has a direct impact on sex drive. Sometimes women with low libido try to self-medicate by imbibing. They think that a drink or two will help them relax and feel turned on. Although this may be true for a social drinker who consumes a single cocktail or glass of wine, it usually backfires for a woman who relies on alcohol more regularly.

In fact, most women begin to feel sluggish and less interested sexually after a second drink. This is because alcohol acts as a depressant. Regular consumption has a sedating effect on both physiology and mood.

In general, experts advise women to limit their alcohol intake to one or two beverages a day. That amount of alcohol doesn't appear harmful and may have some benefits. But if you routinely consume more than that, it likely is depleting your libido.

Incidentally, when experts talk about alcoholic beverages, they mean 12 ounces of beer, 5 ounces of wine, or 1½ ounces of 80-proof distilled spirits. Be sure to remember these servings when topping off your own glass.

If you need help relaxing and getting in the mood for sex, we hope that you'll explore the many nonalcoholic alternatives offered throughout this book. Instead of drinking, how about reading some erotica to shift your mind from the events of the day and toward intimacy with your partner? Or think of a sexual fantasy that helps engage and arouse you. Guided imagery can have a similar effect. Any of these techniques will work better than alcohol in leading your mind and body to a sexual place.

Physical Health Makes All the Difference

Our clients at the Sexual Wellness Center often are amazed by how even minor changes in their lifestyle can lead to a major improvement in their libidos. As they come to realize, physical health isn't just about absence of disease—though that certainly is important. It's about feeling energized and alive. Though they may need to work on other issues, focusing on the physical can jump-start their efforts to reinvigorate their sexuality and their sex drives. Helen's story perfectly illustrates this process.

When I (Dr. Brandon) first met Helen, she had a bright smile and greeted me with a perky "hello." She tried to appear comfortable and at ease, but her forced enthusiasm conveyed a different message. I knew she was unhappy.

In my office, I encouraged her to drop the façade that she was hiding behind. I explained that it would prevent me from knowing her, and thus prevent her from getting what she needed from therapy. At that, Helen burst into tears. Clutching a handful of tissues, she described how she had been struggling with low libido for more than 10 years. She couldn't remember the last time she and her husband, Phil, had made love.

Helen came to the Sexual Wellness Center because she was afraid Phil would leave her. Recently, he had begun dropping not-so-subtle hints that he was tired of masturbating. Though Helen didn't want to have sex with him, she didn't want to lose him, either. She had been divorced once already, and she had promised herself that it wouldn't happen again.

I asked Helen what she thought was behind her dislike of sex. "I have no idea," she responded. She was copping out. I decided not to let her off the hook that easily. She obviously was intelligent, and I knew that she could generate some hypotheses about her behavior. I waited. Helen became uncomfortable with the silence and finally decided to open up. "I hate my body," she said. "I hate being fat. I can't even look at myself in the mirror, let alone allow Phil to look at me." More silence.

It was true that Helen was overweight. She probably weighed 30 pounds more than what would be considered healthy for a woman of her height and age. "Do you ever speak about this with Phil?" I asked, wondering whether her size was off-limits for discussion between them. "No," she said emphatically. "I'd die if he told me to lose weight. He knows I hate my body!"

"It must be difficult to enjoy sex when you hate your body so much," I replied. "Perhaps this would be a good place for us to start."

Helen and I explored whether she really wanted to lose weight. We identified the pros and cons of changing her body in this way. On the pro side, Helen readily recognized that slimming down would improve her health and self-esteem. She could wear more-attractive outfits rather than clothes that only masked her body. She'd be able to ascend the stairs at work without getting out of breath. She hated having to suggest taking the elevator if she wanted to talk with colleagues when walking between meetings. Most important, she could go to the beach again. She loved relaxing in the ocean waves, but she had given that up years *ago when she decided she could no longer wear a bathing suit in public.*

With all of these benefits, Helen said she couldn't imagine a negative reason for achieving a slimmer physique. But when I offered a few possibilities, Helen agreed with each one. For example, I explained that many women use their excess weight as "protection" from men's sexual advances. Some men, including her husband, might be less interested in her sexually if she is fat. On a subconscious level, this may leave her feeling safe by keeping Phil at a distance.

Further, Helen realized that she was probably relying on food as a coping mechanism. To lose weight, she would need to deal more directly with her feelings, rather than numb them with the comfort of eating.

For Helen, losing weight might also mean facing higher expectations from her family members and friends. She was accustomed to people cutting her some slack because of her low energy. She expressed concern that if she looked fitter and healthier, people might want more from her than she could deliver.

These realizations gave rise to a period of self-awakening for Helen. She wanted to feel good emotionally and physically. She wanted to reinvest in her marriage for reasons other than preventing a second divorce. She wanted to feel comfortable in her body. She searched within herself to determine what she needed to change.

That's when Helen decided to launch an exercise program. Weight loss and physical fitness were part of her plan to enjoy her life and her sexuality in ways she previously had avoided. Over time, she learned to find comfort in outlets other than food. And as she opened herself to pleasure, she discovered that eating healthfully felt less like deprivation and more like a reward for living well.

This process was not always easy for Helen. But she knew that caring for her body was necessary if she wanted to recover her sex drive and truly enjoy sex, which she hadn't been able to do before.

Feeling Good All Over

We encourage you to follow Helen's lead by conducting a thorough and honest self-assessment of your physical health. Make changes in those lifestyle factors that may counteract your efforts to reinvigorate your sex drive. The impact of these changes on your sexuality and on your general health may surprise you.

By practicing basic health maintenance, you will get more from virtually every other aspect of your life. You'll notice improvements in your mood and energy level. You'll feel better physically and psychologically. These benefits further enhance your interest in and desire for sex.

CHAPTER 5

IN TOUCH WITH
PHYSICAL PLEASURE

- To improve your libido, you must be sensitive to the sexual and nonsexual sensations that your body experiences.
- Women who are emotionally detached from their partners or are otherwise struggling with intimacy may not realize when they're physically aroused, even though they are.
- Exploring your sensuality—what feels good to you—can provide valuable insight into your sexual desire and response.
- Through nonsexual contact with your partner, you can reestablish the physical connection that's vital to fulfilling sexual encounters.
- Restoring your sex drive takes time. And even a healthy libido will wax and wane.

Reviving your sex drive is a process that requires a deliberate renewal of sexual awareness. Simply going through the motions of having sex is not enough.

A woman with low libido may not realize that she has dissociated from her physical self and thus her sexuality. She must become reacquainted first with her body, then with her sensuality, and finally with the sexual thoughts and feelings she has rejected over time. Through this exploration, she may discover that what turns her on now isn't the same as what turned her on before. That's the case for most women.

Sexuality is dynamic; it evolves as your body matures and your life circumstances change. If you have disconnected from the physical sensations of sex over time, you must relearn how to feel when you make love and experience pleasurable touch. Remembering what used to arouse you is a good starting point.

Reconnecting with your sexuality is a conscious choice. It also is an opportunity to rediscover a part of yourself that is not dead. It simply has been in hibernation for a while.

Why Women Dissociate from Their Sexual Selves

The self-examination that's necessary for embracing your sexual identity can be uncomfortable at first, especially if you've already dissociated from this part of yourself. One of our clients, Amanda, found this to be true when she came to the Sexual Wellness Center for help with her low libido.

Amanda was in her early forties when she called my (Dr. Brandon's) office for an appointment. Although she and her husband, Trent, were sexually active, she couldn't recall the last time she actually wanted to make love. She appeared demoralized and pessimistic about her apparent lack of sexual desire.

Amanda interpreted her predicament in purely hormonal terms. She believed that because her body's hormonal balance had changed as she had gotten older, her libido had disappeared forever. But Dr. Goldstein's physical exam and hormone tests found no indication that Amanda's health was somehow standing in her way.

Amanda and I began our work by exploring what had turned her on in the past. At first she said she couldn't remember. She was aware of feeling intense desire and excitement with Trent (as well as with other men before him) but was unclear as to her role in that process. In her mind, her sexual feelings had just flowed naturally.

After much contemplation, Amanda spoke about a time in her life when she had been more receptive to her sexuality. Back then, she thought about sex quite a bit. She routinely planned romantic or erotic sexual escapades that she and Trent could share. She dressed in provocative clothing, clearly reveling in the fact that Trent wanted her. She was tuned in to her sexual self on many levels—her thoughts, her feelings, her behaviors, and her physical sensations.

The two of us then compared that period in Amanda's life with the current state of her sexuality. Although she had bought sexual props and toys in an effort to reignite her sex drive, her use of them lacked any spirit of inspiration or exploration. She admitted that she would get out her vibrator when she and Trent were making love because she could climax quicker, not because she enjoyed the sensations it provided. She seemed to approach their sexual encounters with one overarching thought: "Let's get this over with." Beyond that, if sex ever crossed her mind, it usually had some negative connotation—as in "I hope Trent won't want to make love tonight."

Amanda noticed something else, too: She no longer appreciated the more subtle aspects of life that had once stimulated her. For example, she could remember when she made a point of playing sexy music during her weekend dinners with Trent. And she used to enjoy swimming naked in their pool at dusk, relishing the sensation of the cool water on her skin. Yet she couldn't name a single instance in her current life in which she enjoyed being sensual and experiencing her body in an erotic way.

Rather than creating situations to enhance her sexual awareness, as she had done regularly in the past, Amanda seemed to be subverting her sexuality. We discussed how she was attempting to deal with her low libido by dissociation, and how this coping mechanism—though a popular one— is rarely successful in helping women overcome their sexual difficulties.

Amanda had disconnected not only from thoughts of her sexuality in her daily life but also from the physical sensations of her sexual encounters with Trent. She described her experience of being touched by her husband in clinical, cold terms. She essentially shut down her body and mind when he made sexual advances to her. While they were making love, her thoughts often drifted to matters completely unrelated to sex.

Even when Amanda managed to stay focused on the moment, she didn't have a positive reaction to her sexual interactions with Trent. Without deriving pleasure from Trent's touch, Amanda understandably felt little desire for intimate contact with him.

Eventually, Trent joined Amanda in therapy. But first, she realized, she needed to do some work on her own. She understood that she had turned off sexually. Now her task was to figure out why.

In our experience, women like Amanda tend to dissociate from their sexual selves when they repeatedly experience negative emotions. In other words, whenever they tune in to how they're feeling, sexually or otherwise, they become uncomfortable. So they subconsciously decide that they're better off not feeling at all. Their emotional and physical responses go numb.

Women who resort to dissociation as a coping mechanism often struggle with the quiet moments in their lives, such as time alone, because they're more vulnerable to turning inward then. But introspection and dissociation don't mix. These women will resist opportunities to know themselves more intimately, because they want to avoid evoking the negative emotions buried inside.

This is why they may try to speed up or skip over foreplay during sexual encounters. Because foreplay tends to be slower and more introspective than intercourse, the risk of connecting with themselves, and with their partners, in a deep and meaningful way is too great. Instead, these women will put their energy into the "active" part of sex. Unfortunately, intercourse probably won't be all that enjoyable, because they haven't had enough time to warm up. Of course, if they continue repeating this pattern of bad sex, they won't want sex at all.

When the Mind Disconnects, the Body Follows

If you are like most women with low libido, you probably would say that you never think about sex or feel sexual in any way. You may question whether you are even capable of experiencing sexuality again. Sometimes you chalk up your lack of desire to growing older, and you try not to think too much about it. But you have moments when you wonder whether you are giving up too quickly.

A research team at the University of Texas at Austin, led by psychologist Cindy Meston, Ph.D., is conducting some interesting research on this topic. Specifically, they are looking at women's self-perceptions of sexual arousal. In these studies, female volunteers are presented with a sexual stimulus, perhaps an erotic video. While they watch the video, special instruments record their bodies' sexual responses, such as vaginal lubrication and degree of genital engorgement. The women also rate how sexually aroused they become.

The results of the studies are fascinating. Women repeatedly underestimate their level of sexual arousal. That is, they have little awareness of how much they're turned on. Generally, they rate their bodies as sexually unresponsive, even when their vaginal lubrication is adequate and their genitals are engorged in a typical arousal state.

What does this research mean? It tells us that women base their perceptions of what arouses them on their emotional reactions, rather than on their physiological responses. In other words, most women who believe that their bodies don't react "normally" to sexual stimuli in fact are not tuned in to what's going on physically. It seems that their emotional experience of a sexual stimulus is overriding their physiological experience of it. Even when a woman's body arouses normally, she can block the physical feedback with her emotions.

This suggests that if a woman is ambivalent about her sexual partner or his lovemaking style, she will perceive that she is not aroused, even when all the relevant physical measures show that she is. Making use of this research in therapy means that we must focus more on a woman's emotional reactions to sexual stimuli. If she is not engaged or satisfied emotionally, physical arousal will be relatively meaningless for her.

At the Sexual Wellness Center, we advise women who have disconnected from pleasurable physical sensations to tune in to their bodies whenever they feel anything emotionally. This follows the theory that all emotions are experienced on both psychological and physical levels, so one can help increase awareness of the other.

Thus, if you feel sad, finding the place in your body where you harbor that sadness can help increase your perception of physical sensations. You can do the same with happiness, anger, or virtually any emotion. Conversely, you might ask yourself, What emotions lie behind my back pain? My migraines? My irritable bowel syndrome?

You also can explore the connection between physical sensations and emotions with help from, oddly enough, a tennis ball. Lie on top of the ball so that it rolls up and down your spine. You'll be amazed at the tension that's harbored there and the emotions that arise as you manipulate those muscles. These exercises may seem strange, but they work. As you increase your understanding of how your emotions and your body interact with one another, you'll become more sensitive to your sexual response. This is not a small point. Your sexuality is as much an emotional experience as a physical one. Thus, the better you understand the connection between your mind and body, the more you will be able to facilitate pleasurable sexual sensations.

Pathways to Rediscovering Physical Pleasure

If you want to reconnect with the physical side of your sexuality, your first step is to define what is sensual for you. This involves becoming aware of your most subtle sexual thoughts and feelings. Many of our clients say that their lives are too hectic to pay attention to such subtleties. The fact is, the chaotic pace of their daily routines probably has contributed to the depletion of their sex drives in the first place.

Once you tune in to your sensuality, you probably will find that you've maintained more of it than you give yourself credit for. Contrary to how you may feel at this moment, you are not asexual. You simply need to reawaken that part of you. Bringing back your sensuality will require effort, but it also can be fun.

The exercises in this section can be powerful, though they may seem relatively innocuous on the surface. We know that you may be tempted to skip over them in search of more-potent solutions to your low libido. Perhaps you are interested in what will deliver the biggest return for your time and energy investment. We certainly don't blame you.

But these exercises are a particularly integral part of your healing process. Besides, you need to slow down. You probably have been moving so quickly through your life that you are missing out on the more delicate aspects of your sexuality. And you must reacquaint yourself with these subtleties in order to rediscover and revitalize your sexual desire. We invite you to relax and take pleasure in this process. It involves the type of homework that you actually can enjoy completing!

Try to approach the following exercises with an attitude of curiosity and openness to learning new things about yourself. As human beings, we are constantly growing and changing. Our sexual selves are no different. And you've been out of touch with yours for a while.

WASH AWAY INHIBITIONS

A wonderful way to ease into the process of becoming re-acquainted with pleasurable bodily sensations is to take a warm bath. Be sure to have massage oils and a soft washcloth or sponge available. You may choose to light some candles or play music to enhance your sensual experience. Take the phone off the hook and let others know that you are not to be disturbed. Expect to spend at least 30 minutes with yourself. You're going to use this time for relaxation and exploration.

Familiarize yourself with what your body responds to and how it likes to be touched. Move slowly and deliberately from one body part to the next, massaging your throat, breasts, underarms, inner elbows, belly, inner thighs, buttocks, back of your knees, and feet. Notice when you start to lose interest in what you're doing. What is going on that leads you to dissociate from this experience? Can you make any connections between this experience and your tendency to shut down when you are with your partner?

Experiment with a variety of touching styles—a light, feathery caress; a deep, slow rub; a quick circular motion; or whatever else comes to mind. Which is sexiest to you? Massage oil onto your skin. How does this change the experience for you? Pour water over various body parts, or if you have a shower massager, experiment with different water pressures against your skin. Which feels best to you?

As you perform this exercise, pay attention to what makes you feel sexy and what methods of stimulation spark your sexual energy. See how deeply you can relax and let go.

STOCK UP FOR SENSUAL INDULGENCE

Now that you've gotten a taste of the sort of self-exploration that you'll be doing, you're ready to move on to your next assignment. It involves an activity that many women enjoy: shopping!

First, take a trip to a lingerie shop. Once you are comfortable, choose a few sexy things to try on. You may be attracted to a particular style, or perhaps a color or type of fabric. Find something that feels sensual when you wear it. This is not for anyone's eyes but yours. If you later decide to share your selection with your partner, that's fine. But right now, you are pleasing only yourself. Try to purchase at least one item that challenges your impression of yourself sexually. That is, get a little crazy!

Next on the agenda is a trip to the grocery store. Your task is to identify at least four or five foods that feel sensual when you eat them. As with your choice of lingerie, your selections need to appeal only to you. Look for foods that have an alluring appearance, a seductive taste, or an erotic consistency. Imagine what you will feel as you eat them. Perhaps you derive the most sensual pleasure from sweet, juicy seasonal fruits such as cherries, strawberries, and peaches. Chocolate always is a favorite, as is ice cream. Wine and cheese definitely can create a seductive, sexy mood. Or maybe a steak on the rare side does it for you. Have fun and a sense of humor when filling your basket.

Finally, you'll want to visit your local bookstore. There you will find a selection of erotic literature. Yes, you are in search of pornography. The civilized folks at the store probably label it "erotica"; they have shelves and shelves of it. Your task is to locate this section and choose something wonderful from it. Among my clients, the books with short stories written by women for women seem to be especially popular. Try not to be concerned about what the people at the checkout will think of your purchase. They probably have discovered this tantalizing reading for themselves!

Once you've stocked up on the necessary supplies, schedule an evening alone at a time when you won't be interrupted. Make the final preparations for your own seduction. Consider what music you want to hear. Are scented candles in order? Indulge in whatever will enhance your efforts to feel sexually alive.

You may want to begin your evening with a warm bath or relaxation exercise to help distance yourself from the day's events. Then combine your lingerie, food, and erotica in ways that please you. Be slow and passionate about it. Your goal is to make yourself feel good. Savor your sexiness. Welcome this part of you back into your life.

DEVELOP A FANTASY LIFE

Many women with a diminished sex drive have lost touch with the sensual pleasure available to them through fantasy. This is unfortunate because fantasy can assist in reawakening sexual desire by reestablishing a connection to your body's sexual response. What's more, your particular fantasies can offer clues as to what you and your partner could do so that you feel more engaged in your sexual encounters.

Women can be self-conscious about developing an active fantasy life. Sometimes, they feel that their fantasies actually keep them from connecting with their partners. This can be true if a woman uses fantasy obsessively. That is, if it becomes her only method of sexual release, or if she depends on it when she is with her partner, she probably has taken it to an unhealthy level.

For most women, however, fantasy is a normal part of a healthy sex life and a valuable tool for enhancing libido. Anyone can further develop her use of fantasy, should she so choose. Even those who don't visualize well can invent sexy story lines for themselves.

A first step in developing or enhancing fantasy is to create—preferably on paper—a scenario that you might find sexually interesting or exciting. You can use yourself as the main character, but if that feels too awkward, dream up a fictional heroine. Then write something risqué. You won't have to show it to anyone, so why not experiment a bit? Make the story rich with detail. Consider what the key players look like, wear, and say to each other, and of course, how they act. Fine-tune your story to suit you perfectly. The beauty of fantasy is that it isn't reality-based, so you can exercise some creative license. If you have difficulty coming up with your own plot, you may want to borrow a sexy scene from a book or a movie as a starting point.

Once you have your fantasy in writing, set aside some private time to enjoy it. You may want to begin your session with deep breathing and then move on to full-body muscle relaxation. (For descriptions of these techniques, see chapter 11.) Once you've achieved a focused, relaxed state, you can immerse yourself in your fantasy. As you do, touch yourself in any way that feels pleasurable. Adding this sensory experience can make your fantasy more sexually stimulating.

Some women have difficulty using fantasy for sexual enjoyment. Imagining a sexual encounter feels dirty or disgusting to them. They may struggle to think up plausible scenarios for themselves or to re-create their scenarios in their minds. More than likely, these women perceive something threatening about having fantasies, so they prevent themselves—albeit subconsciously—from doing so. Guilt, shame, and other negative emotions can complicate the pleasure of fantasizing.

We are unaware of a woman ever being unsuccessful at creating and enjoying her sexual fantasies if she is motivated enough to experience them. Common scenarios include making love in a new or risky environment, making love to more than one person at the same time, and being seduced by someone. We'll explore the possibility of sharing your fantasy with your partner a bit later in the chapter.

EXPAND YOUR REPERTOIRE FOR STIMULATION

Ready for more shopping? This time your assignment is to acquire some new sex toys. Regardless of how many (or how few) toys you already own, you can always find something different to experiment with. And thanks to the Internet, you no longer have the excuse that you are too embarrassed to go to a sex shop, or that you can't find such a store in a safe neighborhood. (The resource section on page 312 includes several Web sites that you may find helpful.) Still, many women prefer to shop in person, so they can see what they're purchasing.

When choosing your toys, remember that you are looking only to please yourself. Here again, we encourage you to challenge yourself. Allow yourself to be more adventurous than you are initially inclined.

A few words about vibrators are in order, as many women find them valuable in their efforts to reconnect with their sexuality. With a vibrator, you can experience constant stimulation at a level of intensity that is most pleasing to you.

Most women use vibrators externally, on the clitoris, though some also use them inside the vagina. Because the majority of nerve endings are located in the lower third of the vagina, focusing on this area may be most pleasurable. If you enjoy lots of stimulation, you might look for a vibrator that works internally and externally at the same time.

If you are just learning to climax, your best bet is an electric vibrator, which offers variable speeds. The advantage of variable speeds is that you can control the amount of stimulation you're receiving. Generally, electric vibrators are more expensive. But because they don't rely on battery power, they are more reliable, and they tend to last longer. They plug into any wall electrical outlet.

Keep in mind, too, that vibrators are made from different materials. Some are soft and feel more like a penis, and others are hard plastic. Usually, the hard plastic ones are less expensive, but they may not feel as comfortable. Also, because the plastic is porous, it could harbor bacteria. Vibrators made from silicone are not porous and thus may be considered safer from the standpoint of bacterial transmission. Regardless of the material you choose, you should clean your vibrator after each use.

For your first time with a vibrator, you may feel more comfortable trying it over your underwear. The fabric will buffer the intensity of sensation, allowing time to adjust to the stimulation.

EXPERIMENT WITH PLEASURING YOURSELF

Masturbation, with a vibrator or without, can be a valuable tool in reconnecting with your sexuality and reviving your sex drive. You can learn a lot about your sexual response by pleasuring yourself.

Many women with low libido masturbate on occasion. But most report a decline in their desire to masturbate—which is not a surprise, because they've experienced a decline in their desire for sex.

As with all of these exercises, you will need time and privacy to masturbate comfortably. We suggest that you begin by looking at your genitalia in a mirror. Perhaps you've done this before, but why not do it again? It will help familiarize you with your clitoris and clitoral hood, your vagina and labia, and your anus. Appreciate the beauty inherent in your body and the complexity of your sex organs. Notice how you feel as you study yourself. You're collecting more information about how you experience your sexuality. If you're uncomfortable, then you have work to do. You won't be at ease sharing your body with your partner if you're not at ease with yourself.

Masturbate when you feel comfortable and ready. Do not worry about whether or not you have an orgasm. Just concentrate on stimulating your genitals in a way that feels good to you. You may wish to involve other body parts, such as your breasts or other erogenous zones that seemed pleasurably sensitive during your self-massage. Make use of your new sex toys, your erotica, or anything else that may help engage you in the experience. Be as creative and free as you can.

You may want to take this opportunity to explore your G-spot, particularly if you haven't discovered this erogenous zone before. It's located through the upper front wall of your vagina. When you are aroused, the G-spot swells with blood and becomes even more sensitive. Some women report a sensation of having to urinate.

You can find your own G-spot by inserting a finger into your vagina while imagining that you are trying to massage your belly button. As with any part of the female anatomy, massaging the G-spot is more pleasurable for some women than for others. Some experience orgasm from this type of stimulation.

If you happen to climax, luxuriate in your sexual expression a while longer. Women too often assume that the "goal" of masturbation is orgasm, and once that's achieved, the event is complete. Your sexual exploration need not be so regimented.

If you have difficulty reaching orgasm, or if you've never had one, a variety of issues may be at play. For example, hormones, medications, and physical illnesses may inhibit your ability to experience physical sensations. So, too, can your emotions, if they affect your willingness to give in to this type of pleasure. A number of self-help books provide a systematic and highly effective approach to becoming orgasmic. We've listed a few of our favorites in the resource section on page 309. You also might consider consulting a qualified sex therapist.

Before wrapping up our discussion of masturbation, let's take a moment to explore multiple orgasms. Not all women have multiple orgasms, but most women can teach themselves how, if they want to. If you would like to have more than one orgasm at a time, you may want to practice without your partner first. Later on, you can teach him what you learn about yourself.

The key to multiple orgasms is constant stimulation. Some

women are uncomfortable continuing with high levels of stimulation after they climax. If they're masturbating, they stop touching themselves immediately. We suggest that you try touching yourself more gently for a while after your first orgasm. If you are using a vibrator, turn it to a lower speed. After a few moments, you may notice that you're becoming aroused again.

The Physical Aspects of Intimacy

As you continue the process of rediscovering your sexual self, you may decide to take a closer look at the physical connection between you and your partner. The two of you should begin your exploration on a nonsexual level, just as you did on your own.

First, consider the quality and frequency of the physical contact between you and your partner. How often do you touch each other? Do you hug, hold hands, rub each other's back, or sit close together, enjoying your physical bond? Are both of you comfortable with the amount of physical interaction in your relationship?

Some women with low libido show no interest in nonsexual physical contact with their partners. They fear that their partners will interpret a positive response to any kind of touch as a desire to make love. They may feel that, having lost their libidos, they no longer want any degree of physical closeness with their partners.

For other women, the opposite is true. They believe their partners have no interest in sharing nonsexual touch with them. They attribute their low libido to a general lack of physical intimacy in their relationships.

In both cases, the cycle of limited physical contact must change for a mutually satisfying sexual relationship to take shape. Engaging in nonsexual touch that is pleasurable for both partners is a necessary step toward eventual sexual reconnection.

TAKE A BREAK FROM SEX

At this point, some couples agree to a sexual hiatus, during which they practice mutual nongenital touching over a period of time (perhaps a few weeks) without making love or experiencing orgasm. Therapists refer to this technique as sensate focus. It removes the pressure or expectation to perform sexually, allowing more freedom to engage in and concentrate on physical contact.

If you and your partner decide on a sexual hiatus, be sure to use the time in a healing way. You may be tempted to view it as a welcome reprieve from sex and not make an effort to engage your partner in physical exploration. This, however, essentially constitutes a manipulation of your partner, which will only increase the tension in your relationship. Approaching a sexual hiatus with this mindset is not in your best interest.

To make the most of a sexual hiatus, you and your partner should set aside a number of hours per week to experiment with touch. If you don't schedule dates and times for this homework, other life issues are likely to take priority. Gather lotions, pillows, candles, feathers, a selection of music, and whatever else comes to mind that may help you and your partner relax and enjoy your experience together.

Be creative in the ways you touch each other. Try using physical contact to convey a variety of intentions, letting your mood set the tone for your interactions. You might be intense one evening, playful the next, loving or romantic another. Observe how these variations affect your response as well as your partner's. Don't limit yourself to one type of touch. Experiment with licking, biting, kissing, squeezing, and kneading each other's bodies as well.

Also take the opportunity to find ways to reawaken each other's senses. For example, just as you used food to tap into your own sensuality, consider a similar exercise with your partner. Take turns blindfolding each other and feeding each other a variety of luscious treats. Or climb into the tub for a sensual bath together. Or practice the art of couples massage, enrolling in a class or buying a video to explore various techniques. Obviously, these exercises require willingness on the part of both partners to evolve together, sharing new, intimate experiences in order to grow their sexual relationship.

Disclosing personal fantasies is an intimate activity that many couples find both risky and rewarding. Telling a partner about a particular fantasy is an act of trust and vulnerability. But if it upsets or threatens the partner, it can strain the relationship even further. If you would like to reveal a fantasy to your partner but you're unsure of his response, you could "test the waters" first. For example, rent a movie that depicts a similar scenario and watch it together. You might gather some clues about your partner's receptivity to what you're fantasizing about.

If you continue to resist any physical connection with your partner, take some time to explore why. Addressing these feelings is important. If you force yourself to move further in your relationship than you feel comfortable, your situation will likely become more intolerable.

CHANGE YOUR APPROACH

When you and your partner feel ready to move toward more sexual intimacy, you still may want to refrain from intercourse, at least initially. Instead, your next step is to engage in genital stimulation, without the goal of orgasm. Use your scheduled sessions to experiment with and experience a variety of genital touches. Don't try to avoid or force an orgasm, as climaxing is essentially irrelevant at the moment.

See if you can open yourself to sensations that you previously considered "off limits." That means taking some risks, so you are touching and being touched in ways that may intrigue or challenge you. By pushing your own boundaries, you allow yourself to be vulnerable with your partner. This likely will translate to a level of intimacy that the two of you haven't previously shared.

When you and your partner are ready to resume making love, try to bring that same sense of adventure to the experience. It is exceedingly easy to fall back into old, tired habits. Make an effort to change your sexual patterns. This can be anything—the environment you make love in, the clothes each of you wears, the sexual positions you use, the way your partner thrusts, the way you move and speak while receiving him, the level of eye contact the two of you maintain. Role-playing different scenarios can add intrigue to your interaction.

Try introducing an element of risk and excitement into your lovemaking sessions. This may mean different things to you and your partner. If you're stumped for ideas, reflect on your sexual past, the moments in your life when you found sex exhilarating. What experiences stand out in your memory? Recall as much specific information about those occasions as you can. Where were you? What were you feeling in those moments of ecstasy? What was your partner doing to your body? What were you doing to your partner's body? Now think about your favorite fantasies and answer the same questions.

These thoughts and memories can offer important insights into what can help spark your sexual desire now. Are you comfortable sharing similar experiences with your current partner, exposing yourself emotionally and physically in the same way? If you are unwilling to take such a risk, why? The answer to this question may reveal what is interfering with your libido.

Be aware that these exercises inevitably will create challenges for you and your partner. This is not a bad thing, because challenges present opportunities for change and growth. Use these points of disconnection to get to know each other better.

We also encourage women to speak up during their love-making sessions, especially when they become aware that they're uncomfortable. For example, if you notice that you stiffen up when your partner moves from massaging your back to touching your breasts, talk with him about it. Explore what he can do to help you feel more at ease. By telling your partner when you are struggling, you ultimately have a much better chance of using that moment in a healthy, healing way. The alternative of not speaking up leads only to further distress and disconnection.

REESTABLISH PHYSICAL CONNECTION

When couples enter therapy in an attempt to reconnect sexually, both partners usually must put forth significant effort to get this part of their relationship back on track. Linda and Chuck, an attractive couple in their early thirties, provide a perfect example of this process.

Linda and Chuck came to the Sexual Wellness Center seeking help for Linda's low libido. Both were motivated to improve their sex life, although Chuck seemed reticent to discuss it in any specific way. Linda's enthusiasm and motivation won him over, and he became a more willing participant after several therapy sessions.

Linda and Chuck described a sexual history that I (Dr. Brandon) had heard so many times before. They obviously valued their relationship from the word "go." Linda described sex in the initial stages of their relationship as "simply incredible." But in a quiet moment, she admitted that she had lost interest in sex even before she and Chuck had married.

Linda recalled that time in her life with pain in her eyes. She disclosed that she had been struggling at work, questioning her choice of career. She was depending on Chuck probably more than she should have been to keep her head above water. Because of this, she never told him about her dwindling sex drive. She tried to ignore it, hoping the problem would resolve itself over time.

Through the first few years of their marriage, Linda struggled to conceal her lack of sexual desire from Chuck. But eventually, that became too difficult, and the two of them began having sex less and less. When they made love, Linda didn't enjoy it as much, and she considered faking orgasms to "speed things up." She even tried it once, and it scared her. She decided to be honest with Chuck and seek help through therapy.

Chuck's description of their sex life was less complicated. In his view, sex between him and Linda had been good at one time, but he had been feeling dissatisfied for several years. It seemed that Linda always avoided intimate contact with him. She was passive in bed, usually motionless and cold. She rarely touched him, and never initiated sex. Chuck's polite observation was that Linda had a problem, and he wanted to support her in fixing it. He appeared hopeful that I would see this truth and "dismiss" him from couples work. I acknowledged Chuck's comments but encouraged him to stay. On Linda's insistence, he did.

As Linda became more comfortable in therapy, she had lots more to say. She described Chuck as being "lazy" sexually. Although he could be counted on to make sexual advances to her with some regularity, he was mechanical and uninteresting in bed. His approach was always the same, and Linda wasn't even sure that he really enjoyed making love to her. She wondered out loud if he had sex simply because "it's what married people do."

Linda looked more and more angry. Chuck looked more and more confused. Between them, they were telling a story of two sexually disconnected human beings. Each was able to observe this tendency in the other, but neither was able to see it in themselves. I had faith that over time, both of them would see their own contributions to the dysfunction in their sex life.

Chuck needed some help with his sexual technique. Like most men, he had learned how to make love to a woman mostly from adolescent banter and pornographic movies. The sexual wisdom shared in these venues is minimal, not to mention the fact that most porn movies are intended to appeal to men, not women. Neither of these sources struck me as particularly insightful, and Chuck agreed.

Chuck's homework was to read a book about how to sexually please a woman and enhance the lovemaking experience. (There are several great books on the subject, a few of which we've listed in the resource section on page 309.) I encouraged Chuck to pay attention to what turned him on as he read. He needed to become more aware of not only what Linda would enjoy but what he wanted as well.

As for Linda, I challenged her to become more interested in discovering what might please her. I suggested that she purchase an erotic video made exclusively for women. Generally, these deal with sex in a more loving context, and the actors engage in activities that appeal more to women than to men. (You can order such videos through the Web sites under "Sexual Aids" on page 312 of the resource section.) Linda was shocked by this assignment, though Chuck seemed pretty pleased with it. For the first time, he looked as though he was enjoying therapy. I also encouraged Linda to purchase some erotica written by women and make mental notes of which stories she liked and which she didn't.

When they returned for their next session, Chuck was decidedly enthusiastic to be there. Linda, however, seemed more skeptical. She hadn't noticed any improvement in her libido, despite following through with most of the homework I had given her.

I asked Linda to describe a typical sexual encounter with Chuck. It became clear that Linda still was physically stiff, expecting to hate or at least not enjoy sex. She said that they always stopped making love as soon as Chuck climaxed. For many couples, the man's orgasm serves as a subconscious signal that sex is complete.

I started Linda on a course of relaxation training. She would never be able to fully enjoy a sexual encounter if she couldn't relax her body. We also worked on changing her expectations about sex from "I'm sure I'm going to hate this!" to "I wonder how this is going to feel." This cognitive technique assisted her in becoming more open to experiencing sex differently, rather than replaying the same old scenarios in her mind.

I challenged both Linda and Chuck to become less rigid about the end point of sex. They were to experiment with continuing their sex play after Chuck climaxed. Some creativity was called for.

When Chuck finished his book, we explored his sexual passivity from an emotional perspective. As an adolescent and young adult, he had gotten the message that sex would lead only to trouble. His parents believed that if he got a woman pregnant, it would ruin his life. His religion also denounced sexual relationships out of wedlock. Though these warnings about sex were intended to be in Chuck's best interest, he was unable to let go of them as an adult, even when they no longer served him.

We also discussed Chuck's tendency, if not obsession, to please others before himself. He felt safe in relationships only when he was taking care of others. Subconsciously, he believed that it would prevent people from leaving him. This approach to relationships negatively affected his sexuality, as he shut down his awareness of what actually pleased him. As a result, he was less able to enjoy making love to Linda, who in turn interpreted his passivity as disinterest.

The irony is, in an attempt to please Linda, Chuck wound up having the opposite effect. This is true for so many of us: What subconsciously drives our behavior often creates what we most fear.

Chuck wasn't alone in contributing emotional baggage to their failing sex life. Linda was engaged in her own dysfunctional dance, the result of poor self-confidence. She realized that she had been depending on Chuck to make her feel good about herself, emotionally and sexually. This was an impossible task for Chuck, as much as he may have wanted to do it for her. Over time, Linda became angry with Chuck for not meeting her expectations of him. Because this anger was largely subconscious, she expressed it indirectly by not wanting to be intimate.

Linda and Chuck's therapy had a happy ending. Both were moti-

vated to understand themselves, and their relationship, in a clearer light. They were able to get not only their sex life but also their emotional connection back on track. They worked hard and felt proud of their accomplishments.

Time Heals a Low Libido

We've noticed that as women rediscover their sexual selves, they tend to expect a sudden return of their sex drives. But it isn't like flipping a switch that allows your sexual energy to flow freely once again. Instead, you likely will experience a more gradual return, with many peaks and valleys. This means that some days you will feel more sexually interested, and other days you will feel as though you are slipping back to square one. This is the normal ebb and flow of becoming reacquainted with your sexual self.

Keep in mind that your libido always will remain sensitive to your physical and emotional experiences, as well as to the state of your relationship. This is not necessarily a bad thing. Being mindful of your degree of sexual interest offers regular opportunities to "check in" with yourself and your partner and to take care of any simmering issues. For most women, the sooner they attend to such issues, the easier they can stop a return to stuck sexual territory.

Fluctuations in your sexual interest, and in your partner's, are to be expected throughout your lifetime. We urge you to talk about any changes you notice, so they're out in the open. Keeping such information private generates only confusion and misunderstanding between partners.

CHAPTER 6

THE HORMONE FACTOR

- Your hormones are responsible for determining whether or not you want sex and how you act on that desire.

- The hypothalamus fuels your basic sex drive, and the neocortex governs your thoughts and behaviors in response to your sex drive. Both brain structures are under the influence of hormones.

- Estrogen, progesterone, and testosterone are vital to your sexuality. Each interacts with a host of other hormones to determine how you experience your libido.

- The vast majority of hormones have an antagonist, or a hormone that produces the opposite effect. This helps your body maintain balance.

- If you run low on estrogen or dopamine (the pleasure-seeking hormone), you will not want sex.

I don't know what came over me. I shouldn't have had sex with that guy I met at the party last weekend. After all, I'm already dating someone I'm crazy about. I wasn't even drunk. He was just so hot, and once he kissed me, I had to have him. Life would be so much less complicated if my behavior was controlled by my brain instead of my hormones!"

At some point in our lives, all of us have suspected that our actions are determined not by our brains but by our hormones. If we haven't felt that way recently, we certainly did when we were teenagers.

It isn't necessarily comforting to think that our behaviors, and our moods, might be under the influence of a force that's beyond our control. And though we do not want to minimize the role of "free will" in the choices we make, we must acknowledge the ability of hormones to push us in one direction or another.

So what are these superpotent things called hormones? And why do they have so much power over us?

Simply put, hormones are chemical substances that allow the body's organs to communicate with each other. They are synthesized in special cells in one organ of the body and then carried by the bloodstream to other organs. In effect, a hormone is like a message in a bottle being tossed into the ocean.

Suppose you decide to go for a jog on a hot summer day. After a couple of miles, a part of your brain called the hypothalamus senses that you are becoming dehydrated. In response, it releases two hormones. One goes to the kidneys, instructing them to make less urine to help conserve fluids. The other goes to a part of the brain called the limbic system, which causes the sensation of thirst. The limbic system also releases another hormone, which travels to a part of the brain called the neocortex. Your neocortex allows you to form the thought, "I'm thirsty. I need to find water to drink."

This example is interesting, because it demonstrates how a physical condition (dehydration) can cause you not only to feel a certain way (thirsty) but also to act in a certain way (you search for water). Thus, hormones work together with the brain to influence what you think and feel, as well as what you do.

Sexual Desire Starts Here

By now you may be wondering, How does all this affect my libido? As illustrated by the above example, hormones can interact with the cells of the brain, called neurons, to trigger changes in our moods and behaviors. But wanting to drink water is a lot different, and a lot less complicated, than wanting to make love to someone. To explain this phenomenon, we need to look deeper into our wonderfully complex brains.

At the base of the brain, right behind the eyes, lies the hypothalamus. It is responsible for monitoring the body's most basic and essential functions: temperature control, blood pressure, heart rate, water and food intake—and sex drive. But the hypothalamus doesn't act alone in determining whether or not we want sex. It answers to the neocortex, the complex structure of the brain that separates humans from the rest of the animal kingdom. Thanks to the neocortex, we're able to store memories and form thoughts. We're also able to control our drives and desires.

To understand how the neocortex works, let's look at another example: a woman named Mary and her cat, Paws. Both Mary and Paws are hungry, and two fish are lying on the kitchen counter. Paws jumps up on the counter and eats one of the fish. Mary, on the other hand, thinks, "The fish would taste great if I poached it with some white wine, mustard, and dill. Maybe John would want to come over and have some, too."

Both Mary and her cat are hungry, but only Mary can control this basic drive and postpone immediate action. Her neocortex allows her to determine that the fish will taste better if she cooks it, and that she'll have a more pleasurable meal if she combines eating with a social interaction—inviting John to join her.

Although the hypothalamus controls our basic drives (often called instincts), these drives are regulated by the neocortex, the higher brain center. The catch is, even the neocortex is under the influence of hormones.

This brings us back to the question of how all this affects your libido. Hormones direct both the hypothalamus, which is responsible for your basic sex drive, and the neocortex, which is responsible for the thoughts and behaviors related to your sex drive. Because so many different hormones get in on the act, you experience corresponding variations in your sex drive.

Women have known this intuitively all along. Sometimes you may want fast, aggressive sex; other times you may want slow, passionate lovemaking. The differences in your desire can be explained by which hormones are "in charge" at any given moment.

Hormones You Need to Know

The late Theresa L. Crenshaw, M.D., a pioneer in sexual medicine, once described four distinct categories of female sex drive: aggressive, receptive, seductive, and aversive. And though we know that libido—just like people—doesn't always neatly fall into one category or another, this is a useful starting point to examine how various hormones influence sex drive.

The hypothalamus starts the process by directing the pituitary gland to release follicle-stimulating hormone (FSH) and luteinizing hormone (LH). In turn, they instruct the ovaries to produce estrogen, progesterone, and testosterone. All three of these hormones are major players on the sexual stage and are important to your sex drive. Let's take a closer look at each one.

ESTROGEN: IT FLIPS THE SWITCH FOR SEX DRIVE

Estrogen is the Marilyn Monroe in all of us. It is the hormone in the diaphanous dress, the chemical with the cleavage, the molecule with the glowing skin and ruby lips. It gives women their curves, their softness, their rounded breasts and moist inviting vaginas. When estrogen is in power, [women] signal, "Take me, I'm yours."

—From *The Alchemy of Love and Lust*, by Theresa L. Crenshaw, M.D.

If one hormone defines womanhood, it is estrogen. When a girl enters puberty, her breasts grow, her hips widen, the mucosa of her vagina thickens and starts to secrete lubricants, and a layer of body fat develops—all because of estrogen.

The production of estrogen is the responsibility of special cells in the ovaries, called granulosa cells. Ironically, the granulosa cells use a special enzyme to convert testosterone—usually thought of as the male hormone—into estrogen.

After directing the magical transformation of the female body during puberty, estrogen continues to play a major role in a woman's sexuality. The following two scenarios show how.

Debbie arrived home from work earlier than usual. She expected Ted to be home soon, too, and she wanted to be there to greet him. After all, he'd be turning 40 tomorrow. Perhaps they could celebrate tonight.

When Ted walked in, Debbie was searching for their favorite wine glasses. He seemed delighted that she was home and held her warmly for a bit longer than usual. Debbie wished she had picked up his birthday present early.

Ted suggested that they change into more comfortable clothes, lest they confuse the Chinese-takeout deliveryman by actually looking presentable for once. Debbie followed Ted upstairs to their bedroom, then walked into her closet. To her surprise, Ted was right behind her. She looked at him quizzically, and he laughed out loud. He wrapped his arms around her and kissed her neck. She could feel him harden as he pressed against her. She wanted him to make love to her.

Sara was getting ready for a dinner party—an elegant, formal affair. She moved slowly, almost seductively. Instead of showering, she had taken a bath infused with aromatic oils. She loved the way her skin felt afterward—warm, almost like silk to the touch. It glowed a pale golden color. Now she was ready to pick out her lingerie. She paged through her extensive collection of intimate apparel, another of her indulgences, before deciding on a beautiful pair of French-cut black lace panties. She laughed at the contradiction—the incredibly sexy underwear that she would be covering with the conservative velvet dress that she favored for these occasions. Sara loved the way the velvet felt, and the way the dress dipped down deep to expose her pale cleavage.

As she took the elevator to the lavishly furnished apartment that overlooked the lake, Sara felt a tingling sensation in her skin. In a few moments, she'd be walking into a room full of good-looking men, all of them wanting her. She relished the power over them that she effortlessly maintained.

Looking around the room, Sara spotted a man staring out the window. He was handsome, though his hair was too long and his bow tie was escaping from his collar. Sara immediately knew whom she intended to seduce.

On her way to introduce herself, she stopped for a glass of wine. From the first sip, her mouth came alive with fruit and the warmth of alcohol—another wonderful sensual experience. And the night had hardly begun.

Sara coyly slid next to the stranger, and the two stood silently for a few moments. Then she caught him looking up and down her body from the corner of his eye. "Beautiful view," he finally stammered. "A perfect night for a boat ride," she replied, keeping him off guard. "I suppose it would be quite cold," he thought aloud. "I'm sure we could find a way to keep warm," she teased.

Both Debbie and Sara are under the strong influence of estrogen. Yet they behave very differently.

Dr. Crenshaw would categorize Debbie's sex drive as receptive. Although she wants to make love, she won't initiate it. She is neither aggressive nor seductive. Through her body language and behavior, and through chemicals in her sweat known as pheromones, she sends the message that she is available and willing if Ted is.

Debbie wants to feel close to her husband, to touch and be touched. She wants to be penetrated, because when Ted is inside of her, she feels as though they are one person. Of course, she wants to enjoy sex, but achieving orgasm is not her main goal.

Sara, on the other hand, is not at all passive about her desire for sex. In Dr. Crenshaw's terms, Sara's sex drive is seductive. She wants physical intimacy, but unlike Debbie, she is going to turn on all her charms to get it. She uses obvious signals to lure her potential partner. She shows him that she not only is available, she is ready for sex in bed—or on any available surface, for that matter.

Sara needs physical contact. It's like a hunger with her. During sex, she enjoys lots of foreplay—the more sensuous, the better. Like Debbie, Sara wants to enjoy sex. But the erotic touching is what she really craves.

If both women are under the strong influence of estrogen, what accounts for the variations in their sex drives? For them, as for all women, estrogen acts at the level of the hypothalamus. As we said before, the hypothalamus is responsible for the basic sex drive. Think of it as an on-off switch: "Do I want sex or not?" In the hypothalamus, estrogen and testosterone turn on sex drive, and progesterone turns it off.

To understand why Sara and Debbie behave so differently, we must look beyond the hypothalamus to the neocortex. Another set of hormones acts at the level of the neocortex to determine how a woman experiences her sex drive.

Debbie's receptive sex drive results from a relatively high level of the hormone serotonin in her neocortex. According to Dr. Crenshaw, serotonin "facilitates [a] calm, warm sociability that promotes continued intimacy." It also decreases anxiety and aggressiveness and increases relaxation. Thanks to the combination of high estrogen and relatively high serotonin, Debbie is open to sexual contact, though she won't actively pursue it.

Incidentally, we say "relatively high serotonin" because too much of the hormone actually depresses sexual desire. It can even inhibit orgasm. We will examine this effect in chapter 8, when we talk about the antidepressant drugs Prozac and Zoloft, which improve mood by increasing serotonin but severely blunt libido in the process.

By comparison, Sara's seductive sex drive can be traced to high levels of the hormones dopamine and oxytocin in her neocortex. Dopamine inspires and motivates the pursuit of pleasure. It provides an emotional high and positive reinforcement of pleasurable activities. Not surprisingly, excessive amounts of dopamine are responsible for almost all addictions. Whether someone is addicted to gambling, cocaine, chocolate, or sex, the common denominator is that the person gets a dopamine rush when she engages in that activity.

Also not surprisingly, too little dopamine can contribute to mild depression. People who run low on the hormone may be apathetic even toward activities they once enjoyed. Because of dopamine, we are able to anticipate and pursue pleasure. Without it, we won't seek out gratifying experiences such as sex.

Oxytocin—dopamine's partner in shaping Sara's seductive sex drive—is secreted by the pituitary gland in response to a stimulus from the hypothalamus. Oxytocin increases sensitivity to touch and allows pleasure in being touched. It also encourages the pursuit of activities that involve touch, such as sex and grooming. In Sara's case, oxytocin makes her want physical contact, and dopamine makes that contact feel pleasurable.

Oxytocin is released in pulses during orgasm, causing the rhythmic contractions of the uterus that you may feel as you climax. Oxytocin also is released during breastfeeding, triggering the discharge of milk and reinforcing the loving bond between mother and child. Many new moms are uncomfortable admitting that they occasionally become sexually aroused while nursing. But it is more common than they realize and certainly nothing to be ashamed of. It is a natural response to a wonderful hormone that encourages them to seek and enjoy physical contact.

For Sara, the high levels of estrogen, dopamine, and oxytocin in her brain make her feel desirable and voluptuous. This specific mix of hormones gives her the necessary confidence to be overtly sexual and seductive. Of course, it also makes even strong-willed men weak in the knees when they are around her.

PROGESTERONE: ESSENTIAL TO REPRODUCTION— BUT AT A PRICE

Susan felt miserable. She had endured a terrible day at work. She couldn't concentrate on anything, and she had made some stupid mistakes. After her boss flew into a tirade, she went into the bathroom and cried. She hated herself for doing it, but she was just so emotional.

By the time she got home, even the feeling of her clothes against her skin was bugging her. And she craved a pint of Ben & Jerry's.

Her boyfriend, Mitch, was annoying her, too. He kept asking her to go out and "have some fun." And if he wasn't asking her to go out, he was pressuring her to have sex. She would rather be tortured than have sex tonight. "Why doesn't everyone just leave me alone?" she thought.

The hormone progesterone is produced by the ovaries. It is responsible for regulating a woman's menstrual cycle when she isn't pregnant and for supporting her pregnancy if she conceives.

Though progesterone plays a crucial role in a woman's reproductive ability, it also is behind some common "female" unpleasantries. For starters, it interferes with sex drive by depleting levels of testosterone and dopamine and by reducing sensitivity to oxytocin. What's more, it promotes weight gain and water retention and aggravates PMS (premenstrual syndrome). It can have a profound impact on mood by causing emotional instability, irritability, and depression.

This raises the question: If progesterone is so awful, why do women need it in the first place? As mentioned above, the hormone is essential during pregnancy. It maintains the lining of the uterus so that an embryo can implant after fertilization. It also slows the contraction of the smooth muscle in the uterus, preventing the expulsion of the embryo. (Unfortunately, this slowing also affects the smooth muscle in the intestines, which is why moms-to-be are prone to morning sickness.)

Postpartum, progesterone has another important task: It acts on the neocortex to increase prolactin, the hormone responsible for milk production during breastfeeding. The combination of high progesterone, high prolactin, and high oxytocin fosters nurturing and protective behaviors in women after childbirth. It encourages new moms to bond with, protect, and nurse their newborns.

Prolactin, however, is an antagonist to dopamine. Most hormones have at least one antagonist—in other words, a hormone that produces the opposite effect. This is your body's way of maintaining balance. Think of it as a seesaw: When one hormone is up, the other is down, and vice versa. In this case, high prolactin is responsible for low dopamine, which may lead to postpartum blues and depression.

Similarly, progesterone acts as an antagonist to estrogen during the postpartum period. This is a major reason that—even after the pain of childbirth has faded, her vagina has healed, and her baby is sleeping straight through the night—a new mom still will not want sex. It is simple: *You are not going to have a strong sex drive if you're short on dopamine and estrogen.* The longer you breastfeed, the longer your prolactin and progesterone stay high, and the longer your dopamine and estrogen stay low.

Please don't get us wrong. We are strong proponents of breastfeeding; it is the healthiest way to feed your baby. We just want you to be aware that while you breastfeed, you won't be very interested in sex. And that's perfectly normal. (We will address this issue in more depth in chapter 20.)

TESTOSTERONE: NOT JUST FOR MEN

Jamie needed to blow off some steam. She had spent the better part of 2 months holed up in the library, studying 12 or more hours each day for her bar exam. So she decided that she would fly to Aspen to visit her younger cousin, Kim, who worked as a ski instructor in the winter and a windsurfing instructor in the summer.

Jamie was waiting for her bags at the airport when Kim walked up to greet her. "You must be exhausted," Kim said. "Let's go home, so you can get some rest."

"To hell with that," Jamie replied. "I'm here to party and to get to know some of your sexy ski instructor friends. Let's go to the hottest place in town."

The pair ended up at Jack's Barn, a nondescript bar popular with the locals. After one or two drinks, Jamie was out on the dance floor grinding to the music. Soon she was drinking stomach shooters off the flat abs of Jody, a friend of Kim's. When Jody invited Jamie to join him in the hot tub, she didn't hesitate to take off her clothes and climb in.

The two of them ended the night in bed together. Jamie was on top of Jody, and she was being very vocal. She had one goal: orgasm. Jody would get her there.

Although we tend to think of testosterone as mainly affecting men, it plays an important role for women, especially for their sex drives. Testosterone begins to exert its influence on the female body during the phase of puberty known as adrenarche. This is when the adrenal glands, which lie on top of the kidneys, release hormones that are similar to, but weaker than, testosterone. These hormones cause young girls—who were "made of sugar and spice and everything nice"—to grow pubic and underarm hair, to sweat, and to develop body odor.

Later in puberty, and for the next 40 years, the pituitary gland—under direction from the hypothalamus—releases follicle-stimulating hormone and luteinizing hormone. They direct the ovaries to convert cholesterol into testosterone, the majority of which then changes to estrogen. But about 25 percent of the testosterone stays as is. This "leftover" hormone has a profound impact on women and their sex drives.

Testosterone is responsible for sexual assertiveness. It stimulates the need for orgasm as well as the urge to masturbate. It causes the nerves in the clitoris and nipples to become especially sensitive.

Testosterone influences nonsexual behavior as well. In moderate doses, it improves self-confidence and cognition, reduces depression, and creates a sense of vitality. But excessive amounts can cause destructive aggressiveness and interfere with cognition. After all, nobody in their right mind would say that a teenage boy going through puberty is "thinking clearly."

In women, a decline in the sensitivity of the clitoris and nipples and a diminished interest in masturbation may be the first signs of testosterone deficiency. Later manifestations include the loss of vital energy, an inability to focus or to think clearly, and an overall passivity about life.

Of course, other hormones can influence the sexual assertiveness that comes from elevated testosterone. For example, a woman who has high dopamine and high oxytocin to accompany her higher testosterone is more likely to try to quench her sexual thirst through a sexual encounter, whereas a woman who has lower oxytocin is more apt to masturbate to relieve sexual tension.

Getting the Upper Hand on Your Hormones

As you have seen from the examples in this chapter, hormones profoundly affect your behavior and your sex drive. Moreover, the complex interplay of various hormones is largely responsible for your wanting or rejecting sex.

This isn't to imply that your sexual behavior is completely at the mercy of your hormone levels. It still involves conscious decision-making on your part. You may feel a strong sense of sexual desire and choose not to act on it. Or you may choose to have sex even though you aren't especially interested in it.

Of course, you also can override your natural hormone-driven sexual tendencies by altering levels of certain hormones. At the Sexual Wellness Center, we often advise women with low libido to take steps to replenish their dopamine and testosterone. Without adequate amounts of these two hormones, you're unlikely to recover your sex drive, no matter what else you may try. The next two chapters will outline your options for determining whether you're running low on dopamine or testosterone, and how to boost your supply of each hormone.

CHAPTER 7

TESTOSTERONE FOR YOUR SEX DRIVE

- Testosterone is the dominant hormone in the female body, surpassing even estrogen. A shortage of testosterone is a common factor in low libido.
- Other androgens indirectly affect sex drive by providing the raw material from which your body can manufacture testosterone.
- Certain medical conditions, medications, and surgical procedures—especially an oophorectomy, or removal of the ovaries—can deplete your supply of testosterone.
- The best way to find out if you have an androgen deficiency is to check the amount of free testosterone—the active form of the hormone—in your blood.
- Some forms of androgen supplementation work better than others and cause fewer side effects.

Testosterone belongs to the family of hormones known as androgens. Although they are often called male hormones, that is a complete misnomer. True, men have significantly more testosterone than women do. But women have 10 times more testosterone than estrogen.

In fact, almost all the estrogen in the female body starts out as testosterone. An enzyme called aromatase converts the testosterone in the ovaries to estrogen.

Besides testosterone, the androgens include dehydroepiandrosterone sulphate (DHEAS), dehydroepiandrosterone (DHEA), androstenedione, and dihydrotestosterone (DHT). Only DHT and testosterone are biologically active. In other words, they can bind to the androgen receptors in cells to produce a particular effect, such as increased sex drive or muscle mass. DHEAS, DHEA, and androstenedione are more like prehormones, in that they must be converted to testosterone to be biologically active. Otherwise, they don't fit the androgen receptors.

Yet these three hormones are no less important than the rest of the androgens. DHEAS and DHEA, for example, serve as the body's testosterone reservoir. If they run low, a testosterone shortage will develop. Conversely, if DHEAS and DHEA rise, testosterone will follow suit.

DHEAS and DHEA are manufactured in the adrenal glands, which lie on top of the kidneys, and are secreted into the blood. Once there, the hormones travel to all the major organs, where they can be converted to testosterone. Though the majority of a woman's testosterone is made in the ovaries, some of it comes from the adrenal glands as well as from the conversion of DHEAS and DHEA in other bodily tissues.

We need to discuss just one more piece of the testosterone puzzle so you have a complete picture of how the hormone works in your body. A good amount of testosterone binds to a protein called sex hormone binding globulin (SHBG). When this happens, the testosterone becomes biologically inactive. The active form of the hormone, called unbound or free testosterone, accounts for only a small percentage—approximately 2 percent—of all the testosterone in your body. As we will discuss later, measuring your free testosterone level is the most accurate way to determine whether your low libido has a hormonal cause.

Why Androgens Run Low

Now that you have an understanding of androgens, let's talk about androgen deficiency. As we mentioned earlier, DHEAS and DHEA are manufactured by the adrenal glands. In women, DHEAS and DHEA production peaks in the midteens, then begins a lifelong decline. By the time a woman reaches her forties, her DHEAS level is only 60 percent of what it once was. From there, it continues to drop at a rate of about 5 percent a year. A 70-year-old woman has only about 20 percent of the DHEAS that she had when she was younger.

Likewise, testosterone peaks when women are in their midtwenties and declines steadily thereafter. A woman in her forties has only half as much circulating testosterone as she had in her twenties. Although levels of the hormone continue to drop throughout a woman's life, menopause does not speed up the process. The same cannot be said for estrogen, which falls precipitously during menopause.

Because a woman's androgen supply dwindles with age, it makes sense that her libido might lose some steam, too. This may be natural, but it isn't necessarily desirable—or healthy. Though the sexual changes tend to occur gradually, they can be emotionally damaging in the long run.

REASON TO RETHINK OOPHORECTOMY

Maria is a 46-year-old surgical recovery-room nurse at a world-renowned medical center. When she started having heavy, long, irregular periods, she knew that she could ask for advice from the dozen or so gynecologists she had met in the operative suite. Maria chose the best surgeon of the bunch. He suggested a vaginal hysterectomy. "After all," he joked, "to cut is to cure."

Maria was familiar with the procedure; she had taken care of dozens of women who had undergone the same surgery. As she was so sick of her periods, she quickly agreed. "Can we do it tomorrow?" she asked.

Her gynecologist also offered to remove her ovaries as a prophylactic measure to prevent ovarian cancer. "You may as well," Maria replied. "I'm finished with them."

The operation was successful. Maria went home the next day and was back to work in 3 weeks. Little did she realize that her sex life would never be the same.

Besides aging, a woman's androgen levels can decline because of certain medical conditions, medications, and surgical procedures. The most common procedure that reduces both testosterone and estrogen is an oophorectomy, or removal of the ovaries. Gynecologists often perform oophorectomies to treat benign ovarian cysts. Or they may take the ovaries out if they remove the uterus. This procedure, called a hysterectomy, is the second most common medical operation among reproductive-age women. The usual justification for removing healthy ovaries during a hysterectomy is that it may prevent ovarian cancer.

Unfortunately, too many women don't realize that an oophorectomy amounts to surgical castration. Urologists are much less likely to remove a man's testes to treat benign growths or as a preventive measure. So why have oophorectomies become so routine? We suspect that many gynecologists simply ignore their clients' sexuality, or they're unfamiliar with the importance of testosterone to the female libido.

Sometimes an oophorectomy is necessary. Still, we believe that before any woman agrees to this procedure, she should discuss all the alternatives with her physician and opt to preserve her ovaries, if possible. Removal of both ovaries causes an immediate 50 percent reduction in circulating testosterone, with a more than 80 percent reduction in circulating estrogen. The abrupt drop in both hormones may profoundly affect not only a woman's libido but also other aspects of her health.

The Maryland Women's Health Study, which surveyed more than 1,000 women before and after their hysterectomies, showed that those who had undergone concurrent oophorectomies were two-thirds less likely to experience orgasm 12 months after the procedure. In another retrospective study of 100 women, those whose ovaries were removed during their hysterectomies reported more anxiety and depression, reduced psychological well-being, and diminished sex drive as compared with those who kept their ovaries.

A third study, recently published in the medical journal *Menopause*, found that women who underwent oophorectomies experienced a global decline in their sexual function. This included a reduction in sexual thoughts and desires, diminished arousal, decreased frequency of intercourse, fewer orgasms, and less satisfaction with their intimate relationships.

We should point out that the precipitous drop in testosterone that accompanies an oophorectomy does not undermine libido in all women. Why might this be so?

As we explained in chapter 6, testosterone, estrogen, and dopamine affect libido in different ways. A woman whose sex drive is more testosterone dependent may enjoy sex because of the intense physical pleasure that it provides. For a woman whose sex drive is more estrogen dependent, the main motivation for sex could be the emotional bond that she feels with her partner. A woman whose sex drive is more dopamine dependent likely is drawn to the "psychological high" that she gets from sex. In the latter two cases, even a large drop in testosterone may not cause a significant decline in libido.

Of course, most women do not fit neatly into one of these

three categories. So a drop in testosterone may not diminish their libidos as much as change their experience of sex. In fact, most women find that as they mature and their androgen levels naturally decline, they are less focused on physical pleasure and orgasm. Instead, they perceive more value in the emotional aspects of making love to their partners.

A SIDE EFFECT OF THE PILL

Jessie is a 36-year-old mother of two and a stand-up comic in the comedy clubs of New York City. This is her story in her own words.

"A few years after the birth of my second child, my periods started to get out of control. Every month for the week before my period, I would become severely moody. I alternated between laughing, crying, and screaming—sometimes in the same sentence.

"On the first day of my cycle, my cramps would be so bad, all I could do was crawl into bed with a heating pad on my stomach. I would get migraines. I was miserable.

"My gynecologist suggested birth control pills to smooth out my hormones. I had been on the Pill before—from the time I started college until I missed a couple of pills, had a few too many drinks, and got pregnant with my first child. I though it was a great idea.

"The Pill worked almost immediately. By my third pack of pills, I felt much better. But by my sixth pack, I felt neutered. No sex drive—none, nil, nada. I got more thrills from my electric toothbrush than from my vibrator.

"I ran back to my doctor. Something was wrong, very wrong. I begged her to fix me. She suggested that it might be the Pill. 'No way, it couldn't be the Pill,' I told her. 'I had been on the Pill in college, and I had a very healthy sex drive!' She changed my prescription anyway. Within a few months, my sex drive was back. Thank God!"

Many women are surprised to learn that birth control pills can have an adverse effect on their libidos. Taking oral contraceptives reduces free testosterone by increasing SHBG. The elevated SHBG does not change a woman's total testosterone, but it decreases the amount that's biologically active.

Incidentally, this is why oral contraceptives have been approved for the treatment of moderate acne. A reduction in free testosterone will help prevent breakouts because free testosterone and DHT are partially responsible for sebum secretions by hair follicles on the surface of the skin. Sebum is an oily substance that bacteria thrive on. Less sebum means fewer bacteria, which in turn minimizes infection in the hair follicles. A woman is less likely to develop acne as a result.

So why doesn't every woman who takes birth control pills report a decline in libido? First, a woman's desire to have sex actually may increase when she is protected from unwanted pregnancy. Second, the drop in free testosterone may not be enough to alter the sex drive of a woman in her twenties, because she has a naturally high level of testosterone at that age. It would be a different story for a woman in her early forties, whose testosterone and DHEAS have dropped significantly. Taking birth control pills might push her free testosterone below the threshold necessary for a healthy libido. Third, as we mentioned before, libido isn't always testosterone dependent.

Incidentally, menopausal women on hormone replacement therapy also will experience a decline in free testosterone. Just like oral contraceptives, hormone replacement therapy increases SHBG, thereby reducing free testosterone.

Screening for Androgen Deficiency

Most physicians are not well-versed in androgens or androgen deficiency. If you want to check your levels of these hormones, you may need to ask for a test. You have several options, though some are more reliable than others.

As we discussed earlier, although total testosterone is important, free testosterone is the most clinically significant value. Unfortunately, measuring a woman's free testosterone is difficult. The tests currently offered by the major commercial laboratories in the United States were developed for men, because men have much higher levels of circulating testosterone. This means that what's considered "normal" for the tests is based on the testosterone levels of men, not women. Any test loses accuracy when measuring levels far beyond its normal range.

This becomes a more significant issue when you consider that free testosterone accounts for only about 2 percent of a woman's total testosterone. In other words, free testosterone is even further outside the normal range that the tests are designed to measure.

Most experts agree that the test most often recommended for women, the analog free-testosterone assay, is not especially reliable. Better tests exist, but often they're available only to women who are taking part in research studies. Still, with a little perseverance, you may be able to obtain a more accurate reading if you work with your doctor to send your blood sample to a specialty lab.

The best of the available tests are the equilibrium dialysis assay and the bioavailable testosterone assay. If you are unable to obtain either of these, your next choice should be the calculated free-testosterone method, also known as the free-androgen index or free-testosterone index. Actually, this is a combination of two tests—one for total testosterone, the other for SHBG. From these results, a lab technician can calculate your free testosterone index using the following equation: total testosterone $\times$ (100/SHBG).

Before scheduling a test of your free testosterone, we suggest that you consider three important issues. First, your physician may want to measure your salivary testosterone, because a saliva sample is easier—and less painful—than a blood sample. But most experts agree that salivary testosterone is not accurate enough to identify a testosterone deficiency. Second, some experts believe that a woman's testosterone production varies throughout the day, peaking in the morning. For this reason, we recommend that you schedule your test between 8 A.M. and noon. Third, you may want to ask your doctor to check your DHEAS and DHEA as well. Later in this chapter, we'll explain how you can raise your testosterone by taking supplemental DHEA.

What the Numbers Mean

Once you have the results of your test, you'll need to know how to interpret them. Before we explain our guidelines, we must acknowledge that few published studies have examined normal androgen levels in women. Because these data are lacking, we do not have a set level below which we automatically prescribe supplemental androgens.

The good news is that large-scale studies to determine normal androgen levels for women are under way. Until the results of these studies are available, we suspect androgen deficiency if we see a total testosterone reading of less than 25 nanograms per deciliter (ng/dl) in premenopausal women or less than 20 ng/dl in postmenopausal women. Free testosterone of less than 1.5 picograms per milliliter (pg/ml) in premenopausal women, or 1.0 pg/ml in postmenopausal women, is another red flag. So is a DHEAS reading of less than 150 ng/dl.

Of course, every woman is unique, even in terms of her androgen makeup. But in general, if a client's androgen levels are even slightly below what we consider normal, *and* she is showing other symptoms of androgen deficiency, we may try low-dose androgen supplementation to see if it helps her libido.

Bear in mind that many symptoms of androgen deficiency are nonspecific and could just as easily be linked to other medical problems. This is why we never recommend supplementation to a client until we have performed a thorough physical and psychological evaluation.

Your Options for Raising Androgens

If we diagnose androgen deficiency in a client, our next step is to review the treatment options with her. Many are available, but unfortunately, none of them is ideal. Scientists are working to develop a safer and more effective alternative. In the meantime, we have a couple of treatment protocols that we feel comfortable recommending, and several that we do not.

THINK TWICE ABOUT THESE TREATMENTS

On the pharmaceutical front, the FDA has given its blessing to only one androgen medication. It's a combination of estrogen and methyl testosterone, sold under the brand name Estratest. For decades, postmenopausal women have taken Estratest to get relief from recalcitrant hot flashes. The drug is not approved as a treatment for low libido, so its use for this purpose would be off-label.

The methyl testosterone in Estratest is a derivative of the hormone, rather than the natural form. We advise our clients to steer clear of methyl testosterone for several reasons. First, the hormone alters a woman's cholesterol profile by lowering her HDL, the "good" cholesterol that prevents heart disease, and raising her LDL, the "bad" cholesterol responsible for facilitating the artery damage that can lead to heart attack or stroke. Second, the tests mentioned earlier cannot measure methyl testosterone, so monitoring levels of the hormone is difficult. Third, research has shown that large doses of methyl testosterone can harm the liver.

In Europe and Australia, researchers have developed a method of implanting testosterone pellets under the skin. It requires a surgical procedure, which raises the risk of infection. In addition, the pellets last only a few months, which severely limits their convenience for general use. Currently, the FDA has not approved this treatment for women in the United States.

The intramuscular injection of testosterone esters is a well-established and widely accepted treatment for men. Now physicians are offering the injections to women, albeit with much smaller doses of the hormone. After an injection, the amount of testosterone in the blood remains high for a number of days. The huge downside is that it can climb well above the normal range for women, leading to side effects such as permanent clitoral enlargement, male pattern baldness, acne, and deepening of the voice.

THE BEST BETS FOR BOOSTING ANDROGENS

So now that we've identified which forms of androgen supplementation we don't like, you may be wondering which forms we *do* like. One is oral DHEA, which has been the focus of recent research. The idea is that if you increase a woman's supply of prehormones, her body will convert them to testosterone. Oral DHEA is available in health food stores, pharmacies, and supermarkets without a prescription.

We follow a protocol established by André Guay, M.D., at the Lahey Clinic in Boston, starting with 50 milligrams of DHEA each morning. In 2 months, you should check your levels of total and free testosterone. If your free testosterone is between 1.8 ng/ml and 2.2 ng/ml, you can stay at the current dosage. If the hormone is below 1.8 ng/ml, you should increase your dosage to 75 milligrams of DHEA a day. Continue checking your testosterone every 2 to 3 months. If necessary, you can take up to 100 milligrams of DHEA a day.

We have one very important caveat about using DHEA that you should be aware of. Because DHEA is classified as a nutritional supplement and not a medication, it is not subjected to FDA regulation. As you might imagine, product quality varies widely. In fact, a recent analysis of 17 different brands found that three brands actually contained *no* DHEA. Most had between 60 and 80 percent of the amount of DHEA listed on the label, but one exceeded its stated dosage by 149 percent.

For this reason, we recommend sticking with one brand of DHEA—we prefer Vitamin Shoppe or Natrol—and monitoring your free testosterone every 3 months, if not more often. We also recommend checking your cholesterol profile every 6 months and your liver function once a year. Most important, you *must* use effective birth control while on DHEA or any other form of androgen supplementation, as these hormones can harm a fetus.

Besides oral DHEA, we often prescribe a 0.2 percent testosterone gel or ointment (compounded in a penetrating base) to our clients with androgen deficiency. The advantage of this preparation, which can be made by a compounding pharmacist, is that it can be combined with estrogen (0.01 percent estradiol) and applied directly to the vulva and clitoris. Although no one has published research on this preparation, our clients who use it typically notice improvement in clitoral sensation and vaginal lubrication within about a month. It seems especially helpful after pelvic surgery.

Our regimen is an adaptation of one developed by Judith Reichman, M.D., a nationally known gynecologist who teaches and practices at Cedars-Sinai Medical Center and the University of California, Los Angeles. We recommend applying 1 gram of the hormone preparation every night for 4 weeks, then cutting back to twice a week. While using the preparation, you should check your total and free testosterone after the first 2 months, then every 3 months. As with oral DHEA, we suggest testing your cholesterol profile every 6 months and your liver function once a year.

As a side note, our Sexual Wellness Center is one of several dozen clinics around the world conducting a large-scale clinical trial for a testosterone patch designed especially for women. Smaller studies of the patch have produced promising results. We hope that it will be available to all women with androgen deficiency in a few years.

Hormones Aren't the Whole Picture

Liza met Cole on a beach in sunny southern California. She was an 18-year-old college coed. He was 24, a blond James Dean type—completely different from the yuppie wanna-be's that populated the campus at Southern Cal. He even drove a beat-up '67 mustang convertible. Though he was quiet and often sullen, Liza imagined that he had grand, exotic dreams.

Their relationship was not much more than sex on the beach or in the back of Cole's car. But after one memorable lovemaking session in front of a raging bonfire (and a few other amorous couples)—combined with the intoxicating effects of a few beers and a couple of joints—they drove all night to Las Vegas and got married.

Liza's vision of an exotic and adventurous life with Cole quickly began to fade. He made a few halfhearted attempts to land small acting parts in Hollywood, but he was easily discouraged. He spent more time on the beach drinking and hanging out with his buddies. Liza had to work two jobs to support the family, which grew to include twin girls.

Even though sex had been the foundation of their relationship, Liza noticed that she wasn't all that interested anymore. She mentioned her declining libido to her gynecologist, who diagnosed a low testosterone level after running some tests. Liza received a prescription for a testosterone cream to help restore her sex drive.

Ever the optimist, Liza believed that if their sex life improved, Cole might change his behavior—spending time at home rather than with his friends, becoming a more attentive father and husband, maybe even getting a job. Though she used the cream religiously, her libido did not improve.

Then Liza caught Cole having sex with another woman on the beach, only a few blocks from where she had met him 3 years before. Devastated by his betrayal, she realized that their marriage would never be what she had hoped for. She filed for divorce.

Did Liza lose interest in sex because of low testosterone? And shouldn't testosterone supplementation have helped her sex drive? In our opinion, the answer to both questions is no. Low testosterone was the *result* of Liza's poor marriage, not the cause of it.

From the beginning, Liza had mistaken Cole's dark, brooding nature for adventurous sophistication. In truth, it revealed a fundamental inability to communicate effectively and to form deep emotional attachments. Liza realized this subconsciously long before she acknowledged it consciously. This is why her sex drive waned long before she filed for divorce.

To understand the impact of all this on Liza's testosterone level, we must acknowledge the mind-body connection—that is, the interplay between our emotions and our physical health. Modern medicine long ignored this relationship, but compelling new research is changing many opinions. For example, one recent study found that women who are under stress are more susceptible to infections. Another confirmed that people who are depressed have a lower survival rate after a major illness.

Findings like these clearly illustrate how our minds can affect our bodies. This is another reason why we feel so strongly about conducting a thorough physical and psychological evaluation before we consider androgen supplementation—even if a client has low testosterone.

Supplementation to the Rescue

As we've said throughout this book, our experience has taught us that low libido generally results from a host of factors, not just a single problem like androgen deficiency. Still, we've seen androgen supplementation make a dramatic difference for many women. In some cases, it's all that's necessary to restore a healthy sex drive. That certainly was true for Carla, one of our clients.

Both Carla and Charles had been married before. Though neither of them had any intention of ever marrying again, they eventually moved in together and settled into a comfortable and loving partnership.

Carla and Charles admitted that their life was rather mundane. Still, they could say with all honesty that they felt content. They also agreed that their sex life was not nearly as tepid as other aspects of their relationship. In fact, Carla described sex with Charles as "explosive and hot." So both of them were surprised when her sex drive began to wane.

At first, Carla almost completely stopped masturbating. Even when sex had been plentiful, she had enjoyed the pleasures of self-stimulation. Over time, she initiated sex less frequently. And if Charles made advances, Carla often would perform oral sex instead of having intercourse.

Because the changes happened so gradually, and because Carla found other ways to be intimate with Charles, her diminished libido never became an issue. Then one day, she found a videotape of the two of them making love. They had made the tape a few months after moving in together.

Carla sat on her bed sobbing as she watched the video over and over. She realized how far she had fallen from her sexual prime. And at that very moment, she resolved to become that sexy woman again—no matter what it took.

First, she needed to figure out what had happened to her sex drive, which had been so strong for so long. She found some health references at the local library, but they weren't very helpful. Then she tried the Internet. Searching on the words "decreased libido," she came across our Web site at www.sexualwellnesscenter.com. Even though our clinic was 400 miles away, she couldn't make an appointment soon enough.

After performing a thorough medical evaluation, I (Dr. Goldstein) concluded that Carla's low libido had resulted from an androgen deficiency. Her free testosterone, measured by an equilibrium dialysis assay, was 0.3 pg/ml; her DHEAS was 77 ng/dl. As she was not taking any medications and had no underlying medical conditions, I suspected that the decline in her hormone levels was age-related.

I prescribed a compounded testosterone-estrogen gel, which Carla began using right away. Within a few weeks, she noticed an improvement. She even dreamed about sex, something she hadn't done in several years.

When we checked Carla's free testosterone 2 months into her treatment, it measured 0.7 pg/ml—an increase of more than 100 percent. As Carla lived about 8 hours from the Sexual Wellness Center, her regular gynecologist continued to monitor her free testosterone every 3 months. It stabilized at around 1 pg/ml.

Carla did not experience any adverse effects from the hormone supplementation. Her cholesterol profile and liver function remained healthy. This is exactly what we expected, as her free testosterone was well within the normal range.

A year and a half later, I received an invitation to a book signing for Charles's latest work. Attached to the invitation was a handwritten note: "Charles took much longer to write this than usual. We had forgotten how much time we used to spend in bed (wink, wink). This was an accommodation he was all too happy to make. Thank you so very much!"

CHAPTER 8

BOOSTING DOPAMINE FOR BETTER LIBIDO

- Running low on dopamine impedes sex drive by dampening the anticipation of a sexual encounter.
- Breastfeeding and sleep deprivation are key risk factors for a dopamine shortfall—which is why many new moms aren't interested in sex.
- Regular physical activity helps replenish dopamine, as do certain medications.

It was an unseasonably warm day in June, with the temperature hovering in the high 80s. Sandy thought it might be cooler by the waterfront. So when she finished breastfeeding her 7-month-old daughter, Haley, she put the baby into the stroller and headed down to the water.

As Haley slept, Sandy sat on a bench, letting the gentle breeze sweep over her body and watching the sailboats and jet skis go by. It seemed like a metaphor for how she had been feeling lately.

Ever since she'd had the baby, Sandy was nothing more than a spectator in her own life. She hadn't gone out with friends, or her sister, in weeks. She couldn't remember the last time she enjoyed a good laugh or was really excited about anything.

Despite her mood, Sandy convinced herself that she wasn't suffering from depression. After all, she wasn't weepy, and she hadn't lost

her appetite. Sometimes she enjoyed sex when her husband, Kevin, ini-
tiated it.

After more than an hour lost in thought, Sandy decided to head
home. As she and Haley passed in front of the local ice cream parlor, she
heard a voice call out, "Sandy, you stranger! Where have you been?" It
was Julie, her neighbor. "Come in and join me for some ice cream. I just
ordered a sundae, and I can't eat it all."

"No thanks, Jules," Sandy found herself saying. "Kevin will be
home soon."

Sandy continued up the hill to their apartment, contemplating the
excuse she had just given. Sandy wasn't surprised that she hadn't wanted
to hang out with Julie, whom she found too self-centered. What did sur-
prise her was that she had turned down ice cream. She never turned down
ice cream! Sandy didn't know why, but that day, she just wasn't interested.

Judging by Sandy's story, she is not suffering from severe depression. The classic symptoms—feelings of hopelessness and anxiety, changes in sleep patterns, a desire to self-inflict harm—result
from a deficiency in the neurotransmitter serotonin. (You'll find an
in-depth discussion of various forms of depression a bit later in the
book, in chapter 12. For now, if you are experiencing the symptoms
described above, please seek help from a physician or mental health
professional as soon as possible.)

Instead, Sandy has mild depression, brought on by a deficiency in dopamine. This neurotransmitter is responsible for anticipatory drive—that is, the pursuit of pleasure. Clearly, Sandy isn't
interested in pleasure. She doesn't think about what would be fun
or feel good. She can't see that if she'd go out with her friends or
sister, she might have a good time. She even passes up ice cream,
something she relished in the past.

Surely, Sandy doesn't have much of a sex drive, either—even
though she enjoys sex when her husband initiates it. What we call

sex drive or libido is, after all, a specific kind of anticipatory drive. If Sandy doesn't look forward to sex, of course she won't want it.

Risk Factors for Low Dopamine

What causes dopamine deficiency? Doctors can't always pinpoint the cause. But in Sandy's case, she has two major risk factors: breast-feeding and chronic sleep deprivation that started with the birth of her daughter.

As mentioned in chapter 6, breastfeeding increases production of the hormone prolactin. Levels of prolactin and dopamine are inversely proportional. That is, when prolactin is high, dopamine is low, and vice versa. Dopamine may not return to normal for several months after a new mom stops breastfeeding.

As for sleep deprivation, it has a profound effect on the biochemistry of the brain. Altered sleep patterns, such as those that follow childbirth, not only reduce dopamine but change the levels of almost all neurotransmitters. In fact, in women with a prior history of depression, one of the most significant risk factors for a recurrence is sleep deprivation.

Can your doctor measure your dopamine level to see if you're running low? Not easily. Researchers have studied dopamine using positron-emission tomography (PET) scanners and radioactive labeling, but generally, these diagnostic techniques are not available outside of a laboratory setting. You and your doctor must rely on symptoms of diminished anticipatory drive to identify a dopamine deficiency.

Replenish Your Supply with Exercise

For the fifth time in 7 years, Janet made a New Year's resolution to join a gym and lose some weight. This time, however, she seemed to get over the hump. She continued her workouts well past mid-February, when she had given up before.

By mid-May, Janet was 10 pounds lighter and much firmer. She felt comfortable parading around the gym in her Lycra shorts and sports bra. She drew plenty of leering glances from the hard-bodied regulars, but she didn't mind. In fact, she enjoyed it.

Janet felt better outside the gym as well. She showed more confidence at work. Her concentration improved, and she wasn't as restless as before. Her relationship with Brian, her semiserious boyfriend, also heated up. Their sex life burned with a new fire.

Janet always had been a willing participant in bed. She enjoyed sex, and more often than not, she experienced an orgasm. But recently, she noticed that she was thinking about sex more. She had frequent sexual fantasies, and she didn't hesitate to initiate sex with Brian. "I can't remember when I felt so . . . so horny," she confided to her best friend, Lauren.

If you suspect that you may be running low on dopamine, how might you go about increasing the hormone? In Janet's case, she stumbled onto one of the most effective treatments: exercise. Regular physical activity stimulates production of dopamine as well as other hormones called endorphins. They are responsible for the "high" that comes after physical exertion.

Of course, exercise has other benefits that improve the quality of your life both inside and outside the bedroom. It can enhance your fitness level, muscle tone, and stamina, all of which can pay dividends for your sex life. If you are overweight, it can help melt away the extra pounds and possibly improve your body image. (We discussed this in much greater detail in chapter 4.)

Help from the Medicine Chest

If exercise by itself doesn't do the trick, your doctor may prescribe one of several medications to increase dopamine. The most common of these is Wellbutrin (bupropion), a dopamine reuptake inhibitor approved for the treatment of depression.

Several studies have shown that Wellbutrin improves libido and orgasmic potential both in depressed and in nondepressed women. In addition, the drug appears to reverse the negative sexual side effects of SSRI antidepressants such as Paxil (paroxetine), Prozac (fluoxetine), Zoloft (sertraline), and Celexa (citalopram). Up to 75 percent of women who take SSRIs report a decline in libido, and 35 percent either have great difficulty achieving orgasm or don't climax at all. If a woman who is suffering from SSRI-induced sexual dysfunction adds Wellbutrin to her treatment regimen, she likely will regain her libido, as well as her ability to experience orgasm. She also may notice improvement in her energy level and motivational drive, both of which can be blunted by an SSRI.

Two new dopamine-like medications—Dostinex (cabergoline) and Uprima (apomorphine)—have shown great promise in treating low libido. In a study published in the *International Journal of Impotence Research*, researchers gave Dostinex to 60 healthy men. Before taking the medication, the men needed 19 minutes, on average, to regain an erection after ejaculation. With Dostinex, they were able to climax several times within a few minutes.

Usually, the amount of the hormone prolactin in the brain rises after orgasm. This acts as a negative feedback mechanism, inhibiting intercourse for a while. Dostinex prevents the increase in prolactin, thereby allowing the men in the study to quickly regain their libidos and experience multiple orgasms in rapid succession. Even better, the drug produced no noticeable side effects. This research supports the theory about dopamine steering sex drive and orgasm.

Researchers are in the process of testing Dostinex in women to see if it has the same benefits for libido and orgasm. In the meantime, it has been approved by the FDA for the treatment of Parkinson's disease, a neurological disorder caused by a deficiency of dopamine-producing neurons in the part of the brain that controls movement.

Uprima also increases dopamine. It has been approved in several European countries for the treatment of male erectile dysfunction. Uprima is different from most medications because it comes in sublingual tablet form. In other words, the tablet is placed under the tongue, where it quickly dissolves and gets absorbed into the bloodstream. This delivery system speeds the effects of Uprima, allowing men to achieve erections in less than 20 minutes. (By comparison, Viagra may take up to 90 minutes to produce results.)

Uprima had been under FDA review, but the manufacturer, TAP Pharmaceuticals, retracted its application for approval because clinical trials showed two significant side effects: Up to 20 percent of men taking Uprima experienced nausea, and 0.6 percent reported fainting—neither of which can be good for sex drive! The manufacturer is working to modify the drug's formulation to help limit these side effects. Research focusing on women also is under way.

For the sake of completeness, we should mention Sinemet (carbidopa/levodopa), another medication that's prescribed for Parkinson's disease. Once ingested, Sinemet is converted into dopamine. It has been shown to increase libido in Parkinson's patients. Unfortunately, it can cause significant side effects, including low blood pressure, cardiac arrhythmias, severe nausea, and vomiting. These limit its potential use in treating low libido.

Before we wrap up our discussion of medications that can elevate dopamine, we must acknowledge that none of these pharmaceuticals has received FDA approval specifically for the treatment of low libido in women. For this reason, we recommend trying them only under the close supervision of a health care provider who's familiar with them as well as their potential side effects.

CHAPTER 9

APHRODISIACS FROM MEDICINE AND NATURE

- For centuries, cultures throughout the world have attached potent sexual powers to an array of natural substances.
- Modern medical research is attempting to formulate a pharmaceutical aphrodisiac, but with mixed results to date.
- Many herbs contain compounds that can enhance sexual desire and performance. But like conventional medications, they must be used with care.

April is a daughter of the sixties. As a young woman during that tumultuous decade, she made "sex, drugs, and rock 'n' roll" a motto for her life. Actually, although she experimented with some of the psychedelia popular at the time, she was much more into the music and free love. She proudly attended at least one concert on every Rolling Stones tour beginning in 1968. She even partied with the Grateful Dead's Jerry Garcia near Haight and Ashbury Streets in San Francisco.

After a few years of drifting in and out of college, April realized that she lacked the financial means to continue supporting her lifestyle. She had to find work. But she could not imagine being stuck in the suffocating confines of an office. Instead, she took a position that would satisfy her wanderlust: She became a flight attendant. She always wanted to explore the world; now she had the opportunity.

Other than the piggish behavior of an occasional drunk passenger, April loved her job. And like the sailors of times past, she had a lover in every port—Hong Kong, Greece, Nairobi, Ecuador, and Marrakech.

Through her many years of travel, April developed two hobbies. Despite never wanting to settle down and raise a family of her own, she was fascinated with fertility symbols. She collected dozens of them: statues from Africa, amulets from Asia, necklaces from South America. Her second hobby, which she put to more personal use, was finding the perfect aphrodisiac.

Over the years, April tried dozens of herbal teas, powders, and creams—all promising to enhance her already strong libido and sexual response. Some of them were stimulating, others did next to nothing, and still others caused nausea, vomiting, and diarrhea. To this day, she hasn't given up her search for the ideal "love potion."

Every culture—civilized or primitive, rich or poor, modern or ancient—has searched for the perfect aphrodisiac. The word *aphrodisiac* comes from Aphrodite, who happened to be the Greek goddess of love. Aphrodisiacs are substances that stimulate sexual desire, heighten sexual awareness, or improve sexual function.

Through the centuries of their existence, aphrodisiacs have gone from being the stuff of folklore to the subject of medical research. Thanks to technological advances, scientists can test whether certain substances have any real effect on human sexuality. Guess what? Some of these "love potions" really work.

Until relatively recently, the vast majority of aphrodisiacs came straight from nature, as herbs were the sexual elixirs of choice. Now pharmaceutical labs are attempting to isolate the compounds in herbs that can enhance our sexual experiences or fix our sexual problems. A company could make millions, if not billions, if it successfully synthesizes these compounds into pill form—an aphrodisiac in a bottle.

In this chapter, we'll take a closer look at a selection of sexual "remedies" from conventional and herbal medicine. All promise to reinvigorate your libido—and improve your sex life in general. But as you'll see, some support this claim better than others do.

Drugs That Work, Drugs That Don't

To be honest, most women who come to see us at the Sexual Wellness Center are hoping for a pill to solve their sexual problems. As we explain to them, and as we stress throughout this book, low libido is much more complex than that. Though medication may help, it seldom is a cure-all. Until any underlying emotional, intellectual, or spiritual issues are addressed, libido most likely won't bounce back.

With this in mind, let's explore the aphrodisiac offerings from the pharmaceutical front. We'll start with the medication that helped launch a sexual revolution all its own: Viagra (sildenafil).

VIAGRA: PROMISING, BUT NO MIRACLE CURE

It was Friday afternoon, and Mindy was looking forward to the weekend. Her 16-year-old daughter, Samantha, had just left for a school band trip and wouldn't be back until Sunday night. With dinner already made, Mindy relaxed with a glass of chardonnay.

To pass the time until her husband, Steve, came home from work, she decided to tidy up their bedroom closet. Hidden under a pile of old T-shirts, she found Steve's prescription bottle filled with Viagra. About a year before, he had developed a problem maintaining an erection—a side effect of the Paxil that his doctor had prescribed in the aftermath of his father's death. He stayed on Paxil for almost 6 months. But once his doctor said that he could discontinue treatment, he did. His erections returned to normal soon after.

Mindy was feeling playful. "What's good for the gander may be good for the goose," she thought as she held the bottle. "Wouldn't this make for an interesting evening when Steve gets here?"

You may be wondering why we haven't mentioned the infamous drug Viagra before this. When we first began planning our book, we were following at least a dozen clinical trials involving pharmaceuticals that we hoped would solve many of the problems that women routinely encounter in their sex lives. Unfortunately, the results of these studies have largely been disappointing. This is especially true in the case of Viagra.

Viagra was the first in a class of drugs called phosphodiesterace 5 (PDE5) inhibitors. The PDE5 inhibitors increase blood flow to the vagina and clitoris by raising the concentration of nitric oxide, a very potent chemical that causes relaxation and dilatation of blood vessels. In fact, nitric oxide is so important that in 1998 the Nobel Prize was awarded to the three American pharmacologists who discovered the chemical's role in regulating blood flow.

We fully expected Viagra to help treat the most common sexual complaint among women (and the focus of this book): low libido. Unfortunately, the drug—which has become extraordinarily important for treating male sexual dysfunction (specifically erectile dysfunction)—does not improve a woman's sex drive. It does, however, play a limited role in treating two other "female" sexual complaints.

One of these conditions, called female sexual arousal disorder (FSAD), is analogous to male erectile dysfunction. Doctors define FSAD as a persistent or recurring inability to attain, or maintain, sufficient sexual excitement. It is associated with the same health problems that can cause male erectile dysfunction: diabetes, hypertension (high blood pressure), and high cholesterol. It also can occur after pelvic surgery. All these result in decreased blood flow to the vagina and clitoris. This leads to reduced vaginal lubrication, diminished vaginal and clitoral sensitivity, difficulty climaxing or inability to achieve orgasm, and less intense orgasms.

In studies, Viagra has improved the quantity and quality of orgasms in women with FSAD. It also can significantly improve the quality of their sexual response. And although scientists have not studied Viagra in women with "normal" sex lives, many women like Mindy have experienced more-intense orgasms after trying their partners' pills. (For your own safety, you should never take any kind of prescription pharmaceutical—especially someone else's—without first consulting your doctor.)

Viagra also has proven effective in helping women with impaired sexual response, a common side effect of SSRI antidepressants. As we mentioned in chapter 8, more than one-third of women who take SSRIs either cannot climax or have trouble doing so. For the vast majority of these women, Viagra—or either of the two new PDE5 inhibitors, Levitra (vardenafil) and Cialis (tadalafil)—can restore orgasm. Unfortunately, it does not enhance the desire for sex.

OVER-THE-COUNTER LIBIDO ENHANCERS

Kelly was surfing the Internet when, for what seemed like the millionth time, a pop-up ad came on the screen. Usually, Kelly would close the ads without giving them a thought. This one, however, grabbed her attention. It was for a product called Viacreme. The ad promised better orgasms and a stronger libido.

"What the heck," Kelly thought to herself. "I spend a ton of money at Victoria's Secret to turn Jed on. Why not get something to turn me on?" A few mouse clicks later, Kelly hoped she was on her way to a whole new world of sexual pleasure.

You probably have noticed the recent explosion in both topical and oral over-the-counter products that promise to fire up sexual response in women. Almost everyone who gets e-mail has seen the ads for products such as Viacreme, Dr. K's Dream Cream, Please Her V-gel, and ArginMax. All have one thing in common: Their active ingredient is L-arginine, a naturally occurring amino acid that is a precursor to nitric oxide.

All of these products promise a more satisfying sexual experience because they contain L-arginine. But with the exception of ArginMax, such claims have not been substantiated by controlled medical studies.

TREATMENTS ON THE HORIZON

We want to mention a few other medications that one day may be prescribed for low libido in women. Two different drug companies are investigating alprostadil, a powerful blood vessel dilator, as a treatment for FSAD. Clinical trials have shown that when women apply alprostadil to the clitoris and vagina, the majority report increased vaginal warmth, tingling, and lubrication.

The oral medications phentolamine and Melanotan also may help in cases of FSAD. The injectable form of phentolamine already has earned FDA approval as a treatment for erectile dysfunction in men. It works by dilating blood vessels, just like alprostadil. Melanotan was intended to be a sunless tanning agent, until researchers discovered that it causes spontaneous erection as a side effect. Now it is being tested as a treatment for erectile dysfunction. It may work for FSAD as well.

From Mother Nature's Medicine Chest

As pharmaceutical companies continue their quest for the perfect synthetic aphrodisiac, more and more people are experimenting with natural alternatives to enhance their sexual experiences. Much of their interest has focused on herbs, though some cultures prize animal parts for their suspected aphrodisiac powers. (Tragically, this pursuit has contributed to the near extinction of several animal species—including the black rhinoceros, whose horn is believed to enhance sexual prowess.)

Plants in general are a rich source of compounds that can alter our physiological and psychological states. In fact, an estimated 60 percent of conventional medications come from plants. And that's after scientific study of just a relative fraction of the world's plant population. Realistically, then, many more herbs than the ones presented here may possess potent aphrodisiac powers. They just haven't been discovered yet.

A number of our clients at the Sexual Wellness Center have tried herbs to improve their libidos, with excellent results. But as we always remind them, herbs are medicines. Like conventional pharmaceuticals, they can cause serious side effects if they are not used according to directions or if they're taken with preexisting medical conditions such as hypertension.

In addition, the herbal industry—like the supplement industry—isn't subject to FDA regulation. This means the quality, safety, and effectiveness of herbal products is not guaranteed. As we mentioned in our discussion of DHEA in chapter 7, what is on the label is not necessarily what is in the bottle. And DHEA, which is synthesized, is much easier to control than herbal preparations, which are grown.

The potency and quality of an herbal preparation depends on the same variables that affect all crops, such as rain, sun, temperature, and soil conditions. As an analogy, consider wine. Some years, the weather cooperates and the grapes grow well, so the wine is full-bodied and robust. Other years, too much rain, or not enough, takes a toll on the grape crop, producing a thin and not especially tasty vintage. Herbs are just as vulnerable to environmental factors, if not more so.

Keep in mind, too, that we do not intend for this section to be an authoritative text on herbal aphrodisiacs. Dozens, if not hundreds, of herbs can claim prosexual properties. We have chosen to recommend only a handful at the Sexual Wellness Center, because they have been scientifically studied, their side effects are well-known, and they are widely available.

As you'll see, we've not included specific dosage information here. Your best bet is to consult a qualified herbalist or a physician who specializes in herbal medicine, who can recommend an appropriate dosage for you.

YOHIMBE: A PROVEN "LOVE POTION"

Manzambi and her husband, Remmy, moved from their native Zaire to the United States 7 years ago. At first, they lived with Remmy's brother and his family in a cramped, dark Brooklyn apartment. Remmy worked 12 hours a day, 6 days a week driving a cab. It certainly was not paradise, but it was a much safer place to raise their daughter than in their war-torn country.

Like generations of immigrants before them, Manzambi and Remmy stayed in New York for a few years to get acclimated to the wonders and fast-paced life of their new country. Then they moved to Cleveland, where another relative had settled some years before. There Manzambi made many friends, who openly admired the relationship between Manzambi and her husband. While their husbands often went out to bars after work, Remmy headed straight home and showered affection on his wife.

Her new friends wanted the same type of relationship with their husbands that Manzambi had with Remmy. So they asked her advice. "The secret," she told them, "is to keep your man happy in bed." She continued: "Every night we drink a tea that we have sent from back home in Africa. The tea causes a pleasant fire in my vagina, and Remmy can make love like a man 15 years younger. Good sex keeps my husband home."

A traditional herbal remedy in West Africa, yohimbe has a centuries-old reputation for its libido-enhancing properties. The herb, which comes from the bark of the corynanthe yohimbe tree, plays a role in tribal fertility celebrations, marriage ceremonies, and mating rituals. Spurred by yohimbe's effects, some of these ceremonies involve sexual activity that may go on for days, or even weeks.

Since the late 1930s, researchers have been studying yohimbe to substantiate the prosexual claims for the herb. No less than 30 scientific articles have shown that the active ingredient in yohimbe, the alkaloid yohimbine, increases blood flow to the genitals and stimulates the central nervous system as well as the nerves of the genitals. Together, these physical changes set the stage for sexual arousal.

Researchers at Valparaiso University in Indiana confirmed that yohimbine increases the frequency of sexual activity and heightens sexual arousal. In fact, the FDA already has approved the compound as a treatment for erectile dysfunction in men. Further studies have shown that yohimbine can counteract the negative sexual side effects of the widely prescribed SSRI antidepressants.

As yohimbine works to stimulate the nervous system, it can enhance blood flow, metabolism, and alertness. On the downside, it can raise blood pressure and heart rate and cause heart palpitations, restlessness, and insomnia. For these reasons, we do *not* recommend yohimbe or yohimbine for anyone with a history of coronary artery disease, stroke, heart arrhythmias, high blood pressure, migraines, panic attacks, schizophrenia, or bipolar disorder. Even if you don't have one of these conditions, we advise trying yohimbe only after a thorough physical exam.

You have several options for using yohimbe. You can brew yohimbe bark to make a tea—we suggest adding honey to mellow the slightly bitter taste—or buy the powdered form in capsules. Yohimbine also is available as a concentrated tincture.

DAMIANA: FIGHTS LOW LIBIDO ON MANY FRONTS

Damiana is a wild shrub that grows in parts of Mexico, Central and South America, and the West Indies. Recently, it has been cultivated in Texas and California. Its botanical name, *Turnera diffusa aphrodisiaca*, hints at its reputation as a libido-enhancing plant. The ancient Mayans used damiana for its prosexual properties. And for centuries, Mexican women have been brewing tea from the plant's leaves to improve their sexual satisfaction.

Though much less studied than yohimbe, damiana has been the subject of some research that's worth discussing here. In one trial, researchers gave a damiana extract to impotent or sexually sluggish male rats, which showed marked improvement in their sexual activity. In another, an herbal preparation called ArginMax for Women—which combines damiana with other reputed sex-enhancing herbs—boosted sexual desire, reduced vaginal dryness, increased the frequency of sexual intercourse and the frequency and intensity of orgasm, and improved clitoral sensation in women who took it.

In fact, almost three-quarters of the women in the study showed positive changes in these sexual variables, compared with only slightly more than one-third of the women who took a placebo. The results are all the more significant because they come from a double-blind placebo-controlled study, considered the gold standard in clinical research.

Damiana leaves can be brewed as a tea or taken in powdered form in capsules. You also can buy Damiana Liqueur, a light herbal-based liqueur that is made from damiana grown in Baja California. It comes in a bottle with the shape of a pregnant woman, modeled after the Incan goddess of fertility. According to Mexican folklore, the very first margarita was made with Damiana Liqueur. The Damiana Margarita remains popular in the Los Cabos area of Mexico.

GINKGO: SLOWLY BUT SURELY, IT WORKS

Chinese culture is rich in the study and use of aphrodisiacs and sex-enhancing herbs. For centuries, the Chinese people have relied on the nuts and leaves of the ginkgo tree to help improve their sexual vigor, as well as their mental acuity.

Though limited, recent scientific research suggests that ginkgo may benefit sexual function by increasing blood flow. Two separate studies involving men with erectile dysfunction found that the herb helps to restore erections without side effects. In a study involving women, a preparation of ginkgo mixed with other herbs improved orgasms and overall sexual satisfaction.

Most herbalists agree that the effects of ginkgo are gradual. A woman who's taking ginkgo may notice increased genital sensation and more vivid orgasms, along with sharper memory, over a period of several months. Ginkgo can be found in most health food stores in extract form or as a powder in capsules.

GINSENG: GOOD FOR MIND AND BODY

Perhaps the best known of the Chinese herbs is ginseng. It has been used in Asia for more than 5,000 years to boost energy and alertness. It also is known for improving sexual response, increasing sexual energy, and reviving libido.

There are three different types of ginseng: Asian, or "red," ginseng (*Panax ginseng*); American, or "white," ginseng (*Panax quinquefolius*); and Siberian ginseng (*Eleutherococcus senticosus*). The herb is considered an adaptogen. In other words, it helps restore normal function to the human body by increasing all-around re-sistance to stress.

117

Ginseng contains ginsenosides, compounds that stimulate the hypothalamus to invigorate sex drive. It also acts locally on the vagina and clitoris to increase genital blood flow, which enhances lubrication, sensation, and arousal.

In randomized placebo-controlled trials, Asian ginseng has improved sexual response in men with erectile dysfunction. And in combination with ginkgo and damiana, ginseng appears to boost sexual arousal and overall sexual satisfaction.

Look for ginseng in tincture, capsule, or tablet form. Some health food stores even carry soft drinks made with the herb.

BUYER BEWARE

Before concluding our discussion of herbal aphrodisiacs, we must mention Avlimil, an herbal formula that is aggressively marketed on radio and TV. The ads cleverly compare Avlimil with Viagra by saying that women now have their own "little blue pill," just as men do. They also urge potential customers to ask their doctors about Avlimil, which implies that the supplement is available only by prescription and, therefore, has been approved by the FDA. Unfortunately, neither is the case.

As an herbal supplement, Avlimil is not regulated by the FDA. And if it has been studied, the research has yet to appear in any peer-reviewed medical journal.

Avlimil contains a blend of sage, red raspberry leaf, kudzu root, red clover, capsicum pepper, licorice root, bayberry fruit, damiana, valerian root, ginger, and black cohosh. Though damiana may have aphrodisiac properties, there is no evidence that the combination of herbs enhances desire, arousal, or orgasm, as the manufacturers claim. And it's very expensive—$55 for a 30-day supply!

PART III

THE SECOND KEY: EMOTIONAL RESILIENCE

CHAPTER 10

THE EMOTIONAL BUILDING BLOCKS OF LIBIDO

- Wanting to revive your sex drive for your partner is never enough. You must want sex for yourself, too.
- To experience a more satisfying sex life, explore what turns you on—and what turns you off.
- Sharing your sexual preferences with your partner is vital to a healthy sexual relationship. Without this information, your partner can't do what pleases you.
- Your libido needs nurturing to thrive. This means making time for sex in your life.

Most women think of the emotional component of libido in rather straightforward terms. If they love their partners, they reason, they should want to make love. So they can't fathom why they would lose interest in sex. After all, they may get angry or frustrated with their partners from time to time. But the fundamental emotional bond remains healthy and strong. Or, they wonder, have they been fooling themselves about their feelings?

In truth, the emotions that feed libido are much more complicated than "I love him, I love him not." They have just as much to do with how a woman feels about herself as with how she feels about her partner.

Those women who desire sex display certain emotional traits, which we identify as the emotional foundation of a healthy libido. These traits go beyond "pure" emotions like love and hate, happiness and sadness, serenity and anxiety. They're rooted deep in a woman's perceptions of sexuality and of sex itself.

To help illustrate these emotional "building blocks," we will use the story of Laura, one of our clients at the Sexual Wellness Center. Like many women, she came to us seeking help for her low libido.

Laura was a delicate woman in her early thirties. She had been introduced to her partner, Trevor, at a holiday party 5 years earlier. Laura admired Trevor's intelligence and self-confidence. They began a serious relationship almost immediately.

Laura enjoyed their lovemaking at first, but her desire waned over the years. Though they still were having sex several times a week, Laura didn't get nearly as much pleasure from it. She liked being close to Trevor and being held by him. But somehow, she never seemed as enthusiastic about sex as Trevor thought she should be.

In our first session, Laura told me (Dr. Brandon) that she couldn't care less whether she ever had sex again. She was a private, reserved woman, clearly struggling to speak openly about a topic as personal as her sex life. Her subdued demeanor gave the impression that she was content and easygoing in life, never demanding or challenging of others. Laura was an expert at taking up little space in the world, both physically and interpersonally.

From an early age, Laura had learned how to please people. Her father was an alcoholic, and she had become adept at reading his moods to avoid confrontations. Her passive but attentive behavior toward Trevor was a manifestation of a relationship strategy that she had used with her father. She protected herself by being the ultimate "good girl."

As she sat in my office, Laura's eyes became moist, and her chin quivered ever so slightly. Her already petite frame was shrinking into the chair. She seemed to be getting more fragile by the minute. I waited while she composed herself enough to speak. "Trevor has had it with me," she said. "I don't think he's going to wait much longer. I'm afraid he's going to have an affair. And I really wouldn't blame him." Her eyes again became teary. "I do love him; he's a wonderful man. I can't understand why I don't want to have sex with him."

I asked Laura an important question, one that I ask all my clients. "Why do you want your libido back?" She responded without hesitation: "Because Trevor wants to make love." Laura began to explain how much he likes sex, but I interrupted her. "This is about you, Laura, not Trevor. Why do you want your libido back?" Laura wasn't getting my point. With a quizzical expression, she continued to describe Trevor's sexual needs. Again, I stopped her. "If you don't want this for yourself, Laura, I don't expect that we will get very far."

Wanting Sex for Yourself

Laura was typical of many women who come to the Sexual Wellness Center. They want their libidos back to make their partners happy. They see little in it for themselves. We tell them the same thing we told Laura: A woman's success in rekindling her sexual desire will be severely limited if she doesn't perceive herself as the primary beneficiary of her efforts. In other words, if she isn't the big winner in the situation, she will remain lackadaisical about sex, or she'll get angry with her partner. Either way, she'll become even less interested in emotional and physical intimacy over time.

A first step in developing and maintaining a healthy libido is understanding and accepting this: Making love must be for you, not for your partner. You must want it because of what it offers you, or because of what you can take from it for yourself.

Keep in mind that sex offers different things to different people. Most women want sex because of the intimacy, the holding and caressing. On a basic level, humans crave touch. Research has shown that to develop normally, infants require nurturing physical contact. Adults benefit from such interaction, too. Specifically, touch causes changes in brain chemistry that make us feel good. It leaves us feeling loved and connected. It reminds us that we are not alone in what sometimes seems an unforgiving universe. Through sex, we can satisfy our need for physical contact.

Along the same line, a woman may want sex because of the intense physical pleasure that comes from it. The thrill of a warm, wet tongue flickering over her clitoris, the luscious ache of strong hands massaging her inner thighs, the gratification of simply lying naked with her partner—interactions like these produce sensations and experiences unparalleled amid the demands and responsibilities of daily life.

Of course, we can't overlook how sex affords a wonderful and welcome release of tension, as well as a physical means of expressing emotion. A tender encounter demonstrates love for a partner; more-fervid interplay reveals passion or desire. Even a negative emotion like anger can manifest as aggressive, demanding sex. One of our clients found that sex after an argument was especially gratifying, because touching her partner more roughly enabled her to vent her hostility as words never could.

Other women value sex because they are able to give to their partners in a warm, meaningful way. In exchange, they feel good about themselves and about the bond they are helping to nurture.

But sex can be as much about connecting with ourselves as about connecting with our partners. In a world where women risk being chastised for expressing and enjoying their sexuality, the bedroom offers a safe environment for releasing and relishing their female sexual energy. On some level, they might experience sex as a creative outlet—for feeling rather than thinking, intuiting rather than analyzing. In effect, their right brains take charge of the situation, seizing control from their frequently overactive left brains.

Then, too, sex might be all about having fun, something that too often becomes a low priority in adult life. Partners become playmates, making love for the sheer delight of it. In the process, they're able to achieve a new level of connection and intimacy with one another.

No matter what their motivation, women who have healthy libidos want sex because they get something from it. So you need to ask yourself: What do *I* get from it? If you're like Laura, thinking only in terms of your partner's needs, you need to shift your focus to yourself. What happened to your needs? Why did your enjoyment of sex become less important than your partner's?

In sex—as in all aspects of our lives—the better we care for ourselves, the more we can give to others. Consider how this applies to your sexual relationship with your partner. If you want something from sex, you'll be more interested in having it. You probably will be more engaged and interactive while making love. You might become more experimental and adventurous. As you can see, being more selfish has its advantages!

SOMETIMES SELFISHNESS IS NECESSARY

In Laura's case, she seemed to be detached from many of her needs, not just her sexual ones. This became even clearer when she invited Trevor to one of her sessions.

Laura spoke less when Trevor was in the room. Trevor had a strong personality, and when I asked him if people ever saw him as controlling, both he and Laura laughed. I asked Laura how she felt about Trevor's dominance. Usually, his comments were right on the mark, she said, and she appreciated his input and direction. Laura was choosing not to verbalize the other side of the story—that sometimes she felt overwhelmed by Trevor's demeanor. She couldn't see how her tendency to rely so completely on Trevor resulted in her not taking responsibility for her own sexual enjoyment.

Laura seemed to do things because of what other people wanted from her, not because of what she wanted for herself.

We considered how her need to please others might play out sexually. What if she made love only for Trevor's sake? "Oh, he would be ecstatic," she replied. "He probably would spend more time at home in the evenings, rather than at the office." But Laura could see how this might feed into her own self-doubt over time. She would wonder whether Trevor stayed with her just because of the sex. She'd get angry. She'd resent Trevor for expecting sex from her, no doubt to such a degree that she would stop responding to his advances.

Then Laura contemplated a different scenario. I asked her to imagine having sex and caring about how she felt. This was a big leap for her. She had a hard time not thinking about Trevor—whether he was enjoying himself, or worse, waiting for him to bring her to orgasm. We talked about how good sex is a process of give and take. So far, she was just giving, without taking anything for herself.

We also explored Laura's fears. What did she think would happen if she were more "selfish" in her sex life? Laura's subconscious early training to be the good girl clearly was getting in her way. Simply put, good girls aren't supposed to desire sex. Only bad girls do. "You must make a choice," I explained. "What's more important to you—being a good girl in a stressed marriage, or letting go of that image and sharing a rewarding relationship with Trevor?" Laura didn't deliberate very long. She chose the latter.

I suggested that Laura try having sex because she derived pleasure from her own sensuality and from her intimate connection with Trevor. How might things be different? In this scenario, being sexual was about being generous with herself and getting more for herself physically and emotionally. She imagined enjoying sex because she felt closer to Trevor. This was what she wanted for herself and for her partner. Laura became deter-mined to be self-indulgent. "I guess I need to use Trevor for my own sexual gratification," she mused. "It's time that man learns how to please me!"

Over the next several months, Laura worked at bringing this new-found attitude into their relationship and, ultimately, into their bedroom. Her first step was to be more assertive. For example, when they wanted to eat out, Laura would suggest a restaurant rather than saying she had no preference. And when she needed another car, she decided which makes and models to test-drive instead of relying solely on Trevor's opinion of which to lease.

At first, Trevor seemed shocked, even hurt, by Laura's budding as-sertiveness. But as she became more empowered, Trevor realized that he would benefit from her new style. In particular, she was showing signs of becoming a more active and willing participant in sex. Trevor was happy about that.

Discovering Your Sexual Preferences

To desire sex, you need to know not only what you get from it but also what you like about it. Women with healthy libidos recognize their turn-ons and turn-offs. Just as important, they communicate this information to their partners.

This may sound easy enough, but it can be quite challenging. The fact is, most women with low libido are aware only that they aren't satisfied with their sex lives. They've lost touch with what feels good sexually. Even if they wanted to communicate with their partners, they wouldn't know what to say. This certainly was true for Laura.

Laura seemed doubtful that anything could excite or arouse her. She had become convinced that unlike the majority of her female peers, she was im-mune to sexual stimulation of any sort. She felt so strongly about this that she continued to believe it even after a routine gynecological exam ruled out any underlying physical problems.

As I explained to Laura, her mind was overriding her body's ability to respond to sexual stimulation. Instead of holding on to her pessimistic attitude, I suggested she get curious about her sexual preferences and do some detective work on her own. I thought she should start by reading.

More specifically, I suggested that Laura make a trip to the local bookstore to pick up some female erotica—sexual fantasies written for women, by women. Most stores carry a good selection. By observing her reaction to the content, Laura could gain valuable insight into her own sexual preferences.

Laura was ambivalent about the assignment at first. She felt strange reading such blatantly sexual material, essentially soft pornography. But she realized that she needed to become reacquainted with her sexual self before she could share this part of her with Trevor in any meaningful way.

When we met next, Laura admitted that the stories had seemed contrived and silly to her—until she made a conscious decision to "loosen up and get curious." She discovered that the ones with chivalrous leading men most excited her, though she obviously felt uncomfortable sharing this information with me. I wasn't surprised. Nearly every client is self-conscious about her sexual fantasies and embarrassed to reveal them to anyone else.

We considered Laura's favorite stories in the context of her personal history, including her past sexual encounters and her emotional experiences with men. Laura understood how her fantasies fulfilled a need for what she never had gotten from the men in her life—namely, attention and adoration. Invariably in Laura's relationships, the roles had been switched: She took care of the men, focusing on their needs. Her energy went out to them, but they never reciprocated.

Gradually, Laura grew less self-conscious about her fantasies. She could see why they held such attraction for her. She felt more compassionate toward herself, as she realized that she had sacrificed her own needs in her relationships with men.

Laura used her fantasies as a springboard to identifying how she wanted to be approached and touched when Trevor was interested in making love. Their interactions played an important role in determining whether or not Laura felt receptive to Trevor's advances.

Not surprisingly, Laura was more open to sex when Trevor showed that he valued and desired her. She especially liked when he put energy into planning an evening for just the two of them. She hoped that he would recognize how much she enjoyed feeling appreciated and wanted. But she admitted that she never had talked with him about it.

Communicating with Your Partner

Knowing your sexual preferences won't improve your low libido unless you share this information with your partner. But if you're like most women, you probably don't bring up sex outside the bedroom. In fairness to your partner, you can't expect him to anticipate your wants and needs if you haven't told him about them.

Ask yourself why you avoid discussing sex with your partner. Are you concerned about your own discomfort, or your partner's? Sometimes we avoid addressing issues under the guise of shielding someone else, when in fact we are attempting to protect ourselves. If this is true for you, consider what you might be afraid of.

A choice not to discuss your sexual preferences likely will backfire. In our experience, when a woman isn't satisfied with some aspect of her sex life, she becomes angry and resentful toward her partner. Yet he isn't aware of the problem, and he hasn't been given an opportunity to help work toward a solution. He's in a no-win situation. Both partners experience a growing sense of frustration and may withdraw from each other over time.

As Laura and I talked, I realized that she had been withholding a lot of information about her sexuality from Trevor. She considered him a good lover, so left him to figure out her body on his own. When I mentioned this to her, she laughed about how complicated and daunting a task pleasing her must have been.

Yet despite her growing awareness that opening up to Trevor about her sexual preferences would help their relationship considerably, Laura dug in her heels. "I just can't talk to him about this," she said in no uncertain terms. "It's too embarrassing."

I asked why she was reluctant to share this personal information with Trevor. Eventually, she acknowledged her fear that Trevor would think she was "some kind of pervert." I asked if she thought she was a pervert. She smiled wryly, shaking her head no. I said that she didn't strike me as a pervert, either.

We compared Laura's options. She could continue to withhold information from Trevor, allowing him to view her as a sexual cold fish; or she could open up to him and risk being judged a pervert. Was being a cold fish really preferable for her?

We also explored how Laura's silence already had affected her relationship with Trevor. Obviously, she wasn't as interested in sex as she had been. And Trevor was frustrated, because he didn't know how to please her sexually so that she'd be more engaged in their interplay. In effect, she was preventing herself from experiencing better sex, even though that was what she wanted.

I speculated that if Trevor didn't know what aroused Laura, Laura likely didn't know what worked for Trevor, either. When I posed the question, Laura snapped, "Everything works for Trevor!" But when I asked for specifics—what turned him on, what he fantasized about—Laura admitted that she didn't know.

Even though they loved each other, Laura and Trevor clearly had a lot to learn about each other. Laura understood that if she wasn't willing to reveal a more intimate side of her sexual self, she likely was holding back emotionally in other ways. For example, Laura never mentioned that she was uncomfortable with Trevor's repeated late evenings at the office. They reminded her of her father's emotional and physical unavailability. Laura was afraid that she'd be perceived as too demanding if she voiced her concerns. Yet they were affecting her and her desire to be close to Trevor.

After much soul-searching, Laura decided to talk with Trevor about some of the things she had discovered during her sexual self-exploration. She took the risk of telling him exactly what she needed from him. She felt tremendously vulnerable when disclosing this information, but Trevor's attentiveness and graciousness had a dramatic impact on her. She knew that she wanted even greater intimacy with him.

At our next session, Laura obviously was pleased with the progress she and Trevor had made. Her opening up had paved the way to several heart-to-heart talks—not just about their sex life but also about their relationship, Trevor's work schedule, and their expectations of each other. Laura relished the deepening bond between them. Her struggle to know her sexual self, and to reveal her sexuality to Trevor, was paying off.

Making Sex a Priority

Many women who come to the Sexual Wellness Center for help with low libido tell us that they might be more interested in sex if they had more time for it. Even though our society is obsessed with sex, it falls low on our list of priorities. If we don't make room for it in our lives, we can't expect our desire for it to remain strong.

Of course, our clients hate being told to find time for sex. We understand why. After all, they have enough trouble allocating their available hours without worrying about fitting in an activity that they currently don't enjoy.

If this rings true for you, we suggest thinking back to when you felt a strong desire for sex. How were you able to find time for it then? Chances are, you accommodated your sexual relationship because you placed greater value on it in the broader context of your life. Consider the reasons that sex no longer carries the same priority status. If you are putting yourself, your partner, or your relationship on the back burner, that may help explain why you simply don't want sex anymore.

Another of our clients, Marsha, has a story that illustrates just how easily sex can be crowded out of a woman's life.

Forty-year-old Marsha was a self-described exhausted working mother—married with two children, working full-time for a company she loved. Marsha's husband, Ron, also worked full-time, but he tried to help around the house as much as he could.

Marsha and Ron obviously loved each other and enjoyed parenting together. Despite her near-chronic state of fatigue, Marsha was determined to "have it all." That included great sex. She came to the Sexual Wellness Center in the hope that she would learn how to better organize her life to reach her goal.

"I'm not here for sex therapy, though I may need it," Marsha said with a smirk at their first therapy session. "Ron's and my sex life is suffering at the moment." She went on to describe her hectic lifestyle, with its multiple demands and responsibilities.

Like so many women, Marsha was striving for perfection. She wanted to be the perfect wife, the perfect mother, the perfect homemaker, the perfect professional. In the process, she was driving herself crazy.

Actually, she was perfect at one thing: creating stress in her life and in the lives of those she loved. Ron confirmed this fact when he described Marsha as unhappy and difficult. "You try so hard, but you never relax," he gently told her in my (Dr. Brandon's) office one afternoon. "Even when you are trying to climax, you seem distracted and in a hurry. I know sometimes you'd rather not have sex at all."

Marsha admitted that Ron was right. But she was determined to find a solution that didn't involve giving up anything. I invited her to join the rest of us mere mortals. "All of us have our limits," I commented. "And our relationships need time and attention in order to thrive." But only when Ron

angrily described the effects of her behavior on their children did Marsha fi-
nally seem to listen. Clearly, this wasn't what she wanted. Her own suffering
was one thing, but her children's suffering was something altogether different.

What happened next for Marsha was the challenging process of
reprioritizing her life. First and foremost, she had to let go of her perfec-
tionist ideals and learn to accept "good enough" as her standard for living.
She also had to be more willing to ask for help from others. She decided to
hire a cleaning service. And she recruited young women from her neigh-
borhood as babysitters for her kids, so she could attend yoga class with some
degree of regularity. She relied more on Ron, too, allowing him to take care
of her rather than doing everything for herself.

Of course, making all these changes evoked many issues that Marsha
needed to explore. She became aware that she was using perfection to con-
ceal a deep-seated fear that she was flawed or deficient in some way. Her
constant pursuit of perfection left little time for pleasure in any aspect of
her life, including sex. Making love became just one more task to perform
well, rather than an opportunity to experience a loving and gratifying ex-
change with her husband.

Marsha also faced the fact that slowing down meant giving up
things that she valued. Ultimately, she decided to relinquish some of her
responsibilities at work and at home. She perceived this as a deep personal
loss; during our therapy sessions, her pain was palpable. Her growing re-
liance on others felt like weakness, rather than the healthy dependence that
I had described.

Although the path was difficult, the payoff was worthwhile. For the
first time in years, Martha was able to truly enjoy living. Her days felt less
pressured and more peaceful. And because she wasn't so tired, she could give
more of herself to Ron and their children.

Marsha's struggle is fairly typical these days. It's borne largely
of the increasing number of life choices available to women. Being
a wife and mother no longer is the only option.

But this new freedom for women to chart their own life paths is a complicated gift. One unfortunate consequence is the profound sense of having even more to accomplish. Stay-at-home moms feel guilty for not "doing more" with their lives. Working moms feel guilty for taking on too many work responsibilities and not spending enough time with their families. Women who decide not to have children feel guilty for being "selfish" with their lives. All of these negative perceptions take a toll on sex drive.

For women with perfectionist or competitive personalities, like Marsha, the constant pressure of being better and doing more creates further stress in their lives. By letting go of their stringent standards and accepting their limitations, they may be able to accomplish more. This might seem to run counter to logic. Clients often say, "If I don't push myself, I won't get anything done." The truth is, being gentle and understanding with yourself frees up your energy. It is an example of how loss and letting go can bring about fulfillment and abundance.

Unfortunately, in an effort to reduce stress, many women must choose between sex and other priorities. Such decisions are never easy. But consider the alternative. Women who exist in a state of constant stress and self-deprivation inevitably feel the impact on themselves as well as see it in their loved ones. They become less of whom they want to be when interacting with others and with society as a whole. Understandably, they feel cheated and angry. They may take out their frustration and dissatisfaction on their partners or other family members. This sets in motion a devastating cycle in which they feel even more distressed and become even more angry.

As you can see, cheating others is an unavoidable outcome of cheating ourselves. By ignoring our own needs or adhering to unrealistic expectations, we have less to give to the people around us. The solution lies in establishing reasonable priorities in our lives and making choices to support them. In doing so, we free up the time and energy to cultivate a satisfying, rewarding sex life.

CHAPTER 11

CULTIVATING A HEALTHY BODY IMAGE

- How you see yourself in the mirror directly affects whether or not you want sex.

- Our society perpetuates standards of female physical beauty that are not only unhealthy but nearly impossible to attain.

- You can change your feelings about your body by learning to appreciate it in nonsexual ways.

- By making a conscious effort to relax before a sexual encounter, you attain greater comfort and confidence in your physical self, which in turn enhances your sexual desire and response.

All of us are aware of how easily our feelings about our bodies can interfere with our desire for sex. Though women of all shapes and sizes want and thoroughly enjoy sexual intimacy, those with poor body images may try to avoid any kind of intimate contact with their partners. The unfortunate reality is that our society actively encourages women to be uncomfortable in their own bodies. This issue has been getting a lot of attention lately, and it deserves further discussion here.

Our cultural standards ordain that adult women should have the bodies of tall boys and the breasts of no identified species, although we all know that this is a physical impossibility. Someone once said that about eight women in the world look like super-models, and about 3 billion don't. Isn't that the truth!

Nonetheless, the media continue to present starving, skeletal women as the epitome of perfection on TV, in the movies, and on magazine covers. No wonder eating disorders have reached epidemic proportions in this country. Women repeatedly receive the message that they must be young and without visible body fat to be considered desirable. This message can be particularly damaging for mature women, whose curvaceous bodies offer reminders of having lived, loved, and mothered over the years.

The Myth of the "Ideal" Female Physique

Many women feel most vulnerable when they are naked with their partners. If a woman is sensitive about her body with clothes on, she'll be even more self-conscious with her clothes off—so much so that she may find ingenious and creative ways to prevent her partner from ever seeing her completely naked. Some women undress in the bathroom behind a closed door and, when making love, remain covered by the bed sheets. Others remove their clothing only after turning out the lights. Or they never disrobe at all, preferring to wear their nightgowns while making love.

What all of these women have in common is a sense of shame about their bodies. In their view, their physical appearance directly correlates to their value as human beings.

Some intriguing research on this topic has shown that when asked to describe themselves, a majority of women focus first on how they look. Take a moment to consider what this means about the importance of our physical appearance to our identities. Naturally, when our bodies do not match the cultural ideal, it can have a direct and potentially devastating impact on our self-worth.

Here's another revealing research finding: When people were

asked to rate themselves and their partners on perceived attractiveness, men consistently gave themselves and their partners higher scores than women did. In other words, men were more likely than women to judge themselves *and their partners* as physically appealing.

Interestingly, both genders report that they tend to focus more on the woman's body than the man's when making love. This creates a scenario in which a woman is self-consciously and negatively concentrating on her physical appearance during intercourse. She's almost certain to lose interest in sex as a result.

The external and internal pressure to fit a certain physical mold insidiously affects a woman's sex life. Women become self-conscious not only about the size and shape of their bodies but also about the appearance of specific body parts. They fret that their breasts aren't a firm and perfect size 36C, or that their waists exceed the ideal 24 inches. Such standards are nearly impossible to attain. Yet they become ingrained in a woman's psyche, draining her self-esteem and her sex drive.

Women who become moms may be especially sensitive about the physical changes that occur during pregnancy and delivery. Stretch marks and varicose veins are common, as is the softening of the vaginal muscles. These kinds of changes can fuel a woman's self-consciousness, especially if she had a poor body image to begin with.

If you identify with feeling distressed or embarrassed about your physical appearance—or about any aspect of your sexuality, for that matter—we urge you not to ignore it. Anxiety and shame have a way of gaining potency if they aren't addressed. You may be able to work through your emotions by talking with your partner or a trusted friend, or by writing about them in a journal. Psychotherapy can help the healing process as well. On the other hand, choosing to remain silent probably will not provide the kind of relief that you need and deserve.

Fight back against the destructive societal ideologies that seek to subvert your right to a positive body image. Allow yourself to feel sexy and physically content. Revel in the genuine beauty of your body.

Your Body Beautiful

A precursor to reclaiming your sexual desire is being able to experience your body in pleasurable nonsexual ways. If you're like most women, you readily focus on those things that are "flawed" or that don't feel good. You're more likely to be conscious of physical discomfort than physical gratification. But you can change that.

A good place to start is by intimately and lovingly exploring your own body. All you need to do is remove your clothing and stand in front of a full-length mirror. We know this may feel uncomfortable at first. But it's vital to your personal growth and understanding.

Observe with compassion your softness, your firmness, your smoothness, your textures. Admire the curves of your breasts, stomach, buttocks, and thighs. Run your hands over your skin, feeling the uniqueness of each body part. Rather than criticize yourself, as most women readily do, make an effort to appreciate what you see and feel. Your body is an amazing machine. Respect it, and love it for the ways it serves you.

Use this exercise as motivation to love and enjoy your body every day. Create opportunities to indulge in pleasurable physical sensations. Take a deep breath, hold it, and then expel all the air from your lungs. Focus on the release, how it feels when you let go. Experiment with various fabrics in your wardrobe, paying attention to how they caress your skin. Paint your toenails and admire your handiwork. Stretch like a cat.

Be mindful of ways to feel good in your body. As you develop a more positive perception of your physical self, you'll be able to balance and perhaps even set aside any negative thoughts and feelings that may be eroding your sexual desire.

If you continue to struggle to feel comfortable in your own skin, we strongly suggest that you consider what alternative health practitioners refer to as bodywork. Actually, this is an umbrella term applied to a category of disciplines that relax and heal the body through touch and physical manipulation. Examples of bodywork include therapeutic massage, Reiki (a form of energy healing with roots in Japan), acupuncture, chiropractic, and physical therapy.

At the Sexual Wellness Center, we encourage many of our clients to explore the benefits of bodywork in revitalizing their sex drives. Often they get more from their therapy sessions when they receive high-quality bodywork as well. It not only fosters a profound new sense of a woman's physical self, it also seems to encourage the release of emotional pain, which in turn fosters receptivity to physical pleasure.

As in any profession, you'll find considerable variation in the quality of care provided by the practitioners of bodywork disciplines. Be sure to do your homework. Ask for a referral from your physician or local hospital, or seek recommendations from family members or close friends. Once you find someone, get to know her and her practice before beginning treatment. You must have confidence and trust in this person to get the most from your bodywork sessions.

Ways to Unwind Your Mind

To enjoy making love, you must be able to relax and give in to the moment. Otherwise, you may find yourself thinking—and perhaps obsessing—about your body, rather than feeling and enjoying it.

When women have a difficult time relaxing, they might not be as sensitive to the subtle energies of their bodies. This can inhibit their sexual desire and response. In such cases, we recommend practicing some form of relaxation for a few minutes before making love.

Being able to relax is a skill that most of us must learn. A variety of techniques can help. Among the more popular options, which we will discuss briefly here, are deep breathing, meditation, full-body muscle relaxation, and guided imagery. If you want to learn more about any of these, we suggest picking up a copy of Dr. Jon Kabat-Zinn's book *Wherever You Go, There You Are* at your local library or bookstore.

DEEP BREATHING: ON-THE-SPOT RELEASE

Deep breathing is probably the simplest and quickest way to achieve a state of relaxation. Studies demonstrate that your muscles literally can't remain tense when you breathe in a gentle, mindful manner. The key to using your breath to induce relaxation is to concentrate on inhaling and exhaling slowly and deeply. Many people find that counting as they breathe ensures that they maintain a slow, regular rhythm. Holding your breath for a few moments before exhaling can help as well.

If you want to try deep breathing, we recommend that you practice simply inhaling through your nose and exhaling through your mouth. When inhaling, imagine your stomach filling with air. Of course, the air is going into your lungs. But most people find that they are able to take in more per breath when they focus on the sensations in the stomach. Feel the walls of your abdomen expand as the air accumulates, then contract as the air leaves. If it helps, visualize a beach ball in your stomach, continuously inflating and deflating.

To start, inhale for a *slow* count of five, hold your breath for a count of two or three, then slowly exhale. Continue for 5 to 10 minutes. It may feel awkward initially, but with practice, you will notice an improvement in your lung capacity. You can keep adjusting the exercise to your ability and comfort level over time.

We suggest that you practice deep breathing at least once, and ideally twice, each day. Many of our clients prefer to incorporate it into their morning and evening routines. The beauty is, you can do your breathing exercises virtually anytime and anywhere. No one else need even notice. This means you can use deep breathing to control your level of anxiety, even in social or intimate situations.

As with all the relaxation techniques we discuss here, the more you practice deep breathing, the better you will get at it, and the more effective it will become over time. And if you spend a few minutes on your breathing exercises before a sexual encounter, we suspect that you'll derive more pleasure from the experience.

MEDITATION: TUNING OUT NEGATIVE THOUGHTS

Many cultures have embraced meditation in the pursuit of relaxation, spiritual enlightenment, and personal growth. It is among the oldest of the relaxation techniques, with roots in the ancient religious traditions of India, China, and Japan. Popular varieties of meditation include transcendental, zen, vipassana, and mindfulness.

Serious students of meditation will practice for many years under the supervision and guidance of a respected master. But you can reap its many proven benefits by practicing it on your own, as well, with written or taped instruction.

Much of the current research into the physiological and psychological advantages of regular meditation comes from the Stress Reduction Clinic of the University of Massachusetts Memorial Medical Center in Worcester. Founded by Dr. Kabat-Zinn, the clinic teaches mindfulness meditation and yoga techniques to people with a variety of medical conditions. Often these clients receive referrals from physicians at the medical center.

According to studies performed at the clinic, between 29 and 46 percent of the workshop participants show improvements in disease markers and symptoms. This includes 45 percent of patients with heart disease, 43 percent of those with high blood pressure, 25 percent of those with chronic pain, and 31 percent of those with stress-related complaints. These numbers are even more impressive when you consider how many people drop out or don't follow directions in the course of a typical scientific trial.

Other studies—some published in respected scientific journals such as *Science* and the *Journal of Behavioral Medicine*—have linked an equally compelling array of health benefits to transcendental meditation (TM). People who regularly practice TM show increases in energy, creativity, and work performance and satisfaction, along with declines in depression, anxiety, irritability, and argumentativeness. TM also appears to reduce dependency on alcohol and drugs.

By now, you may be motivated to develop a daily meditation regimen for reasons besides improving your libido. We believe that the potentially positive impact on your health and quality of life are worth the necessary self-discipline and commitment.

If you're new to meditation practice, try to set aside at least 10 uninterrupted minutes, preferably at the start of your day—even before eating or showering. Then you won't have been pulled into the momentum of your daily routine. You may want to set a soft alarm to go off after 10 minutes, or play a blank tape that sounds a tone at the 10-minute mark. That way, you won't need to open your eyes to check the time.

As you continue your practice, you may wish to increase your meditation sessions to 20 minutes twice a day. Some people meditate for 45 minutes or longer on a daily basis. Set a schedule that works for you. Just be careful not to overextend yourself, or you may not stick with it.

Most people prefer to sit while meditating, though some walk or lie down. The challenge with lying down, especially if you're a beginner, is that you could fall asleep. With walking, you may have trouble clearing your mind, because of all the possible distractions.

You can improve your concentration by repeating a syllable or phrase, called a mantra, on each exhalation. Common mantras include "peace," "love," and "ōm." Closing your eyes while meditating can have a similar effect, though some people prefer to focus their gaze on a particular object, such as the flame of a candle. Another option is to simply look at the floor, without focusing. Experiment with a variety of approaches, so you can identify what feels most comfortable for you.

We've decided to present a mindfulness meditation exercise here, because this particular technique seems to require the least instruction. The basic idea of mindfulness meditation is to concentrate on your breathing while observing and releasing your thoughts with an attitude of detachment. You can focus on the air entering and exiting your body through your nostrils, or on the expansion and contraction of your stomach muscles with each breath.

Whenever your mind wanders, return your attention to your breathing. You will be amazed at how often this happens when you're meditating. And it's completely normal. After all, your mind is always at work—planning, implementing, reviewing. You can easily become frustrated and question your ability to use meditation effectively. Just try to be patient with yourself.

Remember, too, that your job is not to stop the mental chatter; that may be all but impossible. Rather, you want to observe the chatter in a detached way, redirecting your thoughts to your breathing whenever you realize that they've drifted to something else. This is the key to mindfulness meditation. It's about not letting negative thoughts dictate how you feel.

Through regular meditation practice, you will learn not only how to deepen the relaxation of your body but also how to stay in the present. Many women find this helpful as they become more attuned to their bodies while making love. Although we are not aware of any research examining the effects of meditation on libido, we suspect that as stress and anxiety subside, your mind and body become more receptive to sex.

FULL-BODY MUSCLE RELAXATION: GETTING PAST TENSION

Full-body muscle relaxation is a wonderful technique for attending to your physical self in a loving, restful way. It is best practiced lying down, while wearing comfortable clothing or perhaps nothing at all. The basic idea is to systematically tense and then relax all the major muscle groups throughout your body. By first tensing your muscles, the theory goes, you are able to generate and appreciate a deeper state of relaxation.

Take a moment to turn the lights down and make yourself comfortable, lying on your bed or perhaps a couch. Some people like to precede a session of full-body muscle relaxation with a few minutes of deep breathing, as described earlier.

Begin by focusing your attention on your scalp and forehead, tightening the muscles by forcefully wrinkling the skin in these areas. Imagine the muscles shrinking, their surface rough from the strain. Hold for a count of five. Then let go, and imagine the muscles becoming long and smooth from the lack of tension. Experience and enjoy the feeling of release before moving on.

Next, shift your attention to the muscles in your face, including your eyelids, cheeks, mouth, and chin. Create tension in these muscles by grimacing, holding your expression for a count of five. Imagine how these muscles must look under your skin, all bumpy and shrunken from the strain. Then imagine the smoothness and softness of the muscles as you relax. Bask in the exquisite tranquility of the moment.

After your face, continue working through the remaining muscle groups in the following order: neck, shoulders, right upper arm, right lower arm, right hand and fingers, left upper arm, left lower arm, left hand and fingers, upper and lower back, buttocks, chest, stomach, pelvis, right upper leg, right lower leg, right foot and toes, left upper leg, left lower leg, and finally, left foot and toes. When you are finished, spend some time simply lying still and observing your body in its fully relaxed state.

Expect to spend about 20 to 30 minutes on this exercise. Some of our clients prefer to do it just before going to bed, though others have reported falling asleep and thus never getting to all their muscle groups. Plan to practice regularly, at least several times a week, if you want the benefits of full-body muscle relaxation to ultimately improve your libido.

GUIDED IMAGERY: A MENTAL GETAWAY

Guided imagery presents an opportunity to use your senses—sight, hearing, touch, smell, and taste—to achieve deep relaxation. Often it is paired with deep breathing or full-body muscle relaxation, which further enhances the relaxed state. Your goal is to create a pleasurable mental image that you can "revisit" whenever you need to, particularly if negative thoughts or feelings are interfering with your sex drive.

If you wish to try guided imagery, your first task is to identify a setting that you find particularly stress-free. It can be a place that exists, or one that's a product of your imagination. Often people choose somewhere they have been before, so they can conjure a clear picture in their minds. A few of the more popular locations include the beach, an island, a mountaintop, a forest, or even a childhood bedroom. Choose whatever feels most relaxing, safe, and peaceful for you.

Once you've identified a particular setting, you want to mentally guide yourself through the experience of being there. Begin by focusing on what's around you. Don't just look in front of you; imagine turning your head to the right and left, looking up at the sky or ceiling, looking down at the earth or floor. Create a three-dimensional image of your surroundings. Allow ample time to notice everything.

When you're ready, bring your other senses into the scene. What do you hear? Wind blowing, waves crashing, crickets chirping, music playing? Notice how the sounds vary as time passes. What do you smell? The earthiness of the forest, or the sweetness of flowers nearby? Do you taste anything, such as salt in the ocean air? What do you feel? The softness of the sand beneath you, or the crispness of a breeze on your skin? A soft blanket wrapped around your body, or the sun's warm rays on your face? Continue to immerse yourself in the image, enjoying the pleasurable sensations it produces.

Some of our clients prefer to record audiotapes to help guide them through their favorite images. If you decide to make a tape, be sure to allow a few minutes at the end to luxuriate in the mental space you've created. Once you're comfortable with guided imagery, you may want to move on to a more sexual scenario like the one described in chapter 16. In this way, you can train your body to pair relaxation with sexual desire and response.

CHAPTER 12

DEPRESSION, ANXIETY, AND STRESS: ADVERSARIES OF SEX DRIVE

- Any emotional turmoil can dampen your desire for sex as well as your arousal and response.
- Even severe emotional disorders respond well to treatment. And the sooner a disorder is diagnosed, the more effective the treatment will be.
- Physicians routinely prescribe medications both for clinical depression and for anxiety disorders. But some drugs can diminish your sex drive, and others can enhance it.
- Stress can arise from both positive and negative life events. Either way, it can undermine libido.
- If you're showing symptoms of an emotional disorder, seek professional care as soon as possible. It will improve not only your desire for sex but also your quality of life.

Most women are well aware of the close connection between their moods and their libidos. Though feeling happy doesn't guarantee a healthy sex drive, feeling depressed, anxious, or stressed certainly can take away from one.

In recent years, our country has seen an enormous increase in cases of clinical depression, anxiety disorders, and chronic stress. According to the latest estimates, a woman's lifetime risk for depression ranges from 10 to 25 percent—though some researchers think those numbers may be too conservative. Anxiety disorders are even more common, as is chronic stress. Some 43 percent of adults experience stress-related health problems.

As the incidence of emotional disorders like these continues to rise, the incidence of libido trouble will rise as well. In fact, a significant number of women with low libido meet the diagnostic criteria for some form of depression or anxiety.

You don't need to be diagnosed with an emotional disorder to notice the sexual effects of your distress. Even mild melancholy or irritability can dampen sexual desire. You'll be not only less receptive to sex but also less responsive to sexual stimuli—things like your partner's touch or an erotic movie scene. Simply put, if you're feeling good, you're more likely to perceive a sexual stimulus in a positive light. If you're feeling bad, you probably won't be turned on.

When Emotions Run Amok

When a woman comes to the Sexual Wellness Center for help with her libido, we conduct a thorough assessment of her mood and emotional well-being. Perhaps you've started this process on your own by taking the self-test on page 24.

Now you need to ask yourself: Are you getting what you want from life? This is not about being happy all the time or about existing in a state of perpetual bliss. Generally, though, you know whether you feel content and fulfilled. If you don't, it may help explain why you're not all that interested in sex right now.

Perhaps your reply comes with disclaimers or modifiers, such as "Yes, but . . ." or "I will when . . ." Or maybe it's an outright "No." Either way, it hints at some level of emotional discomfort or dissatisfaction that may be sapping your sex drive.

Like most women, you may choose to set aside your emotional health in order to focus on the demands of family, home, and career. But this can backfire in the long run because of the potential negative impact on sex drive, among other things. Why, then, do so many women ignore their true feelings?

Busy lifestyles bear at least some of the blame. Sorting through even mild emotional upheaval takes time and energy, two commodities that are in extremely short supply these days. So many other things demand attention that tending to emotional health typically drops to the bottom of a woman's to-do list. She may continue to function quite productively, even with the strain. But until she confronts and corrects it, she won't truly be well, and she won't fully recover her sex drive.

What's more, many women have been raised with the notion that they should be able to keep their emotional house in order with relative ease. Our clients at the Sexual Wellness Center repeatedly say that they feel weak when they ask for help with emotional issues. This perception is unfortunate, because it leaves women feeling stuck and alone, too ashamed to talk even to trusted family members or friends about their problems.

In fact, just acknowledging our emotional distress to ourselves can be difficult. As it moves to the forefront of our thoughts and lingers there, it can seem particularly troubling, perhaps threatening. Fortunately, once we take steps to address our troubles, we begin to feel better almost immediately. So why not seize this opportunity to explore your emotional health? Your low libido may be an indicator of a problem that needs healing.

We've chosen to focus on a few of the more common emotional disorders known to affect sexual desire and response. For the most part, they require professional intervention and care. So if you think you may have one of these conditions, please see your doctor as soon as possible.

Clinical Depression: More Than the Blues

Clinical depression is one of several categories of mood disorders recognized by the *Diagnostic and Statistical Manual of Mental Disorders*, fourth edition, text revision (*DSM*-IV-TR), published by the American Psychiatric Association. Interestingly, not all mood disorders negatively affect libido. Those that are part of the bipolar spectrum, also called manic-depression, can have the opposite effect. Their symptoms include extreme euphoria and/or irritability, coupled with high energy and a diminished need for sleep.

Bipolar disorders are serious illnesses that require specialized psychiatric care. Because they're more likely to enhance sex drive than inhibit it, they will not be explored further here. The categories of depression that generally deplete libido, however, include major depressive disorder, dysthymia, and depression with postpartum onset, commonly referred to as postpartum depression.

When a woman is depressed, her energy declines, as does her interest in activities she once enjoyed. No wonder she doesn't want to make love to her partner. Even mild depression may lead to low libido. And when the depression subsides, the sexual effects may linger.

Many women who struggle with low libido can identify a specific depressive episode that seems to have triggered the onset of their symptoms. But this isn't always the case. At the Sexual Wellness Center, we routinely see clients who have no idea that they are depressed. If depression sneaks up slowly, the mood changes may not be all that obvious.

If you have a family history of depression, you are at greater risk for developing the illness yourself. But it needn't take over your life. The sooner you receive proper professional care, the better your chances are for a complete recovery. Most people respond well to treatment involving psychotherapy, medication, or some combination of the two.

MAJOR DEPRESSION

Have you heard of someone experiencing a "nervous breakdown"? That's the common name for major depression. Historically, people with major depression were hospitalized in psychiatric wards and medicated, or perhaps given electroconvulsive shock therapy. More effective and humane treatments are available today.

The most severe cases of major depression may be accompanied by psychotic symptoms, including delusions (for example, believing that one's food has been poisoned) and hallucinations (hearing voices in one's head). Often people who attempt suicide meet the diagnostic criteria for severe major depression.

Of course, the illness can take a milder form. The symptoms are similar to those of severe depression, but they're not as intense. People who have mild major depression tend to be fully functional and may display what seems like a normal mood. Even they may not suspect that they have a treatable disorder. For this reason, they may not seek or get proper treatment.

The symptoms of major depression can be short-term (2 weeks) or long-term (2 years or more). They include sadness and irritability, lack of interest in previously enjoyable activities, disturbed sleep and appetite, low energy, and diminished self-esteem. Some women with major depression experience physiological agitation or, alternatively, slowed body movements. Others report poor concentration and memory, as well as feelings of hopelessness, guilt, and worthlessness.

People with major depression tend to evaluate themselves and their lives in an unrealistically negative light while being unaware of their distorted thinking patterns. They readily blame themselves for issues that are beyond their control. Often they experience symptoms of anxiety, which range from excessive worry to panic attacks. Sometimes they are more aware of somatic symptoms, such as bodily aches and pains, than they are their mood disturbances.

In an attempt to self-medicate, women with depression may turn to alcohol or other addictions, such as food or shopping. Combining an addiction with depression not only complicates the symptom picture but also further diminishes sex drive. This is because the addictions themselves diminish sex drive. For example, women who overeat and gain weight as a result may become so self-conscious about their bodies that they avoid making love. Those who shop to boost their mood may find their relationships with their partners strained by financial problems. And because alcohol is a depressant, excessive alcohol consumption—more than two drinks a day—can leave a woman even less interested in sex. (We've talked about the effects of alcohol on libido in chapter 4.)

Phyllis, a 41-year-old Web page designer and graphic artist, is typical of many women with major depression.

Phyllis ran her own business with style and creativity. She was well-liked and full of energy and enthusiasm. None of her friends or professional contacts would have imagined that she was depressed. But her husband, Ian, knew otherwise.

Although Phyllis was a high-functioning artist by day, she was irritable and socially isolative at night. She would vacillate between remaining quiet and yelling at Ian for rather minor issues. She hadn't initiated sex in months, and when Ian made advances to her, she was unresponsive. For his part, Ian was losing interest in making love because Phyllis was so rude.

Ian wanted to help Phyllis, but he didn't know how. He hoped that if he stayed out of her way, she would return to her old self again. But she seemed to get even more irritable as the months went by. She didn't like the person she had become, either.

Phyllis mentioned her moodiness and low libido to her doctor when she went for her annual gynecologic exam. She was referred to the Sexual Wellness Center, where she finally got the help she needed. Without intervention, her depression would have continued to strain her marriage and likely would have affected her professional life as well.

DYSTHYMIA

Dysthymia is milder but lasts longer than major depression. In fact, some people have dysthymia for most of their lives without ever realizing it. They become so accustomed to feeling a certain way that they don't consider the possibility of feeling better.

The primary symptom of dysthymia is a depressed mood that persists for at least 2 years. To be diagnosed with the condition, a woman also must experience at least two of the following: disturbed sleep, fatigue, poor concentration or indecisiveness, lack of appetite or a tendency to overeat, low self-esteem, and a sense of hopelessness. Although low libido is not among the diagnostic criteria, it is quite common in women with dysthymia. Social withdrawal, irritability, and diminished activity or productivity are other suspected symptoms.

Belinda's story illustrates the effects of dysthymia on a woman's sexuality and on her quality of life.

Belinda had been bothered by a blue mood and low energy for years. She always felt like she could use a nap, even though she was getting adequate rest almost every night. Her husband, Randy, expressed his frustration with her indecisiveness. But the fact was, she seldom wanted to do much anyway. She seemed most content when eating—but this also caused considerable distress because of the resulting weight gain.

A fifth-grade special education teacher, Belinda enjoyed her work. But she had to admit, it wasn't as satisfying as it used to be. The rest of her life seemed even less interesting, but she couldn't think of any way to improve it.

Belinda acted happy in front of her family and friends. Meanwhile, she and Randy grew further apart. She knew he wanted to make love more often, but she just couldn't muster any interest in sex. So he spent more and more time watching sports on TV, and she found escape in her fiction books, reading about women who had passionate relationships and exciting lives.

Belinda didn't see any value in going to therapy. After all, she couldn't erase her past, and she wasn't expecting much from her future. It wasn't until a colleague confided that she had gotten help for depression that Belinda reconsidered treatment for herself. She attended individual and group sessions for almost 2 years. During that time, she achieved a better understanding of herself, and she made positive changes in her life that ultimately resolved her dysthymia.

POSTPARTUM DEPRESSION

A specific form of depression unique to new moms, postpartum depression occurs within 4 weeks after childbirth. It is characterized by unstable moods, including spontaneous, seemingly unprovoked crying spells. Many women who develop postpartum depression also report symptoms of anxiety, such as panic attacks, racing thoughts, and obsessive worrying. They may feel that they aren't able to bond with their babies, which causes further guilt and shame.

At its most severe, postpartum depression may trigger thoughts of suicide and/or harming the baby. This fuels even greater emotional turmoil, as women believe they should be happier than ever, having just brought a child into the world. Unfortunately, they may be too embarrassed to reach out for help, so they won't get the treatment that could make a dramatic difference in their emotional state.

Annie, a 32-year-old first-time mom, described her post-partum depression in these terms.

"I was exhausted and overwhelmed. It seemed like I could no longer think clearly or make even basic decisions. I blamed my baby, resenting her for changing my life so dramatically. When she'd cry, I just wanted to run. Everyone around me acted like I was behaving normally, but inside I felt like I was going crazy. I doubted that I could function as a mother."

Women who have a history of depression are at a greater risk for developing postpartum depression. For this reason, they should stay in contact with a mental health professional throughout their pregnancies. A psychiatrist or psychologist could recognize the symptoms early on and recommend interventions before full-blown depression gains a foothold.

The good news is, symptoms like Annie's respond well to treatment. As with other forms of clinical depression, the sooner postpartum depression is diagnosed, the faster treatment can begin, and the more effective it will be.

HOW ANTIDEPRESSANTS CAN DAMPEN DESIRE

These days, the standard treatment protocol for virtually all cases of clinical depression involves some type of antidepressant medication. In general, antidepressants work by elevating levels of certain neurotransmitters—usually serotonin, norepinephrine, and dopamine—which are chemical messengers in the brain. They influence many of the human body's basic functions, not just mood.

Unfortunately, most antidepressants can diminish sex drive. Often, women who experience this side effect feel uncomfortable talking with their doctors about it. And the doctors may not mention it for fear they'll embarrass their patients. Or they may be uncomfortable discussing sexual issues themselves.

Sex is an important component of healthy human function. Doctors and patients ought to be able to talk about the impact of any medication on sexual desire and performance. But more often than not, these conversations don't take place.

According to research, the most common class of antidepressants—the selective serotonin reuptake inhibitors (SSRIs), which include Prozac (fluoxetine), Paxil (paroxetine), Luvox (fluvoxamine), Celexa (citalopram), Lexapro (escitalopram), and Zoloft (sertraline)—tends to produce the most unwanted sexual side effects. So does Effexor (venlafaxine), which has SSRI-like activity but falls into a different class. Although some people experience no sexual symptoms with these medications, approximately 40 to 70 percent of women who take SSRIs or Effexor report one or more of the following: low libido, inefficient or unsustainable arousal, vaginal and/or clitoral numbness, and difficulty achieving orgasm. These side effects can vary in intensity. Sometimes they spontaneously subside as a woman's body adjusts to the medication.

Physicians tend to prefer SSRIs over other classes of antidepressants, because the nonsexual side effects tend to be less severe. For example, SSRIs typically don't cause as much constipation, drowsiness, and dry mouth as tricyclic antidepressants such as Tofranil (imipramine) and Anafranil (clomipramine). Tofranil works by raising serotonin and norepinephrine; Anafranil primarily targets norepinephrine.

Two other antidepressants, Serzone (nefazodone) and Remeron (mirtazapine), are less likely than SSRIs to cause sexual side effects. But they can cause other side effects, ranging from constipation and skin rash to blurred vision, dizziness, and weight gain. Serzone inhibits the reabsorption of serotonin and norepinephrine; Remeron increases the activity of these neurotransmitters.

The good news is that women who take SSRIs may be able to get relief from some of the sexual side effects. Studies suggest that another antidepressant, Wellbutrin, actually may enhance sex drive. Even in subtherapeutic doses, it appears to counteract the sexual side effects of other medications, including other antidepressants. Some doctors have begun prescribing relatively small doses of Wellbutrin in combination with SSRIs with good results. Wellbutrin works by preventing the reabsorption of serotonin, norepinephrine, and dopamine in the brain.

Another possible solution to the sexual side effects of SSRIs is Viagra (sildenafil), the "little blue pill" commonly prescribed to men with erectile dysfunction. Preliminary research shows that some women who experience sexual side effects with prescription medications can get relief with Viagra. It works by causing blood vessels to dilate and fill with blood, which may enhance sexual arousal for women whose nervous systems are affected by medications. (See chapter 9 for more about Viagra and its effects on female libido.)

Sometimes, too, sexual side effects will subside with an adjustment in dosage or a switch to another medication. This is why open communication between physicians and patients is so important. Your doctor should be well aware of the potential side effects of any medication she prescribes. And if she stays abreast of the medical literature, she will be familiar with the latest options for reducing these side effects, as well as new medications that may be less troublesome.

Please keep in mind that you *never* should alter your dosage or discontinue a medication without consulting your doctor. This is especially true for certain antidepressants, which can cause withdrawal symptoms if stopped abruptly.

Anxiety Disorders: Common and Curable

As a group, anxiety disorders are the most common mental illness in the United States. By some estimates, they affect more than 19 million American adults.

Anxiety disorders tend to be chronic, meaning they don't go away spontaneously. In fact, if left untreated, they may become more debilitating over time.

A number of conditions qualify as anxiety disorders, from social anxiety and panic attacks to obsessive-compulsive disorder and agoraphobia (fear of certain places or situations). For all of these, the primary symptom is excessive anxiety. They may cause low libido as well, though it isn't one of the diagnostic criteria for anxiety disorders. This is because anxiety tends to affect libido more circuitously, by altering general quality of life. In other words, a woman with an anxiety disorder may be less interested in sex simply because she's putting her energy into coping with her emotional distress.

Of all the anxiety disorders, the two that most commonly deplete a woman's sex drive are generalized anxiety disorder and post-traumatic stress disorder. We'll explore each of these in turn.

GENERALIZED ANXIETY DISORDER

An estimated 4 million American adults may suffer from generalized anxiety disorder (GAD). It is twice as common in women as in men, often occurring in tandem with another psychiatric diagnosis. For example, many people with GAD also have some form of depression or a history of substance abuse.

Generalized anxiety disorder is characterized by excessive anxiety and worry occurring over a period of at least 6 months. People with GAD often say that they're unable to relax or control their thoughts. Their days seem filled with apprehension, from which they get little relief. Related symptoms may include difficulty sleeping, low energy, irritability, poor concentration, and general restlessness.

With generalized anxiety disorder, a woman may feel too on edge to make love. She can't relax enough to enjoy the sexual interplay, and she may struggle to turn off her mind and tune in to the pleasurable physical sensations. Essentially, she brings her worries into the bedroom, so concentrating on sex becomes highly improbable.

Unfortunately, these circumstances can trigger what's known as response anxiety. It is quite common among women with GAD, and especially those with low libido. Response anxiety is not a psychiatric diagnosis per se but rather a description of the process by which a person becomes almost obsessed with her sexual response. That is, rather than being "in the moment," allowing a free flow of emotions and physical sensations, she becomes a critical spectator in her own sexual experience. And the more she judges herself, the more her dissatisfaction and self-criticism perpetuates itself. This sets up a vicious self-perpetuating cycle.

As with clinical depression, most cases of generalized anxiety disorder respond to treatment with medication, psychotherapy, or some combination of the two. For psychiatrists, the medications of choice are SSRIs and tricyclic antidepressants. As we mentioned earlier, these medications can cause sexual side effects, including low libido. This is why we often advise our clients with GAD to try relaxation techniques first. They may be enough to manage all but the most serious cases of GAD without pharmaceutical intervention. (For basic instruction in deep breathing, meditation, and other relaxation techniques, see chapter 11.)

POST-TRAUMATIC STRESS DISORDER

Post-traumatic stress disorder (PTSD) is a psychological reaction to a traumatic experience or event. It has been getting more attention in the United States because of the upsurge in cases after the 2001 terrorist attacks. More than 5.2 million Americans between ages 18 and 54 may suffer from PTSD.

Traditionally, PTSD has been associated with exposure to extreme trauma, such as military combat, natural disaster, or criminal assault. Now we know that whether or not a situation is traumatic depends on a number of variables specific not just to the incident but also to the person. For example, a woman's trauma history, her coping mechanisms, her social support network—all of these factors help shape her perception of a particular experience or event. This is why incidents that seem mildly stressful to some people may be quite devastating to others.

Stressful but normal life events such as a death in the family or loss of a job can be upsetting enough to trigger PTSD symptoms in certain women. The disorder also can result from cumulative exposure to low-grade trauma. These days, doctors will consider a diagnosis of PTSD when the aftermath of a trauma interferes with a person's normal level of functioning.

While PTSD symptoms generally appear within 3 months of a traumatic incident, they can have a delayed onset, showing up months or even years later. They include flashbacks or nightmares about the incident; attempts to ignore thoughts or feelings about the incident; emotional and physical numbness, including detachment from others; and physical and emotional agitation, characterized by irritability, angry outbursts, and difficulty falling or staying asleep. Even if a woman's symptoms don't lead to full-blown PTSD, they still can have a negative impact on her libido.

Amy's story serves as an example of how perceived trauma can continue to influence a woman's sex life, even if the incident occurred long ago.

Amy, a 41-year-old medical technician, struggled with PTSD for most of her life. It began in childhood, when her mother developed cancer. At the time, Amy didn't know why her mother spent less and less time at home or why she looked more and more sickly. Because Amy's father worked late hours, she became accustomed to making her own dinner and putting herself to bed, even while still in grade school.

It wasn't until her mother died that Amy learned the truth, wrapped in harsh words from a distant aunt who arrived to assist with funeral preparations. Amy remembers few details about her life back then. But she clearly recalls the extreme fear and grief that consumed her for many months following her mother's death.

As an adult, Amy prefers to keep her life as predictable as possible. Anything that challenges her sense of control, including sexual arousal, brings on anxiety that overwhelms her.

In Amy's subconscious, the excitement of sexual stimulation feels similar to the panic of losing her mother. Both cause increased heart rate, altered breathing patterns, and physical tension. As a result, Amy tries to avoid sex with her husband, without understanding why.

In Amy's story, you can see how perceived trauma affects the body as well as the mind. Researchers have made some interesting findings about the body's response to trauma that help clarify our understanding of female libido.

People who react to trauma with physical hyperarousal—in other words, an adrenaline rush—may come to perceive any form of physical hyperarousal as traumatic. So instead of experiencing sexual arousal as pleasurable, they process it as traumatic and therefore avoid it. This occurs despite the attempted intervention of logic. So even if a woman tells herself that she is safe and not being threatened when her partner makes sexual advances, her body can override these conscious thoughts and react as if it's being traumatized.

Physicians routinely prescribe medication for PTSD, but it's intended more for symptom management than for primary treatment. Antidepressants such as Zoloft and other SSRIs can help, as can antianxiety medications. Often they're recommended in combination with some form of psychotherapy.

Talk therapy has proved helpful for people with PTSD, but

recent research shows promising results with techniques that involve the body as well as the mind. One such technique is eye movement desensitization and reprocessing (EMDR).

Developed by Francine Shapiro, Ph.D., a senior research fellow at the Mental Research Institute in Palo Alto, California, EMDR originally was intended for use by military combat veterans struggling to recover from the trauma of war. It pairs deliberate rapid eye movements with thoughts, feelings, and images associated with the traumatic incident.

EMDR is somewhat controversial, in part because doctors can't agree on why it works. But studies of the technique are yielding promising results. Therapists who use EMDR must receive proper training. You can find a qualified EMDR professional via the Web site www.emdr.com.

Chronic Stress: A Fact of Modern Life

In and of itself, stress is not a psychiatric diagnosis. But that does not diminish its impact on our minds, bodies, and relationships. In particular, the subjective experience of physical or emotional stress can significantly affect sex drive.

Sometimes, stress actually enhances sexual desire and response. This tends to be true for women who use sex as a coping mechanism. For them, sexual interplay is a "timeout," a means of release.

More often, however, stress interferes with a woman's ability to relax and enjoy sexual contact. Staying in the moment takes more effort, as her thoughts easily turn to nonsexual matters—even the seemingly unimportant tasks of daily living. This is a problem, because sexual arousal requires ongoing, relatively uninterrupted attention to erotic stimuli. Otherwise, a touch that previously felt pleasurable can be unstimulating at best, intrusive or uncomfortable at worst. Sex becomes another demand, a responsibility or chore instead of the gratifying exchange it once was—and should be.

To complicate matters, women who are in a state of chronic stress may not care that sex has become a casualty of their high-pressure existence. Quite simply, they are too preoccupied with other things to worry about their sex lives.

These days, you'd be hard-pressed to find anyone who considers herself to be completely stress-free. At the same time, tolerance for stress can vary greatly from one woman to the next. In fact, you can have different levels of tolerance at different stages in your life. What might seem overwhelmingly distressing when you're in your early thirties becomes challenging and stimulating when you reach middle age.

Other factors may increase your vulnerability to stress at certain times. For example, a decline in physical health can make previously mundane tasks seem overwhelming. Your body can communicate what your mind may refuse to acknowledge: You have physical and emotional limits that you must respect in order for it to function optimally.

Incidentally, life events need not be negative to be stressful. Though things like physical illness and financial problems obviously cause tension and anxiety, positive events such as marriage, childbirth, a new home, or a new job also take a toll emotionally and physically. The trouble is, you may be less inclined to seek relief from stress when it arises from something positive. Likewise, you may receive less support from loved ones in these circumstances, because they may not understand why you're feeling the way you are. For these reasons, positive stressors can be more difficult to cope with.

If you feel helpless to control the stress in your life, you will experience it more intensely. Identifying and focusing on how you can change your situation may ease your sense of helplessness during stressful times. But your ability to cope could be at the mercy of your genes. Research suggests that humans have an inherited resistance or susceptibility to the effects of stress.

Many women can point to a specific stressful event that seemed to trigger a decline in their sex drives. In such circumstances, low libido likely is a component of the body's normal stress response. We become concerned when a woman's desire for sex doesn't bounce back even after the successful resolution of a stressful situation. Chronic low libido can cause stress as much as *result* from it. This is especially true in intimate relationships, where the longer low libido lingers, the more stressful it becomes for a woman and her partner.

So how can you protect your sexuality from the effects of stress? Research repeatedly demonstrates that perceived social support is one of the best stress-busters around. When you reveal your problems to others, you feel less alone, and you open yourself to nurturance. Both of these factors weaken the impact of stress in your life.

Maintaining good physical health enhances your ability to handle stress and improves your sex life. Studies have shown that adequate sleep, regular exercise, and minimal alcohol consumption can raise stress tolerance in most people. Sticking with a schedule that includes breaks for relaxation also promotes a sense of calm and control, even in the face of chaos. (For a refresher course on self-care for good health and a strong libido, see chapter 4.)

CHAPTER 13

THE HIDDEN IMPACT
OF SEXUAL TRAUMA

- Sexual trauma takes many forms. Its emotional effects can range from mild discomfort to extreme pain.

- An incident needn't involve abuse to be traumatizing. Even consensual sex can cause trauma, depending on the circumstances.

- Whether an incident is perceived as traumatic is determined by a number of factors, including the woman's age at the time of the encounter, her relationship to her aggressor, and the frequency of the interaction.

- Unresolved sexual trauma can lead to loss of trust and difficulty with intimacy. It also can precipitate persistent negative emotions.

- The first step to healing from sexual trauma is to establish a safety zone for yourself in which you can explore your sexual history without feeling uncomfortable or threatened.

The definition of sexual trauma varies, depending on who's doing the defining. For our purposes, we've chosen to interpret the phrase in the broadest sense: Sexual trauma is any unwanted sexual advance, whether verbal or behavioral, that leaves a person feeling victimized and exposed.

In the United States, as many as one in five girls suffers some form of sexual abuse. The incidence of sexual trauma is much higher, though we don't have the numbers to prove it. The reason: Girls—and women—who've experienced sexual trauma may not even realize it. Incidents that don't meet the legal criteria for sexual abuse still can have a traumatic impact.

We're not suggesting that girls who are subjected to sexual abuse aren't traumatized by the experience. Our point is, a woman's sexual history needn't involve a violent incident like rape or molestation to affect her libido. By approaching sexual trauma from this perspective, we hope to make clear how it can shape virtually all aspects of a woman's sexuality.

When the Past Becomes the Present

If you are like most women, you may have engaged in fully consensual sexual behaviors that left a sense of trauma in their wake. In ignoring this information, you forgo valuable insight into your current sex life—and more precisely, your diminished sex drive.

Adolescent dating relationships offer a prime example of the dynamics of sexual trauma. Research demonstrates that girls in dating situations are at high risk for acquiescing to a boy's sexual advances, regardless of their own level of sexual interest. In fact, most women admit that as adolescents, they engaged in sexual interactions that felt shameful, exposing, or humiliating to them. These behaviors range from petting to giving and/or receiving oral sex to engaging in sexual intercourse.

Many women who come to the Sexual Wellness Center for help with their low libido describe losing their virginity in terms that range from negative to blatantly distressing. That was the case with 43-year-old Audrey, who became sexually active while still a teen.

Audrey remembered waiting excitedly to turn 16, the age at which her parents had decided she could begin dating. She admitted being naïve and unprepared for boys' sexual advances. She hadn't actually spoken with her parents about sex. The only communication from her mother about the "facts of life" involved a library book left on Audrey's nightstand.

When boys showed interest in her body, Audrey didn't quite know how to respond to it. Like her female peers, she had gotten the message that nice girls please people. They are sensitive to the needs of others, and they don't make waves. Yet somehow this didn't jibe with what Audrey had learned about sex—namely, that nice girls are passive sexually. They don't initiate kissing or ask a boy on a date. They certainly don't have sex.

Not surprisingly, these mixed messages helped drive Audrey into a situation that went from bad to worse. It involved Evan, a boy several years older than she was. After they had been dating for several months, Evan began pressuring Audrey for sex. She longed for his attention and affection. And making out with him had always felt great. So Audrey made a decision: She'd have sex with Evan, if she could keep him in her life that way.

In my (Dr. Brandon's) office, with a vacant look in her eyes, Audrey described the night she lost her virginity. Her parents had gone away for the weekend, and she was to spend the night with a friend. Instead, she arranged to meet Evan at home.

Evan arrived looking as handsome as ever. The two made their way up to Audrey's bedroom. But she didn't count on what happened next. What had started as second thoughts about having sex turned into cold fear. But Evan looked so intent that Audrey decided to go ahead with their plan. She shut her mouth, closed her eyes, and let him open her legs. . . .

Audrey's voice trailed off as she finished her story. Nonetheless, she insisted that it was no big deal. How could something that happened so long ago be affecting her sex life now? She hadn't thought about that evening in years. In fact, she was a little put out that I had encouraged her to re-live it in my office. She wondered what purpose it would serve, other than stirring up bad feelings.

I invited Audrey to consider how her early experience with sex could be contributing to her current trouble with her sex drive. Audrey seemed stymied for a response. So I offered an analogy—horseback riding, which Audrey said she had never enjoyed.

As a little girl, Audrey had longed for a horse. The ones on TV looked so lovable and sweet. So her parents took her to a stable and allowed her to rent a horse for an hour. Unfortunately, a horsefly bit the normally mild-mannered steed. Audrey was thrown from the saddle, landing on some sharp rocks. The day turned out to be a disaster. And Audrey swore off riding on the spot. She hadn't gone near a horse since.

I asked Audrey why her experience with sex would be any different from her experience with horseback riding. That is, why would the unpleasantness of her very first sexual encounter have no impact on her desire to make love, when the unpleasantness of her very first attempt at horseback riding permanently snuffed out her desire to own a horse? Audrey got my point.

With determination on her part and support from her husband, Audrey was able to adopt a more open, assertive approach to her sexuality—and to find enjoyment in sex. Sadly, far more women choose to ignore the relationship between their sexual histories and their current sex lives. In doing so, they give up deeper insight into their sexual selves, which could cost their libidos in the long run.

Does Trauma Alter the Brain?

As we noted in our discussion of post-traumatic stress disorder in chapter 12, whether or not we perceive a particular incident as traumatic depends a great deal not only on what happened but also on who we are as individuals. Groundbreaking new research offers fascinating insight into how we process and store difficult experiences, including sexual trauma, in our brains. Although a full exploration of this research is beyond the scope of our book, several key points are worth noting here.

From what scientists can tell, disturbing incidents in our lives—even those that are not necessarily disturbing enough to be labeled traumatic—alter our fundamental brain chemistry. More than likely, these changes result from the release of hormones in our brains during times of stress. Over time, it rewires our brains, so we perceive and respond to our thoughts and feelings differently than before.

We already know that thoughts and feelings cause neurons in the brain to fire. The brain attempts to simplify the constant barrage of information by pairing neurons so that they fire together. This pairing seems to increase the likelihood that the neurons will fire together again. In effect, our brains constantly shape and modify our perceptions and behaviors. Applied to sex, this means that one distressing experience can set the stage for similar discomfort in the future.

Even more intriguing, some studies suggest that children may learn to mimic their parents' neural firing patterns. So, for example, a woman with an unresolved sexual trauma in her past may subconsciously affect her child's neurophysiology. Although this research is new, its potential implications for human sexuality are fascinating. In effect, your sexual perceptions and behaviors may be influenced not only by your own history and brain chemistry but also by your parents' history and brain chemistry.

Factors That Define Trauma

What determines the degree of trauma associated with a woman's sexual experiences? Many variables are at play—some obvious, others more subtle.

One is the relationship between the woman and her aggressor. If this person was important or even vital to her existence, she is at a higher risk for trauma. In other words, a woman who was accosted by a family member probably would be more distressed than a woman who was hurt by someone she cared little for and didn't depend on. Let's consider Brenda's story as an example.

While attending summer camp, Brenda was encouraged by a fellow camper to give oral sex to his friend. Although she wasn't even sure what she was supposed to do, she agreed, as she liked the attention she was getting. She relished having something the boys wanted, at least until she realized what they were asking for. Brenda began choking before running back to her bunk. She spent the rest of the summer worrying that the boys would tell on her, or that her friends would think she was a slut.

Years later, Brenda still hated the thought of oral sex. She came to the Sexual Wellness Center because her husband expressed frustration with what he perceived as her sexual inflexibility. Once she opened up about her sexual history, her husband understood her resistance to oral sex. Then they were able to resolve their differences.

If this incident had involved more prominent people in Brenda's life, how would it have affected the outcome? More than likely, Brenda would have felt even more exposed and ashamed. And she would have developed deeper issues with trust, which is common following any kind of sexual trauma. Thus, the emotional impact of one incident can vary considerably, depending on the relationship of the participants to each other.

Many other factors influence a woman's reaction to and recovery from sexual trauma. Age is one of them. In general, the younger a woman is at the time of a traumatic incident, the more she will struggle to cope with it. Frequency is another. A woman who is called a slut by her neighbor on one occasion probably will suffer fewer long-term emotional repercussions than a woman who is repeatedly subjected to such verbal assaults.

170

How others react to an incident helps determine how deep-seated the resulting trauma becomes. It may not be easy, but openly discussing your experience with a trusted family member or friend can make a huge difference in the long-term impact. A woman who receives assistance and support has a much greater opportunity for healing than does a woman who either remains silent about her pain or, worse, seeks help from someone and doesn't get it. Studies have shown that the quality of support can carry even more weight than the incident itself in predicting the emotional aftermath of sexual trauma.

How Trauma Shapes Your Sexuality

A personal history of sexual trauma can influence sexual behavior in numerous ways. Among these effects, we've identified several themes, all of which can undermine female libido.

We should note that women can develop sexual problems like low libido even if they haven't experienced sexual trauma. They still may identify with certain outcomes of traumatic situations. So we hope that you'll read on, even if you can't identify a traumatic incident in your past.

LOSS OF TRUST

Perhaps the most obvious potential ramification of sexual trauma is difficulty with trust. We can readily comprehend how a woman who has been hurt by a sexual experience would be reluctant to expose herself in the same way again. This is especially true if the traumatic incident occurred at the hands of someone whom the woman had found trustworthy before.

What we may not recognize is how a woman who suffers a sexual trauma may lose trust in herself. For example, she may not have confidence in her ability to fend for herself in sexual situations. As a result, she may avoid sex altogether, or she may feel comfortable only when she is in complete control of the sexual interchange. This is what happened with Natalie, a self-diagnosed "control freak."

When I (Dr. Brandon) first met Natalie, she admitted that her husband, David, was crazed by her attempts to run their lives. Although she wanted to be more easygoing, she had no idea how to accomplish that.

Natalie's need to be in control spilled over into her sex life. She wasn't able to find any pleasure in foreplay. She wouldn't allow David to touch her vulva or clitoris when they were making love. Sometimes she wouldn't even let him touch her breasts.

David obviously was frustrated with Natalie. He said that the two of them could have sex only if he completely skipped foreplay, and only if Natalie was on top. She rarely climaxed, and when she did, it was through self-stimulation. They had been making love that way for years, and David was tired of it.

Natalie clearly loved her husband, and she wanted to do her part to improve their relationship—sexually and otherwise. She came to individual therapy nervous but ready for the challenge. Together, she and I explored virtually every aspect of her life. Once we got into the details of her sexual history, things became clearer for both of us.

Natalie was just 7 years old when her parents divorced. Her father moved out unexpectedly, never even saying goodbye. She had no contact with him until she was well into adolescence. Her mother worked hard to support the family, which meant Natalie often ate dinner with babysitters or distant relatives. She didn't feel the attention and nurturing she longed for.

When Natalie entered junior high, her world changed dramatically. As she began developing breasts, she also began getting noticed by the boys in her class. Suddenly she felt wanted. Although she wasn't allowed to date at that age, Natalie managed to find ways to sneak out of the house—and even to sneak boys into her house through her bedroom window. As long as she locked her door, no one checked in on her.

Natalie was so thrilled with the attention that she didn't realize her behavior was backfiring. It wasn't until she attended a local high school foot-ball game that the truth became clear. None of the boys who had wanted her company in her bedroom would even speak to her. She was crushed.

Still, Natalie continued her late-night rendezvous. But she was learning lessons that she would carry with her for years. She learned to hate her sexual self. She learned not to trust men who wanted to be sexual with her. And she learned not to trust her sex drive to steer her toward healthy relationships.

What's more, Natalie lost confidence in her ability to look out for herself, even in the sexual situations that she helped create. Her solution was to subconsciously switch off her sex drive and to make love in a care-fully controlled fashion.

Another, less obvious issue that's rooted in a woman's loss of trust in herself involves a tendency for her body to respond to phys-ical stimulation even in traumatizing situations. This is particularly common among women who enjoyed a sexual encounter that ulti-mately had a traumatic outcome, or who became physically aroused even if they were emotionally ambivalent or uncomfortable. Healthy bodies can respond to stimulation, even when the stimulation comes from an undesirable source.

Natalie described this phenomenon when she spoke about the physical pleasure of letting boys touch her. Once she realized that they were just using her, she felt emotionally devastated. In a sense, her own body betrayed her. She had to retrain herself to expect something good from physical arousal, because for so long she had paired it with emotional pain.

DIFFICULTY WITH INTIMACY

As with trust, women who experience sexual trauma may struggle with intimacy. We talk about fear of intimacy elsewhere in this book, so we will touch on it only briefly here.

In the aftermath of a traumatic incident, a woman may feel ambivalent about getting close to people, emotionally and physically. This can play out through her sexual behavior. For example, she may repeatedly sabotage sexual encounters moments before she and her partner make love. Or she may pick fights with her partner just before bedtime or on weekends, when he is more likely to make sexual advances. In short, she desires intimacy but at the same time dreads sex. Subconsciously, she looks for ways to derail any sexual contact.

Incidentally, a woman who engages in this type of behavior can be very good at making amends to her partner in situations where resolution probably won't lead to sex. For example, she may speak quite intimately to her partner on the phone during the workday, when she knows they can't be together.

MISPLACING BLAME

Sexual trauma can trigger a whole range of negative emotions, including guilt and shame. These create a level of emotional discomfort that ultimately can shut down sexual desire. In particular, women who blame themselves for their sexual trauma may be less inclined to create positive sexual experiences. We've counseled many clients who feel responsible for their own victimization, even though logic tells them that they're innocent.

In this sort of situation, we advise clients to examine the traumatic incident from another person's perspective. For example, how would you respond to the same incident if it happened to someone you care about? You probably would be much more compassionate and supportive. You deserve this for yourself, too.

Guilt and shame are caustic, destructive emotions. If you've been feeling them, you need to start healing—and the sooner, the better. The strategies presented a bit later in this chapter can help the healing process.

Unresolved anger is another potential outcome of sexual

trauma. By itself, anger isn't necessarily a bad thing. In fact, it can play an important role in healing from a traumatic incident. But if it's misdirected—either inward toward yourself or outward toward your partner or men in general—it is more harmful than helpful. It can take the pleasure out of sex and dampen your desire for sex.

Coping without Recovery

More often than not, women who carry unresolved sexual trauma through their lives subconsciously develop unhealthy coping mechanisms to counteract their pain. They may feel better, but invariably, they lose interest in sex in the process.

For example, some women go numb emotionally or physically, especially when their partners make sexual advances. For them, sex is a chore rather than a pleasurable intimate encounter.

Others may engage in a phenomenon called repetition compulsion. That is, they continually attempt to re-create a traumatic incident in controlled circumstances in an effort to master it. Because repetitive compulsion occurs subconsciously, a woman may be unaware of what she's doing.

Consider Natalie, who would make love to her husband only when she was on top and "in charge." She's practicing repetition compulsion, because she's using her position to conquer the sexual trauma from her past. Unfortunately, this sort of behavior does not resolve the trauma itself. Instead, it only impairs sex drive, because sex becomes so monotonous and unsatisfying.

Sexual Healing, One Step at a Time

To experience true healing from sexual trauma, women need to acknowledge and accept the relationship between their sexual histories and their current sex lives. Once this occurs, they become open to the potential emotional and physical gratification that comes from their intimate relationships with their partners. If you suspect that a traumatic incident from your past may be stifling your sex drive now, we suggest taking these steps to launch the healing process.

STEP 1: ESTABLISH A SAFETY ZONE

Perhaps the most devastating effect of sexual trauma is its erosion of your sense of safety, especially in sexual situations. In order to feel comfortable as you work through your sexual history, you first must establish a safety zone for yourself—physically, emotionally, and sexually. Otherwise, exploring any traumatic incidents from your past may cause further distress.

You can reinforce your sense of safety by not pushing yourself further than you are comfortable. Don't pick on yourself, either; self-criticism will only send your psyche into hiding. Instead, approach your sexual history with an attitude of curiosity and compassion. Having your partner's understanding and support can help as well. Discuss it with him, so the two of you can continue this healing journey together.

STEP 2: OPEN UP TO YOUR PARTNER

Disclosing your sexual history to your partner can go a long way toward resolving sexual trauma. The catch is, you must feel as you speak—accessing the pain, fear, sadness, rage, and any other emotion that defines your traumatic experience. Otherwise, you won't be able to process and integrate the information you're sharing. It's important, too, that your partner be a compassionate listener, or opening up to him may be even more traumatizing.

We suggest finding a time to talk when neither you nor your partner is intent on being sexual. However, if you end up making love, and the negative emotions of sexual trauma bubble to the surface, don't shove them aside. Keeping quiet could complicate matters, as you may disconnect from your partner. Instead, take the opportunity to open up to him, so the two of you can work through your emotions together. Chances are, your partner will appreciate your candor, and he'll want to help.

If you aren't quite ready to reveal your sexual history to your partner, writing about your past experiences can help process and release them. You could even create a script to read to your partner when you're comfortable. And don't overlook other outlets for self-expression. Creative pursuits such as drawing, painting, and sculpting can support the healing process, even if you aren't particularly artistic. In fact, nonartists often create the most poignant works, as their goal is self-expression rather than objet d'art.

Creative pursuits have another benefit: By producing a tangible symbol of your sexual trauma, you can define and quantify the experience in your mind. This may help manage and contain your pain. You can see how to keep it from seeping into your sex life, and your life in general.

STEP 3: PINPOINT YOUR PERSONAL TRIGGERS

Once you've spent some time exploring any traumatic incident from your sexual past, try to identify aspects of your current sex life that could evoke the same negative emotions. For example, when your partner is interested in making love, he may approach you in a way that reminds you of a distressing sexual experience.

Identify as many such triggers as you can, and share them with your partner. Then both of you are less likely to be taken aback by your emotional discomfort in certain situations, because you've previously acknowledged them as risky. Actually, you may be able to limit your exposure to your triggers if you and your partner agree to avoid them.

STEP 4: PLAN AHEAD FOR PROBLEMS

Despite your—and your partner's—best efforts, you may face situations that bring forth the emotional distress of past sexual trauma. You can plan ahead for such occasions by equipping yourself with an arsenal of coping techniques. Use them on the spot to take the edge off your emotions and shape a less threatening perspective on your circumstances.

For example, deep-breathing exercises like the one described in chapter 11 can defuse a rising anxiety level. Positive self-talk also can come in handy for navigating a distressing situation. Mentally reciting statements such as "I am safe now" or "I can say no if I want to" reinforces your sense of calm and control. Positive self-talk may seem simple, but it's a powerful tool for moving past emotional blocks.

If sexual trauma continues to undermine your enjoyment of sex and your quality of life, please consider consulting a qualified therapist. You also can find self-help books devoted to recovery from sexual trauma. But in this case, professional intervention may be best.

Sexual Trauma and Men

We hope you leave this chapter with a better understanding of the potential consequences of sexual trauma in all its forms. As you can see, though some incidents clearly fall at the "abuse" end of the trauma spectrum, many more are in a gray area of seemingly minor sexual interactions—not criminal by any legal standard—that nonetheless have a major impact on a woman's sexual identity and behavior. In our experience, women may not even recognize a particular experience as traumatic until we explore its effects on her sex life, including her libido.

In writing this chapter, we do not mean to imply that only

men are sexual aggressors or abusers, and only women are victims. Nor do we mean to imply that all men are looking to exploit women sexually. Neither is the case.

According to some estimates, as many as one in seven boys will become victims of sexual abuse before they turn 18. As among women, the incidence of sexual trauma among men may be much higher than that. In a society that's so obsessed with the image of a strong, tough, virile male, this type of trauma can be particularly devastating for those who endure it. They tend to feel that they can't tell anyone what they've been through, and so they remain alone with their pain—often for a lifetime.

How does this relate to you and your libido? If your partner is dealing with a sexual problem, such as a past sexual trauma, chances are good that you're dealing with a sexual problem as well. For example, men with a history of sexual abuse (note that we are referring to abuse, not trauma) are more likely to develop erectile dysfunction or premature ejaculation. When a man struggles sexually, his partner may begin to lose interest in sex.

Among married couples, the occurrence of sexual dysfunction in both partners is quite common. If this sounds like you and your partner, the two of you might consider consulting a sex therapist.

CHAPTER 14

THE "BENEFITS" OF NOT WANTING SEX

- If you're hesitant to make the necessary changes to reclaim your desire, it could be because avoiding sex somehow works to your advantage.
- Many women use their low libido to express uncomfortable emotions or to deal with difficult relationship issues.
- Once you become aware of your reasons for wanting to maintain the status quo in your sex life, you can consciously choose if and how they continue to play a role.

All of us have moments when we feel stuck in a rut. We contemplate making a change, somehow charting a different course on our journey through life. But more often than not, we continue on the same path—unfulfilled, perhaps, but comfortable in our routine.

Our tendency to stick with what we know points to a complex truth about human nature: When we hesitate to make a change, it is probably because we are getting something from the existing situation. In other words, being stuck in a rut has its benefits or rewards.

This applies to your sexual desire and response as much as to other aspects of your life. We're not suggesting that you actually are quite content with your low libido. If that were the case, you probably would not be reading this book. What we are saying is that other factors are at play, and you subconsciously perceive yourself as benefiting from them in some way.

Our mission in this chapter is to help identify what these mysterious variables are. Then you can make a conscious decision about what role, if any, they will continue to play in your sex life.

Never Having to Say "I'm Angry"

Let's start our exploration with a few questions: What are the advantages of not doing anything about your low libido? Why would you prefer to maintain the status quo in your sex life? What would you lose if you showed more interest in sex?

For example, many of our clients at the Sexual Wellness Center have realized that they subconsciously use their low libidos to convey their anger toward their partners. In doing so, they're able to release their negative emotions while avoiding direct confrontation.

Unfortunately, our society continues to discourage women from openly expressing their anger. It's considered unfeminine and unattractive. What's more, those who dare to buck the social standard are labeled as bossy or rude. As a result, many women choose to suppress their anger, rather than exploring how to verbalize it.

The fact is, anger is an essential component of any intimate relationship. It will surface eventually. So if you have a low libido, it just might be the perfect medium for communicating your anger to your partner without actually discussing it. On the other hand, if you were to improve your libido, you'd need to adopt other strategies for acknowledging and addressing the emotional aspects of your relationship. And you may not be comfortable with that.

To complicate matters, if you do attempt to convey your anger in a healthy and constructive way, you must be prepared to deal with the inevitable fallout of your forthrightness. You might worry about how your partner will respond to what you have to say. Will he become angry himself? Will he expect you to change something about yourself in return?

As you can see, low libido becomes an easy scapegoat for other, more challenging relationship issues. Sarah and Josh are a great example of this dynamic. They had been in an intimate relationship for 6 years when they came to the Sexual Wellness Center to discuss Sarah's low libido.

Sarah and Josh described an active and satisfying sex life during their first few years together. Then Sarah noticed a gradual but significant decline in her sex drive. At first she thought it was a "stage" that would pass with time. But if anything, she became even less interested in sex. Both Sarah and Josh were sensitive to the changes in their shared physical intimacy.

From the start of therapy, Sarah made it clear that she loved Josh and wanted to spend the rest of her life with him. She believed they were "meant to be together," and outside of sex, their relationship was good and solid. She couldn't understand why this one part of their relationship had gone so bad when the rest was so good.

As Sarah worked in therapy, the subtleties of her relationship with Josh emerged. Like all intimate relationships, theirs was much more complicated than either of them originally thought.

Sarah felt uncomfortable admitting it, but some things about Josh really weren't so fantastic. Often she felt that he didn't respect her. He seemed to think that she couldn't navigate the world without him. He tended to infantilize her, treating her as though she needed someone to take care of her. At the same time, he could get pretty childlike himself, demanding her time and energy.

At first, Josh appeared hurt and betrayed by Sarah's comments. He was shocked that she would find so many faults in him and in their union. But when Sarah didn't back down, Josh was able to speak candidly about his perceptions of her.

Josh believed that Sarah wanted him to be a responsible and guiding force in her life. Hadn't she come to him asking for help with various emotional and financial problems that she couldn't face alone? For his part, Josh was tired of being the accountable one in the relationship, taking care of everything from paying the bills to shopping for groceries.

Although these disclosures proved difficult for both Sarah and Josh, they paved the way to a new level of honesty and understanding for the couple. And through this process, Sarah discovered why she had lost interest in sex in the first place. She wanted Josh's protection, but at the same time, she wanted her independence. Meanwhile, Josh discovered that he liked feeling needed by Sarah, and he resented the responsibility he felt she wanted him to take. Together, Sarah and Josh faced the reality that their relationship wasn't as problem-free as they had wanted to believe.

What's more, Sarah realized that she actually had been benefiting from her low libido. It had enabled her to channel significant relationship issues into a neat, less threatening package, thus camouflaging the negative emotions that she needed to resolve.

As Sarah and Josh disclosed their true feelings, they were forced to confront the fact that Sarah's libido probably would not improve unless they made some changes in how they related to one another. Frankly, they weren't entirely sure that they were up to the difficult and demanding task of making those changes. They were acutely aware of their fear of what lay ahead. But they also welcomed the opportunity to take their relationship to a deeper level.

Exercising Control

Perhaps you have no problem expressing anger and other emotions to your partner. In that case, other issues may be brewing. For example, you may be spurning your partner's sexual advances on the grounds of low libido, when in fact you're punishing him—intentionally or not.

We've counseled clients who admit to enjoying the power that comes with rejecting, or at least not desiring, their partners. Consider the emotional impact of saying to someone, "I don't want you." Even if you don't mean for your words to come across as hurtful or spiteful, your partner nonetheless may interpret them that way.

If you feel disempowered in your life in general, rejecting your partner may present a rare opportunity to be in control of a situation. You're calling the shots, and you won't be coerced into doing anything you don't want to. But you'll forfeit this power if you once again desire your partner sexually. This may feel like a significant loss.

Remember, all this may be purely subconscious on your part. It takes strength and courage to evaluate yourself at this level, to uncover and understand the motivations for your sexual behaviors.

Interestingly, channeling unexpressed emotions through sex may occur at an even deeper subconscious level. In particular, we sometimes make others the target of emotions that really don't belong to them.

As an example, let's say you're unfairly reprimanded by your boss. You're steamed about it, but if you confront him, you risk losing your job. What happens to that anger? Maybe it gets channeled to your assistant; you berate her for a minor mistake just because you have the power to do so. Or maybe it gets channeled to your partner; you may reject his sexual advances—again, just because you can. In other words, you're fulfilling your need for revenge and control. These dynamics can be poisonous for a relationship. Unfortunately, identifying them isn't always easy.

Avoiding Exposure

Some women value their low libido because it prevents them—or should we say protects them—from the vulnerability that's essential to good sex and healthy relationships. Virtually everyone longs for an intimate connection with another human being. But at the same time, we fear that connection.

When we are intimate, we allow ourselves to be vulnerable, to be revealed and known to our partners in a deep and meaningful way. We give freely of ourselves, emotionally and physically. Yet in doing this, we feel exposed and unsafe. We know that when another person gets so close to us, they automatically gain the capacity to hurt us. Thus, we face a dilemma: We must weigh our desire to experience a deep emotional and physical bond with another human being against the risk of opening up to someone on such a personal and private level.

Along the same line, some women use their low libido to control the depth of intimacy that they achieve with their partners. They are able to avoid crossing into a realm of vulnerability that feels unsafe for them. In effect, a fear of being hurt or rejected by another human being ultimately may result in a lack of desire for sex. We may prefer to interpret a fear of intimacy as low libido, rather than leave the safety zone of vulnerability that we have created for ourselves.

Preventing Dependence

Though some women carefully guard their vulnerability with the "armor" of low libido, others respond by not allowing themselves to become dependent on anyone.

We commonly regulate our degree of dependence based on our level of fear. In fact, most women are consciously or subconsciously ambivalent about how much of a connection they want to share with their partners. Perhaps they already have been hurt by someone they relied on, such as a parent or a former spouse. Or they may be trying to avoid the painful goodbye that they know inevitably comes at the end of any relationship. Thus, by maintaining a certain distance from their partners, they feel protected from uncomfortable and sometimes distressing emotions.

A woman can alienate herself from her partner not just sexually but also emotionally and financially. By being so determined to protect herself from being hurt, she never fully embraces the intimacy that is vital to a thriving sexual relationship. So it was with Ellen, a 45-year-old artist and mother of two.

When Ellen came to the Sexual Wellness Center, she and her second husband, Greg, had been married for 5 years. She recalled the two of them making passionate love while they were dating and engaged. She also remembered having an exciting, satisfying sex life before she and Greg met.

But Ellen couldn't recall the last time she initiated sex with Greg or even wanted to make love to him. She felt sad and angry about the decline in her sex drive, which once had been so strong.

In individual therapy, Ellen talked about certain "personality quirks" of Greg's that irritated her. Though she loved her husband, she said, she found herself spending more time dwelling on his less desirable characteristics. She was annoyed by seemingly minor details, such as the intonation of Greg's voice when he spoke and the shoes he wore. She was upset with his tendency to spend so little time with their children; he hadn't been to a Little League game all year.

On a more personal note, Ellen had caught Greg watching other women when they were in public together. He also ignored her when she spoke. She wasn't sure that she mattered to him anymore.

Eventually, Ellen found the courage to open up to Greg about her concerns. In doing so, she allowed him to know her better—an important step toward greater intimacy in their relationship. Ellen was surprised to discover how sharing her thoughts and feelings with her husband brought them closer together.

Greg rose to the occasion as well, explaining to Ellen how her be-

havior affected him. He described Ellen as distant emotionally and physically, and hard to please. She repeatedly rebuffed him when he touched her.

Greg was able to identify what displeased him about Ellen, but he was slower to acknowledge his own errant behavior. Then Ellen asked if he would be happy for their daughter if, 20 years down the road, she married a man who spent no time with their children and watched other women in public. That convinced Greg to clean up his act.

The discussion prompted Ellen to share some of her past relationship experiences. She had been devastated when her first husband left her years before. In the aftermath of their divorce, she had decided that she always would take care of herself first and not become "too dependent" on a man to take care of her.

I (Dr. Brandon) asked Ellen if her feelings might go back further than her first husband. Had she experienced them before? In response, Ellen spoke about growing up in a huge Catholic family, the second of seven siblings. Though her parents clearly loved her, they focused on the younger children, who needed more attention. Ellen's natural reaction was to feel jealous. But in her mind, her jealousy wasn't justified. She feared that expressing it would further distance her from her parents.

This sort of situation presents an evolutionary dilemma for children. They are programmed to figure out how to ensure their own survival. So they learn to "read" their parents, who are their caregivers, and to behave in ways that elicit love and attention. This is why as a child, Ellen decided to conceal her negative emotions from her parents: She didn't want to risk alienating them by needing more than they could give. She carried this tendency into adulthood and into her current relationship with Greg.

The problem is, what worked to obtain nurturance in a family setting doesn't necessarily work to foster intimacy in an adult relationship. The relationship strategies that all of us learn as children usually can benefit from some adjusting as we grow up.

As they cleared the air, both Ellen and Greg could see their individual contributions to the lack of sexual desire Ellen was experiencing.

Ellen no longer focused on Greg as the source of their problems. Through therapy, she was able to understand how her ambivalence about intimacy played a role in her avoidance of sex.

It is easy to blame your partner for any distance in your relationship. Like Ellen, you probably can point to specific aspects of your partner's personality and behavior that are driving the two of you apart. You may believe that you are choosing to keep him at arm's length because of his "flaws." But if you were to ask your partner how you contribute to the distance in your relationship, what might he say? Would it be true?

Most of us buy into the idea that we want emotional and physical intimacy with our partners. It's the reason we pair off into couples—to share a profound connection with another human being. But the truth is, intimacy can be daunting. To be known by another person at such a deep and personal level frightens and intimidates us.

Perhaps you are using your low libido to control the connection between you and your partner. You certainly wouldn't be the first woman to play out your ambivalence about intimacy through your sexual relationship, and you won't be the last. By becoming aware of this behavior, you can make conscious and thus more empowered decisions about the nature of the emotional and physical bond between you and your partner. And it may very well have a positive impact on your sex drive.

Changing for the Better

We encourage you to contemplate how your lack of interest in sex might be working to your advantage in your relationship with your partner. We do not mean to suggest that you enjoy not wanting to make love. Your discomfort with your low libido is real, and it's powerful. Rather, we hope that we can raise your awareness of the more complex picture of opposing fears that all of us share. Just as you can pinpoint why you want to reclaim your desire, consider why you may not feel completely comfortable making the necessary changes to achieve that goal.

The fact is, avoiding change results in stagnation—for you and for your partner. You probably can think of couples who have chosen not to grow in their relationships, and who no longer share the emotional and physical connection they once did. Although their behaviors remain the same, the soul of their bond has faded. When you consider this as the alternative, change becomes much less daunting and much more desirable.

Try to approach the process of change as an adventure. If you expect it to be difficult, with lots of distress and turmoil, it probably will be. You will tend to behave in ways that ensure a bad experience. On the other hand, if you embrace the process with excitement and optimism, you almost certainly will emerge with your relationship—and your libido—stronger than ever.

PART IV

THE THIRD KEY:
INTELLECTUAL
FULFILLMENT

CHAPTER 15

HOW YOUR THOUGHTS AFFECT YOUR LIBIDO

- When you're engaged in and enthusiastic about life in general, you're more inclined to desire sex.
- Maintaining an intellectual bond with your partner is essential to a healthy sexual relationship.
- Your thoughts and beliefs about sex began to form when you were very young, and have been influenced by your parents as well as by society as a whole.
- In general, societal obligations and expectations for women inhibit a healthy sex drive.
- By making changes in your fundamental thought patterns and belief systems, you can foster a more positive mindset about sex and your own sexuality.

If emotions are what you feel, then intellect is what you think. And what you think—not just about sex but about everything else in life—has a direct impact on whether you desire sex.

As you'll see in this chapter, your intellectual health is as much a product of your heritage and upbringing as of your own mind. It encompasses your beliefs and values, your habits and behaviors, your interests and opinions.

Women who are intellectually healthy are engaged in and

energized by the world around them. They have a strong sense of purpose and of self. This permeates all aspects of their lives, including their sexuality. They're aware of their sexual needs and preferences, and they're comfortable sharing this information with their partners.

But these women probably would not be so interested in their sexual satisfaction if they felt ambivalent about the rest of their lives. They manage to maintain a level of stimulation and satisfaction by engaging their minds in positive, productive ways. Boredom, the alternative, does not foster the same sense of vitality. When we feel bored with life, we more than likely will feel bored with sex.

Incidentally, finding intellectual fulfillment does not necessarily involve educational pursuits. We can engage our minds through all kinds of activities—for example, art, music, dance, sports, and other methods of creative expression. As long as something piques our interest, it feeds our intellect.

Rediscovering Your Intellectual Self

Consider what engages you in your world. What draws you, beckoning your involvement? What do you enjoy?

If you have difficulty answering these questions—or if you find yourself thinking "Who has time for this stuff?"—your intellectual self is likely out of balance. Making room in your life for activities that interest you feeds your mind and your soul. You're able to energize yourself, to take something for yourself, so that you are not involved in a perpetual cycle of giving, which can lead to depletion.

Some women haven't felt intellectually stimulated in such a long time that they simply don't know what interests them. In our society, women are so entrenched in caring for others that they frequently lose touch with themselves, their needs, and their wants. If you identify with this dilemma, don't despair. Start by thinking about what engaged you in the past. Consider this question: If you had other lives to live, how might you use them? Your answer may point to a new activity that you could explore.

Perhaps you are aware of what you would find exciting, but you're embarrassed to tell anyone else or afraid to try something new. Keep in mind that taking such a risk will likely pay the greatest dividends for your intellectual self. As a result, you will probably benefit sexually as well. After all, your brain functions as a major sexual organ!

On the Same Wavelength as Your Partner

Just as intellectual stimulation makes you feel engaged in your world, it also makes you feel engaged in your relationship. In general, it is difficult for a couple to share an exciting sex life for an extended period of time unless both partners appeal to each other in nonsexual ways.

To nurture an intimate bond with your partner, the two of you must build an intellectual connection as well as a physical one. This could mean participating in activities that you both enjoy. It could also mean finding pleasure in easy conversation, common parenting goals and values, or vacations together. Essentially any meaningful shared experience can contribute to intellectual bonding.

It isn't unusual for a woman with a diminished sex drive to notice a decline in the intellectual stimulation she derives from her relationship with her partner. As you assess your intellectual connection with your partner, consider how you might cultivate interesting new experiences together. Just as you grow personally, how might you and your partner grow as a couple? What activities have the two of you contemplated but never followed through on? Scuba diving, a travel adventure, or swing dancing lessons, perhaps? Even something as simple as trying an exotic cuisine or restaurant can add spark to your intellectual bond.

As you and your partner contemplate your options, make an effort not to be restrictive by vetoing each other's suggestions. Gently pushing each other to explore something new can help cultivate a renewed interest in your relationship, which in turn can help revive your libido.

The Origins of Your Sexual Mindset

All of us hold complex thoughts and beliefs about our ourselves and our sexual partners that affect our libidos. We may not even be conscious of the myriad ways in which we view ourselves, our partners, and our sexuality. Some of these perceptions developed when we were very young; they've been a part of us for so long that we don't pay much attention to them.

Few of us know ourselves as well as we would like to believe. In order to have an intimate relationship with your partner, you must first have an intimate relationship with yourself. You will let someone else get only as close as you already know and are comfortable with yourself. So let's take some time to explore your thoughts and beliefs more deeply.

But first, a word of caution: Embarking on this journey requires not only curiosity but also a sense of humor. Taking yourself too seriously can shut down the process of self-exploration. By adopting a lighter approach, you can achieve a deeper level of knowing. The more you know about yourself, the better you'll understand why you lost your libido, and what you must change to get it back.

FROM YOUR PARENTS' PERSPECTIVE

Let's begin by examining the thoughts and beliefs that could be preventing you from wanting and enjoying sex. It might be helpful to evaluate your views of mature female sexuality in general, because they influence your desire for sex.

Much of your understanding of your sexual self is rooted in your childhood and the information you accumulated as you grew up. This information carries the bias of the people who provided it—more than likely your parents. Keep in mind that your parents taught by what they said as well as by how they behaved. You know the old adage "Actions speak louder than words"? Well, it certainly holds true with regard to sex.

For example, regardless of what your mother may have told you (or not have told you) about sex, you subconsciously learned how she perceived her own sexuality by observing her. And you will hold her perceptions as your own unless you make a conscious effort to identify your own belief system.

Remember, too, that your mother learned about sex in the same way you did. So, for example, if she was raised to be ashamed of her sexuality—which was not uncommon for women of her generation—chances are she conveyed that same message to you, even if she didn't intend to.

To help understand how your parents' views of sex have shaped your own, consider these questions.

- What did you learn about mature female sexuality from observing your mother?
- Did she seem to enjoy her sexuality?
- How did she dress when she and your father went out for a romantic dinner together?
- Was she comfortable with her body?
- How did she react to sexually confident women? Did she like them? Did she feel threatened by them and put them down?
- How did she relate to her body as she grew older? Did she enjoy her body? Did she complain about aging?

- Did she appear receptive to warm, caring touch by your father?

- Was she comfortable with your changing body? Did she teach you directly and clearly about sex, your period, pregnancy, and childbirth? Did your budding sexuality make her anxious?

- What did you learn about mature female sexuality from your father?

- Did he seem to enjoy your mother and her femaleness?

- How did he react to sexy adult women in public? How did you feel about his reaction?

- What did he communicate to you (through words or actions) about women and sex?

- How did he react to your interest in boys?

- What did you learn about sexuality in a committed relationship by observing your parents?

- Did your parents close their bedroom door at night, giving themselves privacy from you and the rest of the family? Or were they always accessible, leaving you with the impression that your needs came before their intimacy?

- If you have older siblings, how did your parents respond to their budding sexuality? How did this affect your sexual expectations and behaviors?

- Were your parents comfortable touching each other in your presence?

- Did your parents make a point of nurturing their intimacy? For example, did they go away alone together? Did they share hobbies or other pleasurable experiences? Did they make a priority of spending time together?

- How did your parents' intimate relationship develop and change as they grew older? Did they eventually move to different bedrooms? Did they divorce?

By exploring the origins of your current belief system, you may come to appreciate how your past learning has influenced—and perhaps limited—your interpretation of your sexuality and your desire for sex. Then you can ask yourself this: Do these beliefs fit you and work well for you? Or do they really belong to someone else?

ALL GROWN UP WITH NO LIBIDO

Elizabeth's story offers an example of how powerfully the thoughts and beliefs we're exposed to as children can affect our sexual experiences as adults.

From a very young age, Elizabeth had been "taught" that sex is bad. Her parents conveyed this message in both subtle and obvious ways. For example, they never touched each other, or even hugged each other, in their children's presence. They never talked about sex or bodily issues in general. Elizabeth learned about her period—a milestone in her developing femininity—from her gym teacher rather than from her mother.

Elizabeth recalled one particular occasion when her mother accidentally walked in while she was masturbating. They never discussed the incident, but from the repulsed look on her mother's face, Elizabeth knew without a doubt that she had been caught doing something horrible. That night, she prayed that if God would forgive her, she'd never touch herself again.

Elizabeth described her mother's insistence that she wear skirts that fell only well below her knees. She admired her classmates' more fashionable clothes, which her mother considered indecent. Yet she never asked why. She trusted that her best interests were at heart.

Though Elizabeth's mother played a major role in shaping her sexuality, her father was a factor, too. The more womanly her body grew, especially during her high school years, the more uncomfortable he became. She was no longer the little girl he had protected and provided for.

Elizabeth's father grew distant in those years. Her maturing sexuality tapped his deepest anxieties. From him, Elizabeth subconsciously got the message that her sexuality made men nervous, that it made them want to disconnect from her.

Elizabeth claimed to understand that masturbation isn't sinful, and that sex between consenting adults can be a pleasurable activity, but her behavior revealed her true thoughts and beliefs. Tearfully, she acknowledged that she felt dirty when she tried to become aroused with her husband. She believed that respectable women don't enjoy sex.

Elizabeth had backed herself into a corner. She wanted to have a healthy and satisfying sexual relationship with her husband, but she was reluctant to express her sexuality. Under such circumstances, her libido was unlikely to return.

Consider how your own upbringing may be influencing your views of female sexuality and your desire for sex. From observing your mother, for example, you may have learned that women become less sexual as they age, or that a mature woman shouldn't revel in her sexuality. Or if your father showed any discomfort with your mother's sexuality, you may have subconsciously determined that men disconnect from women who are overtly sexual.

Look for any similarities between the current sex life of you and your partner and that of your parents at the same stage in their relationship. You may be surprised by the extent to which couples tend to mimic the sexual behavior of their elders.

SOCIETY'S ROLE IN YOUR SEXUALITY

Just as our parents help shape our thoughts and beliefs about sex, so does our society in general. Unfortunately, it promotes an attitude toward women and their sexuality that is counterproductive to a healthy libido.

In particular, our society continues to perpetuate the notion that women are primarily nurturers. We expect a mature woman to devote herself to giving attention to and taking care of others, as opposed to herself receiving attention from and being taken care of by others. But when she focuses on others, she has little energy to explore and experience her own passions. What's more, if she feels self-conscious about stating her nonsexual needs, she certainly won't feel comfortable expressing her more personal, sexual ones.

Our society defines the "perfect" woman as young, attractive, successful, and nurturing to all. In doing so, it fails to acknowledge the reality of her needs. When girls are taught to care for others before themselves, they learn to make themselves a low priority. Some women internalize this message to such a degree that they understand sex only in terms of giving rather than receiving. They effectively switch off their sexuality and disconnect from their bodies. In doing so, they lose touch with their libidos, as well as their sense of the appropriateness of their desire for sexual fulfillment.

Thankfully, attitudes toward women and their "role" in our society appear to be mellowing with each successive generation. But much work remains to be done in order for experiences and expressions of sexuality to be as acceptable for women as they are for men.

This is not to suggest that men have been spared the burden of societal expectations and obligations. For example, just as women are pegged as nurturers, men are pigeonholed as tough and emotionless. We discourage the display of feelings by our male children, and we ridicule it in our grown men. Instead, we want them to work long and hard to support their families, and we don't want to hear them complain about it.

The point is, both men and women must grapple with stereotypes that don't necessarily serve their best interests. It requires strength of character for all of us to evaluate these belief systems and determine which ones we feel are appropriate and which ones we choose not to adopt for ourselves.

Our society interferes with libido in other ways as well. We tolerate, if not encourage, a pace of life that makes intimacy between partners a near impossibility. We expect adults to work 50-plus hours each week; raise healthy, happy children; keep fit physically; and maintain relationships with family and friends—all while having fantastic sex lives! Choosing to be a full-time mom doesn't make life any less hectic. It's no wonder that so many women find their interest in sex waning. If they lack the energy to nurture and regularly attend to themselves and their relationships, their libidos will suffer.

Consider, too, what our society teaches about the effects of aging on female sexuality. Most of us are painfully aware of the unfortunate and ill-informed notion that women lose their sensuality and sexual attractiveness as they get older. (We discuss this further in chapter 21.) Do you perceive yourself as less sensual now than when you were younger? Do you believe that your sexual attractiveness is dependent upon your chronological age? How has Hollywood's depiction of mature sexy women (or lack thereof) influenced your attitude toward aging and female sexuality?

If you accept these harmful societal ideologies as fact, you are most likely harming yourself by undermining your sexual self-esteem and your experience of sexual pleasure. You need to ask yourself this: Do you feel comfortable with society's constraints? Are you willing to forfeit your sexuality as you mature?

Our guess is probably not. Otherwise, you wouldn't be reading this book! But unless you're able to wean yourself from society's belief system and form your own, it will continue to color your sexual attitudes and behaviors, and your sexual desire.

Changing Your Mind

Recognizing how various outside forces have contributed to your thoughts and beliefs about your sexual self is the first step toward making the sorts of changes necessary to foster a healthy libido. Moving forward with these changes requires a conscious commitment on your part. In other words, you must set your mind to accomplishing change in order to start the wheels in motion. It won't happen without effort and determination.

Once you've acknowledged your intent to make a change, your next step is to decide which thoughts and beliefs to keep and which to discard. This is your opportunity to make your sexuality your own. Ask yourself: What is the reality I want to create for myself? What are the thoughts and beliefs I need to embrace?

To help reinforce your new mindset about your sexual self, we suggest reciting your thoughts and beliefs as affirmations. These simple, positive statements actually help "rewire" your brain, so your thought patterns and belief systems become automatic. As they do, your libido will return, too.

CHAPTER 16

INSIDE YOUR SEXUAL
MINDSET

- How you make love to your partner can reveal a great deal about who you are as a person, both sexually and nonsexually.

- Your frame of mind can influence your enjoyment of a sexual encounter for better or for worse.

- Women with low libido often say that they're bored with their sexual "routines." Yet that sameness fulfills a fundamental human need for safety and security.

- You can learn a lot about your sexual mindset by exploring your favorite sexual fantasies, your preferred sexual positions, and your past sexual experiences.

- Your partner's sexual preferences may have just as great an impact on your libido as your own preferences do.

Any exploration of the intellectual aspects of your sexuality would be incomplete without examining your perception of your personal sexual style. That is, how do you interpret your sexual preferences? What meanings do you attach to them?

Everyone has a unique set of sexual preferences. If you can't readily identify yours, don't worry. You simply haven't discovered them yet. They're revealed through things like the type of partner you're attracted to, the type of sex you enjoy, and the type of fantasies you engage in. Your willingness to delve into your particular sexual preferences, and to share them with your partner, can help revitalize a fading sex drive.

The State of Your (Sexual) Union

Before we talk about what appeals to you and arouses you sexually, let's look at what is going on in your sex life now. Chances are, if you aren't interested in making love to your partner, then you aren't satisfied with the experience on some intellectual level.

You can gain fascinating insight into who you are by exploring how you make love to your partner. This information holds clues to the reasons for your low libido. After all, your sexual attitudes and behaviors are direct manifestations of your personality. The way you interact with your partner in the bedroom corresponds to the way you relate to him outside of the bedroom.

How do you perceive yourself as a lover? Many of the women who come to the Sexual Wellness Center because of diminished sex drive say that they were good lovers in the past, but that they haven't maintained the same level of sexual prowess for their current partners. If this describes you, you ought to explore why you don't want more from your sexual encounters *for yourself*. Chances are, the more you seek to satisfy yourself sexually, the more exciting and giving a lover you will be.

GETTING YOUR MIND IN THE MOOD

Let's consider a typical sexual scenario for you and your partner. Who usually initiates an encounter? If you're contending with a decline in your sex drive, your partner probably assumes the role of pursuer more often than not—simply because you're not interested in sex in the first place.

How does your partner let you know that he wants to make

love? Does he tell you with words, or do you know by his behavior? What do you feel at these times? Many women with low libido say they feel dread, disgust, or anger when their partners come on to them. If your internal reaction to your partner's advances is negative, how might this be conveyed to him? That is, how do you respond to him, consciously and subconsciously? These interactions play a crucial role in the overall flavor of your sexual encounter, which is often rife with power struggles and underlying messages.

When we have a "commodity" our partners want—whether it be attention, approval, or sex—we recognize on some level that we have a bargaining chip we can use to our advantage. It's quite tempting to provide or withhold that commodity in an effort to obtain for ourselves what we want from our partners. In effect, we act out our needs through such interchanges, rather than speaking about them directly and openly. Often we prefer the safety of hiding behind our behaviors to the risk of sharing our thoughts and beliefs with our partners.

Assuming you are receptive to your partner's advances, what happens next? How does your partner know that you're open to sex? Do you smile in a certain way, or respond to his touch? Although that may be your intention, it is probably not what really happens.

If you are like most women with low libido, you may give the impression that you're having sex out of duty rather than desire. Perhaps you shut your eyes and contemplate all the things that you'd rather be doing at the moment. Or maybe you focus on what you perceive your partner to be doing wrong. Is he touching your genitals too quickly? Kissing you too sloppily? Doing that thing to your breasts that you hate?

If you identify with these behaviors, then you probably are using your thoughts to distract yourself from your true feelings at the moment. It may be helpful for you to open up to these feelings and to share them with your partner in a loving way. Ask for his help.

For example, when you notice that your mind is wandering, you might say to your partner, "Honey, I feel like I'm shutting down sexually, and I don't know what to do about it." This may not be easy, but it can counteract your subconscious inclination to distance yourself from your partner and from the situation at hand. It also sets the stage for the two of you to address the underlying problem as a team—which probably isn't how you are dealing with it now. Most couples find themselves in adversarial roles when one partner has a waning interest in sex. Working together toward a solution can make a world of difference.

As you can imagine, going into a sexual encounter with a negative mindset definitely interferes with your interest in and enjoyment of making love. Just consider how the same mindset might affect your experience of an activity you readily enjoy, such as dining out.

Suppose your partner invites you to a restaurant for dinner, but you are tired and distracted after a long and difficult day. If you begrudgingly agree to join him, leave on your work clothes, and dwell on the less-than-attentive waitress, you're almost guaranteed to have a terrible time. On the other hand, if you change into a comfortable outfit, order an interesting new dish from the menu, and make an effort to relax and enjoy yourself, your overall impression of the evening probably will be much more favorable.

Of course, the latter scenario would require more effort on your part. But afterward, you likely would agree that the increased energy expenditure paid off.

The same fundamental rule applies for virtually any activity, including making love: You take from it what you put into it. Expecting bad sex all but ensures an unpleasant and disappointing sexual encounter. But if you open yourself to the possibilities of sexual pleasure and satisfaction, you create a mindset that's more conducive to desire.

BREAKING OUT OF A LOVEMAKING RUT

Let's move on to the "main event": foreplay and intercourse. Who does what? How do you perceive your sexual style, and your partner's? What do you think your partner gets from the experience? Is it what you want for him?

Many women with low libido admit that on some level, they're hoping that their partners don't enjoy sex with them. Then, they say, their partners might expect less of them sexually.

At least part of the reason these women don't want sex is that they and their partners are stuck in a rut, sexually speaking. You may be, too—especially if you and your partner have been together for a while. Chances are, the two of you follow a routine for your sexual encounters. Most couples use the same two or three sexual positions for the duration of their relationships. If this sounds like you, you may be ready to break out of your sexual mold.

Do you ever wonder how the two of you fell into a routine in the first place? The fact is, we prefer to be mired in dry, tired sex rather than risk the honesty and vulnerability necessary to create change. There's safety in boring sex. It's as simple as that.

Human nature being what it is, we tend to gravitate toward safety instead of risk. We *like* things to stay the same. This is true even in our relationships with our partners and in our experience of sex. We are drawn to the security of predictable interactions, both sexual and nonsexual.

Perhaps you're thinking, "That's absolutely not true for me! I love exciting, passionate sex. I had it with my partner at the beginning of our relationship, and I had it with previous partners as well. And I know I want it now." Your reaction is understandable. But generally, sexual relationships are much more complicated than that.

We understand that you want to want sex again. But the fact is, you probably want to feel safe even more. We gravitate toward safety in our long-term sexual relationships. Short-term relationships are different because they are less threatening. We know our partners less intimately. And they don't know us well enough to hurt us.

This explains, at least in part, why people fall into extramarital affairs. It is much easier to engage in passionate sexual encounters when we don't know our partners' faults and defects, and they don't know ours. We can color our perceptions to match our desires more easily with partners we know less well. We can project onto them the characteristics we want to see, as opposed to those they really have.

In affairs, as in new relationships, all sorts of motivations propel two people toward a sexual encounter. Often they're seeking confirmation that they're good lovers, that they're attractive, that they're needed, that they're desirable sexually. So they're on their best behavior, putting their best foot forward, sexually speaking. In long-term relationships, motivations like these give way to the security—and boredom—of predictable sex.

MAINTAINING INTIMACY AFTER SEX

When you and your partner have sex, do both of you climax? If so, who comes first? How do you feel when your partner has an orgasm? Do you enjoy watching him experience sexual pleasure? What is your orgasm usually like? Have you learned ways to make it more or less intense?

Some women with low libido notice that they climax more easily when masturbating than during intercourse. Others feel that experiencing an orgasm isn't worth the effort. Either circumstance points to a fundamental disconnect between a woman and her sexual self, or between her and her sexual relationship. It's interfering with her ability to gain pleasure from her orgasms and those of her partner.

The moment of climax seems to signal the end of a sexual encounter. Most couples stop making love once one or both partners have an orgasm. Do you cuddle, talk, run for the shower, or doze off? Do you switch off emotionally, or savor the intimate connection?

If you're like many women with low libido, you may be relieved that you "survived" the experience. You're content to roll over and fall asleep. But think about the message that your behavior conveys to your partner. Is it the message that you really want to send? Hopefully not. If it is, you may be trying to avoid intimacy with your partner, and you need to figure out why.

By now, you may be wondering what your answers to all these questions really mean. Rest assured, they're not suggesting that you in fact hate your partner, or that the two of you have some fundamental compatibility issues—though sometimes you may be convinced that you do.

It is all too easy to blame your partner for the current state of your sex life. Yes, he may bear some responsibility for your lack of interest in sex, especially if he's predictable or out of touch with your needs. But remember, it takes two to tango sexually. Your thoughts and beliefs have just as great an impact on your sexual desire and response as your partner's actions and behaviors. The purpose of the questions above is to assess your expectations and behaviors in the context of your sexual relationship, so you can see how they may be hampering your sex drive. If you want more sexually, you likely must give more. Do your part to change those worn-out sexual patterns.

Your Sexual Preferences Revealed

In our experience, women who report a decline in their libidos invariably have lost sight of the ways in which they're contributing to the underlying problem. Simply experimenting with more-positive or receptive thought processes or belief systems can help stimulate their sexual interest and response.

One option is to explore personal sexual fantasies and their impact on libido. For example, many women like to imagine being made love to by a sexually dynamic and dominant man. That is, they want a man to take charge of them, perhaps overpower them, and assertively guide them through a sexual encounter. Their fantasies might even involve bondage or forced sex.

Admittedly, these types of fantasies can be frightening. A woman may be uncomfortable opening up to her partner about them. Or she may interpret them as a sign of some deep-seated, perverse desire to be sexually abused. Either way, she's likely to shut down her fantasy and her sexual enjoyment as well.

Like dreams, sexual fantasies can be taken too literally. In this case, a woman's desire for domination more likely simply reflects her latent guilt about enjoying sex, which may be temporarily relieved if she perceives herself as not initiating and thus not being responsible for a sexual encounter. In other words, rather than wanting abuse, she is subconsciously conveying her ambivalence about expressing her sexuality.

Your willingness to reveal your fantasies to your partner can have tremendously positive implications for your libido. First, sharing such private thoughts will likely create a greater sense of intimacy between you and your partner. In general, where there is increased intimacy, there is an increased desire for sex. Second, sexual encounters between the two of you likely will become more pleasurable as your partner learns more about what turns you on.

Disclosing this type of information can feel like a big step. But you won't enjoy the rewards unless you're willing to take the risk.

Like your favorite sexual fantasies, your preferred sexual positions reveal a great deal about your sexual mindset. Do you prefer the missionary position, being made love to from behind, or directing the action from on top? Are you an active participant in your sexual encounters, or do you play a more passive role? What turns you on about that? Are you comfortable with your response? How would you feel if your partner suggested trying different sexual positions?

All of us favor certain sexual positions for various reasons. For example, some women like to be on top because they can climax more easily. In this position, the woman has more control over the rhythm and movement of her partner's penis, and her clitoris is more accessible for her or her partner's stimulation. Other women would rather be on top because they feel in control of their partners' sexual experience, which turns them on.

Think about why you enjoy particular sexual positions. What meanings do you attach to them? Can you appreciate these meanings? Hopefully so, because they reveal vital information about what might help reinvigorate your sex drive.

You also can gain valuable insight into your sexual self by taking a closer look at the best sexual experiences of your past. Many women report that their most pleasurable encounters have involved intense emotion or an adrenaline rush. For example, they may have been overwhelmed with love for a partner or felt a powerful intimate connection with that person. Or they may have tapped into emotions not normally associated with sexual pleasure, such as fear or anxiety.

People who enjoy an element of danger during sex—such as making love in a public place at the risk of getting caught, or being encouraged by their partners to try something new and daring—can attest to adrenaline's power to enhance sexual pleasure. Often, we are turned on by breaking out of old patterns of sexual behavior, even if we feel a certain level of discomfort in doing so.

The Interplay of Sexual Styles

In exploring your own sexual preferences, you can't ignore your partner's. Do you know his favorite positions? His sexual fantasies? His preferences for touching and being touched? How often he wants to make love?

Perhaps you're wondering why we're asking questions about

your partner when we should be focusing on you and your libido. The fact is, your perceptions of your partner's sexual preferences are a powerful force in your own sexual experiences. And obviously, that which influences your sexual experiences also affects your sexual response and your sexual desire.

How do you feel about what turns on your partner sexually? If you like what he likes, the two of you probably are an excellent sexual match. For most couples, however, sex just isn't that simple. What about the woman who is put off or even repulsed by her partner's sexual preferences? Obviously, this situation can be a sensitive one.

Probably the most common point of contention for couples is frequency of intercourse. Stereotypically, men desire sex more often than women. We attribute it primarily to hormones, and to a lesser degree to societal expectations. However, low libido can be a problem for men as well. Preferences regarding frequency of intercourse vary not only between couples but also for the same couple as they move through different phases of their relationship.

Discussing differences in sexual preferences can be challenging for any couple. But if the differences continue to simmer below the surface of the relationship, they can turn destructive over time. Like all differences between two people, those that aren't addressed tend to gain in power and potential for harm.

If you and your partner tend not to communicate with each other about your sexual preferences, it most likely will weaken your sex drive. This is because your level of sexual intimacy is limited by lack of knowledge. Where intimacy is limited, vulnerability is limited. As we discussed in chapter 2, intimacy and vulnerability are essential ingredients in a satisfying sex life and a strong libido.

What if you and your partner discuss the differences in your sexual preferences but the situation stays the same or possibly gets worse? In that case, the two of you may need to examine other, non-sexual aspects of your relationship.

Mental Exercises to Enhance Your Libido

At the Sexual Wellness Center, we encourage women to use their minds to enhance their sexual desire. One way to do this is to identify soothing, engaging thoughts that can help guide your sexual experiences. For example, you might remind yourself why you want a closer relationship with your partner, or make mental lists of what you love about him. Take time every day to consider why you appreciate having him in your life. Focus on your gratitude. In this way, you can open up mentally and emotionally, as you take steps to get closer to your partner.

A second way to use your mind to enhance your sexual desire is through positive imagery, an extremely powerful therapeutic technique that you can practice on your own. Your goal is to mentally guide yourself through the type of sexual encounter you wish to experience with your partner. Imagine enjoying every moment, every sensation. Create in your mind the scenario you want to create with your partner. Practicing positive imagery when you are relaxed will enhance the power of this technique to spark your sex drive.

For example, you might try conjuring a mental image of you wanting to be with your partner, and revisiting it throughout the day. Picture yourself greeting your partner warmly when you reconnect in the evening. Imagine responding positively when he puts his arms around you. See yourself later that night, feeling loved and safe as you crawl into bed. Watch as your mind and body open and become receptive to your partner's touch. Follow this scenario to the end. Envision the two of you making love passionately, lost in moments of intense physical and emotional pleasure.

Using positive imagery in this way can help retrain your mind and body to respond freely and enthusiastically to sex. If you are like most women with low libido, that hasn't happened in a long time. Make an effort to remind yourself of what you are striving to recapture.

PART V

THE FOURTH KEY:
SPIRITUAL
CONTENTMENT

CHAPTER 17

THE SOUL OF YOUR DESIRE

- Each of us has a unique perspective of spirituality that's drawn from our core beliefs and needs.
- We feed our spiritual selves by engaging in activities that reward our sense of purpose and fulfillment.
- When we embrace spirituality in our lives, it creates a more meaningful context for our sexual encounters with our partners.
- Often we lose touch with our spiritual selves. To reconnect, we must free up space in our lives, both physically and emotionally.

Many of us have strong spiritual convictions. But few of us realize how these convictions help shape our sexuality, or how our spirituality helps create a more fulfilling sexual experience. In ignoring the spiritual aspect of our sex lives, we unwittingly weaken our sex drive. And though we may feel dissatisfied sexually, we may not be able to pinpoint why.

A rewarding spiritual life doesn't necessarily involve God or a higher power, though belief in a supreme being is vital for many people. Nor is *spirituality* synonymous with *religion*. In general, religion is more organized and structured, with more clearly defined concepts and more-distinct boundaries—though this varies from one belief system to the next. Spirituality, on the other hand, is more personal. It's defined by each person to satisfy unique individual beliefs and needs.

Although people who describe themselves as religious consider their belief systems to be spiritual, the opposite is not always true. That is, people who describe themselves as spiritual do not always view themselves as religious.

For our purposes, we define spirituality as the process of seeking out life-sustaining and life-enriching experiences. It is a means of feeding your life force. It provides a context for living and opportunities for self-actualization. It adds dimension to your self, your relationships, and ultimately your sexuality.

Seeking the Spiritual in the Ordinary

We express our spirituality in a variety of ways. All present an opportunity to rise above the everyday, to replace the potential mundaneness of human existence with depth and meaning.

In general, any activity or experience that stirs feelings of passion and fulfillment can feed your sense of spirituality. Perhaps the most obvious spiritual rituals are those with religious roots, such as holiday celebrations and prayer. For some people, spiritual expression might involve communing with nature—perhaps through gardening, walking in the woods, or caring for animals. Others get a spiritual lift from practicing meditation or yoga. Those who are parents often describe raising and nurturing children as the most profound spiritual experience of their lives.

Certain professions, such as teaching or caring for the physically or emotionally ill, can provide spiritual rewards. So can volunteer work. Being a Big Sister or teaching adults to read, for example, may have spiritual significance for those who choose to donate their time and effort.

The opportunities for spiritual expression are too numerous to explore in a single chapter. Our goal is to encourage you to identify ways of cultivating your spiritual side, if you feel lacking in this area. Most women find that engaging their spiritual selves dramatically improves their sexuality and their sexual desire.

Sex as a Spiritual Act

The intimacy achieved through making love can itself be a profoundly spiritual experience. People who embrace spirituality in their lives are able to explore and express their sexuality in more-meaningful ways. They also are able to transcend, if for only a relatively brief time, the innate sense of loneliness shared by all humans.

Women who engage in exciting, powerful emotional sex with their partners almost universally describe it as spiritual. And they seldom report a decline in libido. In fact, they are more likely to express love—and lust—for their partners. By comparison, women who don't desire sex often are out of touch with the spiritual aspect of their sex lives. As they develop their spiritual side, they enhance their sexual experiences and reinvigorate their sex drives.

How does sex become spiritual? That depends on how you define your own spirituality. In general, sex that is spiritual is incredibly emotional and soulful. Often women describe a sense of merging with their partners, or with the universe at large. They may speak of transcendence, of rising above loneliness, distance, and pain. When sex is spiritual, it has the power to heal.

Developing the spiritual aspect of your sex life won't happen overnight. It takes time and a commitment to exploring your unique spiritual beliefs and needs. It also requires a profound level of intimacy. If you choose to do this, you will notice a change in your libido over time. Spirituality is not a quick fix for diminished sex drive. But it is an effective one.

Creating Space for the Soul

To experience spirituality in your sexual encounters, you must embrace spirituality in the whole of your life. Reconnect with your soul. What inspires you? What drives you? What makes you feel complete? Answering these questions can help define your spiritual identity, which perhaps has been in hiding for quite some time.

As you become reacquainted with your spirituality, you need to make room for it in the rest of your life. Women have become so frenzied, overburdened, and depleted that they tend to neglect their spiritual side. As challenging as it can be, finding time to foster spirituality is absolutely imperative. Think of it as an opportunity to examine your life, pruning or eliminating those things that demand your energy but offer little reward in return. Through this exercise, you make physical space for the sorts of activities and experiences that will nurture your spiritual self.

Emotional space is important, too. To take full advantage of spirituality in your life, you need to stop channeling your emotional energy into places where it serves little purpose. One way to do this is to identify your addictions.

When we say "addictions," we mean more than the sorts of behaviors targeted by residential treatment programs and 12-step support groups. We're referring to any burden that causes a person to become emotionally stuck or enables her to avoid the real issues in her life.

Most of us have these less-obvious addictions. Work is an excellent example. It's a socially acceptable activity that diverts our attention from any turmoil within ourselves or in our relationships. Eating, shopping, and watching TV can have the same effect. We are addicted to these behaviors when we repeatedly use them to create distance from, or to cope with, difficult or unpleasant emotions.

In other words, addictions are a form of self-medication. They may help in the moment—perhaps by numbing us or distracting us—but they drain our emotional energy over time. The problem is, we need this energy to grow spiritually. So instead of transcending pain, we remain mired in the depths of it.

Letting go of your addictions is a process, and a challenging one at that. As you move through it, you'll get to know yourself on a level you may not have been aware existed. Just be prepared to feel worse before you feel better. We're not kidding! That's because the emotions that have been concealed by your addictions will present themselves full force. As you heal emotionally, you will be able to channel that newfound energy into your spiritual self. Your sexuality and your libido are bound to benefit.

Toward a More Spiritual Life

Better sex isn't the only perk of a stronger spiritual identity. Women who actively cultivate spirituality in their lives find pleasure in even the simplest activities, like walking in the woods or gazing at the stars in the sky. They feel profoundly grateful just to be alive. They develop a deep appreciation for the people in their lives, especially their partners. This fosters a stronger spiritual connection in their relationships, and a stronger desire for sex.

CHAPTER 18

SEX AND YOUR SPIRITUAL SELF

- Turning sex into a spiritual experience takes practice.
- Using Tantrism and Taoism can strengthen your spiritual identity, as well as your spiritual connection with your partner.
- Achieving spirituality in a sexual relationship requires a certain amount of exposure and risk.

Bringing spirituality to your sexual encounters is all about being in the moment. Rather than critiquing your performance (or your partner's) or trying to change your sexual style, you let go and allow the interaction to follow its own course.

This doesn't mean allowing your mind to drift to other things—a looming deadline at work or the pile of dirty clothes in the laundry room. You want to stay present, focusing your attention on each touch, each caress, each kiss. Even if you're following a familiar lovemaking pattern, you might experience new, pleasurable sensations. Seize the opportunity to enjoy them.

Do you and your partner tend to rush through lovemaking, cruising through foreplay to intercourse? Make a conscious effort to slow your pace. This deepens the intensity of the experience as well as the spiritual connection between you and your partner. It also puts greater emphasis on foreplay, which can help if you're trying to revive your libido. In effect, the "appetizer" becomes as spiritually nourishing and satisfying as the "main course."

Making Love Sacred

Achieving spirituality through sex takes practice, especially if you tend to mentally or emotionally disconnect during sexual encounters—a common occurrence among women with a diminished sex drive. In that case, we recommend experimenting with exercises and techniques drawn from the ancient Eastern disciplines of Tantrism and Taoism. Both advocate an awareness and manipulation of one's life force, which in turn fosters an expanded consciousness, a sense of timelessness, and a "oneness" with one's partner and the universe.

Tantrism and Taoism share similar views of sex and sexuality as well. Both describe making love as a divine act in which each partner plays a sacred role. They prescribe rituals to enhance the sexual experience—things like perfuming one's body; wearing beautiful, seductive garments; and creating a sacred space with pillows, candles, and other comforts.

Following Tantric and Taoist teachings, each partner should treat the other with utmost respect and gentleness. And both partners achieve sexual fulfillment by engaging all parts of the body, not just the genitals. For example, Tantra identifies multiple erogenous zones on the female body—the vulva, buttocks, and breasts as well as the eyes, lips, nape of the neck, throat, arms, hands, and feet.

This is why we recommend Tantric and Taoist techniques to our clients with low libido, even if they are not looking to cultivate a more spiritual sex life. These techniques help create a sexual ambience that may pave the way to more and better sexual encounters.

TANTRISM: UNITING ENERGIES THROUGH SEX

Tantrism's roots in India extend thousands of years into the past. It is considered a philosophy as well as a science, an art, and a way of life. The goal of Tantric exercises is to awaken kundalini, the essential life energy. Kundalini lies dormant for most of our lives. Those who are serious students of the tantra typically prepare for years to release the powerful kundalini forces within.

According to Tantric teachings, masculine and feminine energies are both present in all of us. Their healthful expression and interaction leads to liberation from human limitations. Making love is a valued medium for uniting these energies and freeing ourselves.

If you and your partner are open to trying Tantric techniques during lovemaking, we recommend starting with some basic breathing and relaxation exercises, like those described in chapter 11. Once the two of you achieve a calm, peaceful inner state, you will be more ready to connect with each other in a sexual—and spiritual—way.

One gentle but powerful Tantric technique involves matching your partner's breathing, and vice versa. For this exercise, one person lies quietly, breathing at a comfortable rate. Then the other person adopts the same breathing pattern. Looking into each other's eyes during this exercise can increase the spirituality of the experience.

With another Tantric technique, you learn to "open" your heart and mindfully exchange love with your partner. Begin by sitting naked, facing each other. Imagine your heart opening up, so that you are able to give and receive love more freely. Then imagine exchanging this love with your partner while you hold him in your gaze. Many couples find this exercise intensely emotional and spiritual. They say that it heightens their sense of intimacy during lovemaking.

TAOISM: ENHANCING CHI AND SEXUAL PLEASURE

Taoism, like Tantrism, dates back thousands of years. The Chinese developed this discipline to guide people in maintaining or increasing their inner energy or life force, called chi. Taoism uses a variety of techniques to build chi, including physical activity, a balanced diet, proper breathing, yoga, meditation, massage, and eye contact. This, in turn, unites and harmonizes the female (yin) and male (yang) energies found in each one of us.

In Taoism, men learn how to delay orgasm and how to achieve orgasm without ejaculating. In this way, they may effectively maintain their life force while enabling their partners to experience more-satisfying sex.

Taoism also encourages men and women to strengthen their pubococcygeal, or PC, muscle. This is believed to intensify the sexual experience for both partners and to enhance ejaculatory control in men. The PC muscle stretches from the pubic bone to the anus; it contracts rhythmically during orgasm. You can find it by stopping your urine flow in midstream.

These days, the exercises that strengthen the PC muscle are known as Kegels. Most texts recommend starting with 20 Kegels a day, repeatedly tightening and relaxing the PC muscle. You can increase the number of repetitions over time.

Practicing Kegels on a regular basis will enhance your sexual arousal by increasing blood flow to your genitals, intensifying sensitivity in that area. In this way, Kegels can be quite helpful for improving your sex drive and strengthening your orgasms. In fact, we recommend them to all of our clients with low libido.

The Risk of Spiritual Connection

If you choose not to try the Tantric and Taoist techniques described above, ask yourself why. Do they make you uncomfortable? Do you find them bizarre?

People who balk at such intimate exchanges with their partners usually do so for a reason. That is, if you resist the opportunity to achieve a deeper level of intimacy with your partner, you probably are holding back in other aspects of your sexuality.

Why are you reluctant to explore this new sexual territory with your partner? Are you embarrassed to initiate the exercises? Do you worry about how your partner will respond to you or what he'll think of you? Are you afraid of how you will react to the exercises yourself? If you identify with any of these concerns, it likely is interfering with your sexual expression and enjoyment. In that case, you need to address the underlying issues before you can embrace spirituality in your sexual relationship. Celeste's story offers a good example.

A vibrant, intelligent woman, Celeste had been happily married for 13 years to Dennis, a man she described as her soul mate. When she spoke about her husband, her dark eyes sparkled and her face brightened.

Celeste was hoping to use therapy to enhance her sexual experience with Dennis. She felt that something was lacking between them sexually. "No bells and whistles go off when I climax," she frowned. "Shouldn't sex be more than just 'okay'? It just isn't that much fun anymore."

Celeste wanted more for herself sexually. She wanted to want her husband again. She appeared comfortable with her body and was able to answer questions about her sex life with minimal embarrassment. But when we discussed the physical, emotional, intellectual, and spiritual aspects of her life, she came up short on spirituality. "I'm not even sure what 'spiritual' means," she said. "I'm not much into religion, I can tell you that."

I (Dr. Brandon) encouraged Celeste to consider what might be in it for her to further explore her spiritual side. We talked generally about her understanding of life and specifically about the things that bring meaning and purpose to it. We also discussed using Tantric techniques to enhance her sexual experience.

At first, Celeste tried to humor me. She respectfully stated that she would consider such exercises but that she had been hoping for something with a little more impact. "I want to explode sexually, not fall asleep," she said with a smile.

I asked her to bear with me, as what she had learned from society about great sex would not be helpful in her current situation. That is, the American ethos of "faster is better" has limited applicability in the bedroom. Mindful, loving sexual expression would be a more effective means to the explosive end that Celeste wanted. Slowing things down was in fact a surefire way to speed things up again. She looked skeptical, but she agreed to experiment.

Celeste came back a week later looking dejected. Although Dennis was willing to participate in her "homework," she felt too self-conscious to press the issue with him. They tried a few of the exercises, but they quickly came to the conclusion that they were searching for something different.

We explored what was happening for her, why she was reacting so negatively to what could have been a fun experience. Celeste thought for a while before she reached her conclusion: She felt uncomfortable being so intimate with Dennis. Looking into his eyes for a long period of time left her feeling exposed and embarrassed. And she wasn't sure she wanted him looking at her that way. She again petitioned for different exercises. The ones I had suggested simply were not working for her.

I suggested that Celeste bring her husband to our next session. I hoped that Dennis would be less afraid of deepening their emotional and spiritual connection, and hence be an ally in the process.

Dennis turned out to be the warm, loving man that Celeste had described to me. But he, too, was skeptical about embracing this sexual "adventure." We discussed the likelihood that if they continued to limit their homework to what felt comfortable, they wouldn't learn anything new about themselves or their relationship. After all, if it were comfortable, they probably would have tried it already. This made sense to them, and they left my office with new enthusiasm.

Over the next several months, Celeste and Dennis continued with the Tantric breathing and imagery techniques. They even took classes at a local Tantric center.

Their spiritual journey was not without challenges. Both of them

227

struggled with trust and control and with their personal perceptions of "letting go."

But at the end of her therapy, Celeste sat in my office with newfound grace. Her delightful energy remained, but her confidence was stronger than before. She laughed as we reminisced over her initial reluctance to explore a spiritual connection with Dennis. By opening up spiritually, she found the sexual fulfillment she had been searching for.

Practice Is Key

Numerous books provide further instruction in using Tantrism and Taoism to achieve a more spiritual union with your sexual partner. We recommend *The Art of Sexual Ecstasy*, by Margo Anand; you can find others in your local bookstore. Practicing the techniques of these ancient disciplines can increase your awareness of your sexual self and support your efforts to improve your libido.

Be aware, though, that even people who practice these techniques on a regular basis don't find every sexual encounter to be a spiritual one. Some will be more profound than others.

PART VI

LIFE PASSAGES
AND YOUR LIBIDO

CHAPTER 19

FROM INFATUATION TO INTIMACY

- Over the course of a relationship, the expectations of new love give way to the realities of long-term commitment. This transition period requires tremendous adjustment for both partners.

- As you move beyond your initial infatuation with your partner, your perception of this person will change. You may question your feelings for him, when in fact you're judging him through the filter of your life experiences.

- Issues with power and control, trust, independence, and competition influence the dynamics of your relationship. Recognizing and understanding these dynamics is essential to achieving true intimacy with your partner.

- Your concerns about all the changes in your relationship can undermine your interest in sex. But as you become accustomed to the new dynamic between you and your partner, you will feel an even deeper bond that can reignite your sexual desire.

All of us can recall how we felt when we first fell in love. Just thinking about our partners sent fiery shivers of sexual energy up and down our spines. Emotionally, we brushed off issues that normally would have irritated or upset us. Physically, even our biological processes changed; we didn't need as much sleep, but somehow we were more energetic. We had an unparalleled zest for living that resulted in frequent, mind-blowing sex with the fortunate benefactor of our desires.

All of these marvelous by-products came our way because of the unique and glorious blend of molecules surging through our veins at that time. Contrary to the popular romantic notion that our unique sexual chemistry with our partners is responsible for our ecstatic state of being, we actually should thank our biology. That's because when we fall in love, our bodies produce a number of wonderful substances, including one called phenylethylamine (PEA). A natural amphetamine, PEA temporarily triggers many of the psychological and physical changes that we equate with being in love.

This concept is as unpopular as it is important. New couples assume that their passion and lust will thrive for the duration of their relationship. As long as they love each other, they reason, they will continue to want each other sexually. Their idealized view can make for a bumpy, but nonetheless inevitable, transition from romantic infatuation to mature intimacy.

Many women come to the Sexual Wellness Center in the midst of this transition, perhaps spurred by a decline in sex drive or other changes in their sexuality. Invariably, they wonder if they are falling out of love—or if they ever were in love in the first place. As we explain, what they're feeling is normal to the evolution of an intimate relationship. If they can weather this passage, they and their partners can look forward to an even stronger union. Fantastic sex still will be possible, but it will require more effort, as well as a greater appreciation for the complex dynamics between partners.

Great Expectations, Not-So-Great Reality

As you move beyond the infatuation phase of your relationship, you likely will notice a profound change in how you perceive your partner. Suddenly he is completely different from the person you first fell in love with. He may seem less attractive, less interesting, or less ambitious than he once was. He might be insensitive to your needs or inattentive in conversation. Perhaps he has regressed to a childlike state that wasn't apparent before. Or maybe he has become parental, making decisions without consulting you, because he knows what's best.

If you're like most women in similar situations, you resent these changes in your partner. You're less interested in negotiating with him and less motivated to please him. You feel as though someone played a terrible trick on you. This is not how you expected your relationship to turn out!

Chances are, your changing perception of your partner has had an effect on your sex life, too. This represents another significant disappointment in terms of your expectations of your relationship. You may not be as interested in sex as you once were. And when you and your partner do make love, you don't respond to him like you used to. You struggle to stay "in the moment," let alone muster any passion. These changes may lead you to question your relationship even more. Why does your partner no longer turn you on? *What went wrong?*

This is when all the negative emotions about your relationship—the anger, the frustration, the resentment—can bubble to the surface. Acknowledging them isn't easy, because their very existence suggests that what you thought you shared with your partner is dying, or at least is in decay. You may decide that you should just ignore whatever is happening in your relationship, in the hope that it will spontaneously correct itself. You may pretend that everything is great, except that your libido is uncharacteristically low. Or you may determine that you need to do something drastic to reconnect with your partner or to distract yourself. Perhaps if the two of you started a family, or you had an affair, or you threw yourself into your work, you'd feel better.

Probably the last thing you would do is admit to anyone how you're feeling. On some level, you may believe that your emotions are wrong, even though they're very real. You may wonder if somehow you're to blame for the changes in your partner and your relationship.

Yet because you don't understand why you feel the way you do, you have no idea how to go about improving the situation. Your relationship seems to be beyond your control. You may worry about the implications for your future with your partner. You've seen the statistics on divorce, and they aren't encouraging. Is your relationship headed for that devastating end?

We understand just how upsetting all this can be. But we hope you'll find some comfort in knowing just how common it is. The transition out of the infatuation phase of a relationship seldom goes smoothly. If only couples were better prepared for it and had more realistic expectations for the evolution of their unions. Perhaps then they wouldn't feel so overwhelmed by the inevitable changes.

The truth is, any long-term intimate relationship has a way of exposing parts of our psyches that we prefer to ignore both in ourselves and in our partners. But when they reveal themselves, as they usually do, they transform how we relate to each other. If we understand this process, we might be able to use it to our advantage, fostering healthier, more stable, and fulfilling partnerships that can last a lifetime.

When Sex Loses Its Luster

The metamorphosis of a relationship from mere infatuation to mature love is both a biological and a psychological process. It gets its initial jolt from your physiology. As your body's production of PEA naturally declines over time, the fantastic "side effects" of the chemical begin to wane. This is not to say that you no longer can experience the same wonderful feelings. You just won't have PEA to help in doing so. This is why your partner may not interest or excite you as much.

Of course, the loss of PEA isn't necessarily the only explanation for your diminished sexual arousal and response at this point in your relationship. Another involves a disagreeable phenomenon called habituation, which experts define as the experience of becoming accustomed to a stimulus after repeated or prolonged exposure. Eventually, the stimulus just loses its impact.

Sometimes habituation works in your favor—when you learned to drive, for example. At first, your car may have felt out of control, especially as you increased your speed. After several times behind the wheel, however, you became accustomed to the sensations, so they no longer were disturbing. Similarly, habituation allows you to increase the intensity of your exercise routine as your body becomes more tolerant of the workload.

You can blame habituation for making you less receptive to your partner's sexual advances. Research has demonstrated that when we are repeatedly exposed to a particular sexual stimulus, our physiological response to that stimulus will diminish. Translated, this means you'll need to put more effort into becoming aroused by your partner.

Incidentally, your partner will experience habituation, too. Try not to take it personally. Women who tend to be self-conscious about their bodies are particularly at risk for assuming that they are to blame for any changes in their partners' sexual desire and response, when in fact it's habituation at work.

"He's Not the Guy I Thought He Was"

As you get to know your partner without the pleasurable veil of infatuation, your psyche begins to exert its influence. Your perception of your partner changes, but usually not in a positive way. Instead, you see him through a haze of personal history and past experiences.

Although you may feel that you are glimpsing your partner's true nature for the first time in your relationship, that probably isn't the case. Instead, you are subconsciously interpreting your partner's actions and behaviors based on your previous interactions with other important people in your life. Thus, you continue to misread your partner, only now it's because of misdirected emotions and pessimistic expectations. Worse, you may interact with him based on this "filtered" perspective, which in turn encourages and reinforces the actions and behaviors that you most dislike. Jennifer and Kent, clients at the Sexual Wellness Center, offer a perfect example of this dynamic.

Jennifer and Kent, both in their early forties, had been married for 11 years when they came to couples therapy at Jennifer's request. They owned a small but very successful consulting business, and both of them seemed fulfilled and energized by their work.

During their first session with me (Dr. Brandon), Jennifer and Kent described in rich and passionate terms the time they had fallen in love some 13 years before. They had met in business school and had lived together platonically as housemates. "Our friends knew we were in love before we did!" Jennifer said with a grin.

When the conversation turned to their current relationship, however, the mood in my office changed dramatically. Jennifer's voice became tense and tight; her level of agitation rose noticeably. The more she spoke, the less responsive Kent became.

Jennifer had been feeling out of touch with Kent for a long time. He was closed off emotionally, she said, and it infuriated her. She went on to describe what she perceived as years of pointless dinner conversation, boring sex, and a general lack of intimate connection between them. If not for their business, she concluded, they'd have nothing in common.

Kent spoke up only after I encouraged him to do so. He was defensive, countering Jennifer's verbal attack with explanations of his own. In contrast with Jennifer's volatile demeanor, Kent came across as exceedingly calm and levelheaded. He downplayed the emotional distance between them, admitting that the space in their relationship wasn't as troublesome for him. He felt that Jennifer acted like a disapproving parent, always directing and evaluating him. Kent acknowledged that they hadn't been making love very often, and he hoped that couples therapy might improve Jennifer's sex drive.

Jennifer displayed a variety of reactions while Kent was talking. When he finished, she was visibly upset and angry. I seemed to be witnessing the same dynamic that played out between them whenever they attempted to discuss their relationship: Jennifer would grow more vocal, and Kent would withdraw. I noticed, too, that the more emotionally demonstrative Jennifer became, the more disconnected Kent became, and vice versa. Even though I pointed out this unproductive communication pattern, neither partner seemed able to respond differently.

As Jennifer and Kent continued therapy, we explored the origins of their respective takes on how their relationship should work. We looked for similarities between the ways they were responding to each other now and the ways they had related to other important people in their lives. When I brought up their parents, Jennifer didn't see any point in discussing hers; "They have nothing to do with my marriage," she said emphatically. I told her that I'd heard that statement a thousand times from other couples, and that it never held true for any of them. "What have you got to lose by exploring the possibility?" I pushed.

Despite her obvious growing frustration with me, Jennifer decided to answer. "My dad is a kind, generous, loving man. He works really hard. In fact, when I was growing up, he held two jobs to provide for us. My mom ran the house; she was more the disciplinarian. She tried to give me opportunities that she never had. But I guess I'm 'daddy's little girl' at heart."

Jennifer described cherished times with her father—attending local baseball games, relaxing together on weekend afternoons. She admitted that in her eyes, her father could do no wrong. Her perception of her mother was quite different. Although Jennifer knew that both of her parents loved her, her mother didn't seem to hear or understand her. She suspected that her father felt the same way.

Jennifer seemed to have fallen into the same psychological trap that ensnares almost all "daddy's little girls." It's called splitting, which refers to the belief—either conscious or subconscious—that one parent is all good and the other is all bad. The split can go either way: a good mother and bad father or, as in Jennifer's case, a bad mother and good father.

Splitting allows us to simplify our relationships. Rather than dealing with the complexity of everyone being both good and bad—loving and cruel, nurturing and withholding—we categorize each person as one or the other. In mentally casting her father as the good guy, Jennifer had brushed aside his very real flaws—including his tendency to control the family with angry outbursts and his preference for spending his free time with his friends rather than with Jennifer's mother.

Jennifer applied the same flawed logic in her marriage by deciding that Kent was all bad. Again, this is a common phenomenon among "daddy's little girls": Their husbands become the scapegoats for the unresolved emotional issues with their fathers. Jennifer's subconscious decision to ignore her father's frailties didn't erase them. Instead, they became the filter through which she saw and evaluated her husband.

Of course, just as Jennifer brought her family history into the marriage, so did Kent. He realized that he was responding to Jennifer just as he had related to his mother years before.

Kent's parents divorced when he was young. He never knew his father. His mother raised Kent and his siblings on her own. Because she worked hard to support the family, she didn't have much energy left for her kids. She made clear her expectations of them, and she showed little tolerance for bad behavior.

As a result, Kent learned to hide his emotions from his mother. Over time, he became so disconnected from himself that he hardly could recognize his own wants and needs.

Through our conversations about their respective family histories, Jennifer and Kent realized that they were reprising the roles from the dramas they had starred in as children. From her perspective, Jennifer had married an emotionally disengaged man who didn't seem particularly interested in her. She felt as though she was reliving her childhood experience of being invisible to her mother. In a desperate attempt to get Kent's attention, she became more verbally aggressive toward him.

Unfortunately, Jennifer's actions served only to push Kent further away. Perceiving Jennifer to be a domineering, controlling woman just like his mother, Kent responded exactly as he had as a child: He became self-protective and withdrawn. His disengagement prompted Jennifer to treat him in the way he most despised—as a failure, as never good enough.

Although Jennifer and Kent could recognize the cycle they were perpetuating, breaking it required tremendous effort and motivation. Neither of them wanted to be the first to change—they perceived it as "giving in"—so we waited. This type of stalemate is common in couples therapy, because the partner who steps up first is taking the biggest risk.

Relationship Growing Pains

The dynamics between Jennifer and Kent, like those in most intimate relationships, were further complicated by interpersonal struggles over power and control, trust, dependency, and competition. As much as all of us prefer to believe that we don't engage our partners in these ways, we do. Our intimate relationships provide the battlefields for waging such wars—sometimes with huge artillery and heavy weaponry, other times with subtle but equally damaging mind games and manipulation. No matter who "wins," libido can be the greatest casualty.

THE STRUGGLE FOR POWER AND CONTROL

As outside observers, we easily can recognize the struggle for power and control inherent in Jennifer and Kent's communication dance. When Jennifer became angry with Kent, she responded by attempting to gain control of him. She jockeyed for a position of power by being demanding and argumentative.

Kent was just as controlling, but in a very different way. He felt most powerful when he could "make" Jennifer react to his behavior. If she lashed out at him, he felt reassured of his importance to her. Thus, he repeatedly aggravated her by withholding what she wanted most from him: himself.

Both partners knew how to achieve power at the other's expense. But this dynamic always results in a hollow victory. They needed to learn how to feel strong in their own right, each without depending on the other's misery as "proof" of their importance and authority.

When Jennifer and Kent perceived in their own relationship vestiges of the hurtful interactions with their parents years before, they felt helpless. Their instinctive reaction was to make a grab for power and control in their relationship. Subconsciously, they decided that the easiest approach entailed hurting each other, which somehow made them feel safer.

Unfortunately, this approach also was the surest route to creating even more stress in their relationship. Over time, Jennifer became less interested in making love to Kent. The distance between them grew, as did their dissatisfaction with their marriage. As for every couple, the dynamics between Jennifer and Kent evolved slowly over several years. As a result, they were almost impossible to detect.

Why do we seek power and control in our intimate relationships? For many of us, the answer is simple. When we feel we can't change ourselves, we subconsciously decide to focus on changing someone else. It is a variation on the old adage "Your best defense is a good offense." We may become obsessed with controlling something—or in this case, someone—to avoid dealing with some truth about ourselves.

This truth can take almost any form. At the Sexual Wellness Center, for example, we routinely see women who engage in power struggles with their partners in order to distract themselves from some emotion that they find too painful to deal with—be it grief, rage, fear, shame, or something else. As we explain to them, they may be able to subvert these feelings for a time. But eventually, they will resurface, possibly in destructive ways.

Power struggles about sex are just one of the many "creative" alternatives that we may use to channel and express our emotions. All of us are guilty of this dance to some extent. But we can rise to another level of relating. Though our behavior patterns may not be easy to change, the rewards are rich and sweet—and they definitely have a positive effect on libido.

In Jennifer and Kent's case, they worked to develop new relationship dynamics that felt powerful to each of them but at the same time did not undermine the other person's sense of self. Jennifer made an effort to state her wants and needs in less harsh terms. She enjoyed the sense of self-control that grew from learning to express her anger less aggressively and more empathetically. It felt like a more mature way of relating to her husband.

Kent did his part by learning to respond to Jennifer rather than withdrawing from her. He no longer could incite her anger through his silence. Perhaps his biggest breakthrough came when he told Jennifer how much her constant criticism hurt. It was a display of vulnerability that invited Jennifer to know him on a deeper level, which is what she had wanted all along.

When Dominance Turns Destructive

In the context of an intimate relationship, power and control sometimes play out to a couple's advantage. They might even serve as aphrodisiacs. But if they exert too much influence—that is, if one partner gains power and control at the expense of the other—they can turn extremely destructive over time.

To use Kent as an example, many women are drawn to men like him, who act emotionally distant. Their standoffishness may seem mysterious and exciting. In reality, they may be using their independent nature as a cover for maintaining power and control in their relationships. Over time, this can cause trouble—for example, if they choose to assert their dominant status by engaging in extramarital affairs.

Sometimes the quest for power and control leads to the exploration of alternative outlets for sexual expression, such as obsessive sexual fantasies, repetitive masturbation, and Internet sex. By engaging in these behaviors, people communicate—either directly or indirectly—that their partners cannot arouse them as much as something else does. In effect, they use their sexual energies to convey underlying emotions and issues that they ought to address directly.

Can you identify anyone who exerts power and control over you? It could be your partner, or it could be someone else—perhaps a parent, a friend, a boss, or a colleague. If so, ask yourself why you've allowed this person to have so much influence in your life. We tend to blame others for seizing power and control from us, when in fact we give them away. For this exchange to occur, we must be willing participants.

Sometimes we hand off our power and control not to other people but to feelings and belief systems. For example, many women relinquish their authority in their intimate relationships because of low self-esteem. They feel that they can't ask for anything from their partners, because they are unattractive or otherwise undeserving of affection and attention. Other women hand over their power and control to food, to outdated concepts of how they should act, or to worries about what other people will think. Even those who habitually suppress their emotions give away their power and control by disconnecting from their emotional selves.

The bottom line is this: If you perceive that you've lost power and control in your relationship for any reason, you risk creating an unhealthy dynamic with your partner. This could be having a negative impact on your sex life and especially your libido.

Let's consider the opposite behavior—that of abusing power and control in an intimate relationship. Many of our clients at the Sexual Wellness Center admit to rejecting their partners' sexual advances to achieve or maintain dominant status in their relationship. They may disconnect from their emotions as well as from physical sensations, so any sexual contact with their partners clearly isn't pleasurable.

If you identify with this behavior, ask yourself whether it really works to your advantage. Quite frankly, we can't imagine any scenario where one partner wins by hurting the other. It inflicts only further damage on your relationship, which makes healing more difficult.

How to Achieve a Balance of Power

Do you want to change your experience of power and control in your relationship? You can start by keeping a journal. In our experience, clients who see their thoughts and feelings in black and white are better able to analyze any power struggles between themselves and their partners and to take corrective action.

Keeping a journal seems to support a biological phenomenon that psychologists call neural consolidation. By combining a left-brain task (writing) with a right-brain task (experiencing your thoughts and feelings), it can help bring about changes in the way you think, feel, and ultimately behave.

We suggest that you incorporate your journal into your daily routine. Set aside 30 minutes, either upon waking in the morning or before retiring at night, to do your writing. Through this exercise, you are certain to gain a better understanding of yourself and your relationship.

Another effective technique for accessing your thoughts and feelings involves interpreting your dreams. If you haven't done it before, it may seem daunting at first. But don't get discouraged! It can make a tremendous difference in understanding the dynamics between you and your partner, particularly in terms of power and control.

We suggest checking your local bookstore or library for a self-help book on interpreting your dreams. One of our favorites is *Living Your Dreams*, by Gayle Delaney. You'll need to keep a daily record of the content of your dreams; stash a journal or tablet close to your bed, so you can start writing as soon as you wake up. Otherwise, you might forget!

Through your dreams, you can connect with yourself on a much deeper level than you might imagine. What's more, you can use these messages from your subconscious for guidance in all aspects of your life, not just in your relationship with your partner.

You also might try using affirmations. According to many of our clients, this practice of repeating positive statements—verbally or in writing—helps identify and overcome issues with power and control between them and their partners. It might seem too simple to have any effect. But it really works. Essentially, you're retraining your mind to process information in a healthier way.

Let's say you're struggling with a sense of disempowerment in your relationship. You might come up with an affirmation along the lines of "I can feel and utilize my power in a loving, respectful, and constructive way." Write this statement 10 times, then repeat it as necessary throughout the day.

THE EROSION OF TRUST

Another factor that influences the dynamics of a relationship, and the emotional and physical connection between partners, is trust. Our ability and willingness to trust is a barometer of our openness to intimacy. This is because intimacy, both emotional and sexual, requires vulnerability. In fact, we can't have intimacy without vulnerability. And we are unlikely to be vulnerable in situations where we are not trusting of our partners.

Believe it or not, our inclination to trust began to take shape when we were infants, preverbal and helpless. Back then, we had few needs beyond food, water, shelter, and affection. But these were essential for our survival. So as they were met, we learned to trust that our environment—primarily our mothers—would provide for us. If we had been left hungry or wet, we would not have felt as safe and secure, or as trusting.

As we grew up, we continued to build upon this belief system. For example, if we felt well-cared-for and protected as children, we developed a trust in those around us. We understood that they loved us and had our best interests at heart. On the other hand, if we suffered neglect or abuse of some kind, we continued to expect the same treatment from others as we got older. Our rational minds might tell us otherwise, but our subconscious minds are largely responsible for our expectations. This is one reason that family history plays such an influential role in intimate relationships.

Other variables affect your willingness to trust. Time is one, though it exerts its influence in a way you might not expect. Strangely enough, trust becomes *more* difficult with time. That's right: As you pass through the infatuation phase of your relationship and move toward a more mature love, you may be less inclined to trust your partner, even if the two of you have been together for years.

Why does trust become harder the longer you're in a relation-

245

ship? Because you realize that your partner knows an awful lot about you, including your idiosyncrasies and quirks. You might not be comfortable acknowledging some of this information to yourself, let alone sharing it with someone else. And being aware of your partner's oddities doesn't offer much comfort.

Think back to when you and your partner first fell in love. How would he have described you? If he had been asked to list your good and bad qualities, what would he have said? Imagine his responses to the same questions now. Quite different, aren't they?

Over the course of your relationship, your partner has gained unique insight into your "human nature." He can more realistically delineate your assets as well as your liabilities. His familiarity with your true self can make trusting an even greater challenge, because he has more "ammunition" to potentially hurt you. So you feel more vulnerable, and thus more cautious, in your relationship.

Of course, you also know much more about your partner than you did when you first met and fell in love. You could list his good and bad points, just as he could list yours. In short, you know he's human. And that may give you pause. Can you really put your trust in someone who's fallible, just like you? You'll learn the answer as your relationship changes and grows.

Rooted in Self-Doubt

Trust isn't only about our partners. It is also about ourselves. Simply put, if we have difficulty trusting ourselves sexually, it's going to affect our sex drive.

Women who have a strong need for control in their relationships tend to struggle with self-trust. They fear that if they lose control, they won't be able to take care of themselves. For these women, climaxing can be a particularly scary or uncomfortable experience. Obviously, strong, satisfying orgasms involve a willingness to let go. If a woman doesn't trust herself enough to lose control, her orgasms will be much less intense, or perhaps nonexistent.

It is easy to understand how sex can become less desirable if your orgasms are underwhelming. For a truly fulfilling sexual experience, you must choose between self-control and passion. A woman who lacks self-trust invariably opts for self-control, which probably will drive down her libido.

We have one final observation about the connection between self-trust and self-control and its role in sexual arousal. As we mentioned in chapter 12, research has shown that the body's response to sexual stimulation can feel much like its response to trauma. This is because both involve a rush of adrenaline.

If a woman experienced trauma—sexual or otherwise—in the past, she may become fearful of her body's response and thus try to avoid it. Subconsciously, she has paired the sensations of the adrenaline rush with the traumatic incident. So even a pleasurable experience like orgasm may evoke the same overwhelmingly devastating emotions as the trauma itself. As a result, she may try to refrain from climaxing, if not steer clear of sexual intercourse altogether. She may lose all interest in sex over time.

Healing Begins with You

Let's return to Jennifer and Kent for a moment. How did trust play out in their relationship? Initially, neither was aware of any reluctance to trust the other. But as Jennifer struggled to rein in her angry outbursts, she became aware of a fear that Kent would be unresponsive if she quieted down. She discovered that if she held on to her anger, she avoided having to trust Kent to respond to her feelings.

Kent's struggle to trust Jennifer was even more apparent. He was wary of all strong-willed, determined women after repeatedly being hurt and rejected by his mother. He carried the subconscious belief that Jennifer inevitably would hurt him if he let her get too close.

If you don't easily trust your partner, you probably can point to specific reasons why he isn't as trustworthy as you'd like him to be. But this really is about you. Your ability to trust your partner depends on your willingness to trust yourself. Once you trust yourself, you'll feel confident that you can take care of yourself in any situation, even when someone else lets you down.

Your first step in building trust is to figure out what happened to it in the first place. Keeping a journal can be really helpful here. So can working with a good therapist.

Once you've reached some conclusions, your next step is to explore the issue of trust with your partner. Explain how he encourages or discourages your trust, and ask how you do the same for him. Such conversations can help heal emotional wounds and enhance intimacy.

The Drive for Independence

Somehow, dependency has developed a bad reputation in our society. Many couples strive to maintain relationships where each partner functions as independently as possible. This allows for a sort of safety net, in that they know they're able to care for themselves should something happen to their union.

Many people seem to believe that if they are self-reliant, they will suffer less if their relationships take a nosedive. The irony here is that the more independent partners become, the less likely they are to matter to each other over time. As they meet few of each other's needs, the relationship itself loses value. The result is ever-increasing emotional distance, and a greater likelihood of separation—just what these couples were preparing for from the start.

Jennifer and Kent had fallen into the independence trap without even realizing it. As Jennifer felt more and more disappointed in Kent, she withdrew from him emotionally. Instead, she talked with her girlfriends about how she was feeling. In effect, she was shutting Kent out of her life. She certainly didn't depend on him anymore.

Kent was going through a similar process, though in his own way. Jennifer had no idea what he needed from her. They had succeeded in becoming functionally independent, with their emotional distance driving them farther apart.

For a healthier way of relating, consider *inter*dependence, a trademark characteristic of all loving, connected couples. In interdependence, two people rely on each other, engaging in a constant emotional give-and-take. In a sense, each partner has the benefits of his or her own strengths, as well as his or her partner's. These two people depend on each other, openly and clearly revealing their needs and weaknesses to one another. Ultimately, while both partners are able to function independently, they consciously choose an intimate connection of mutual caretaking, which feeds the individuals as well as the relationship.

For Jennifer and Kent to create interdependence out of their existing independence, they had to learn to rely on each other. This was harder than they expected. Kent, for example, wasn't even sure what he wanted or expected from Jennifer. He was so accustomed to functioning independently that he couldn't readily identify his needs.

During one especially emotional therapy session, Kent quietly admitted that he was struggling with another family member, and he asked Jennifer for her emotional support. Jennifer walked across the room and sat down next to Kent, taking his hand in hers. His disclosure marked a major step forward, because he invited Jennifer into his life in a way he previously had resisted. For her part, Jennifer clearly enjoyed her new role in their relationship. She felt important to Kent for the first time in years.

If you and your partner want to cultivate greater interdependence in your relationship, you can start by asking yourselves the following questions: How do you depend on your partner? How is he or she important to you? How does your partner depend on you? How are you important to him or her? Write down your answers and share them with each other.

The goal of this exercise is for the two of you to identify individual and mutual needs, whether they're physical, emotional, intellectual, or spiritual. If some of your answers don't neatly fit into these categories, that's okay. Even help with daily chores qualifies as a need. Ultimately, though, you want to focus on the deeper, more substantial ones that form the foundation of relationships.

As you and your partner review your answers, pay special attention to any categories that seem especially brief or one-sided. This is where you should concentrate your efforts to achieve interdependence. Once the two of you decide on a goal, come up with a plan for working toward it, so you won't feel overwhelmed by the process.

For example, suppose you and your partner notice that you're coming up short in the spiritual component of interdependence. You might choose a goal like "I want to experience greater pleasure with my partner." (Yes, pleasure can be spiritual!) Then think about how you might accomplish it, as a series of smaller, more manageable tasks. You could watch a spiritually empowering and uplifting movie together, or take a weekend camping trip to some secluded beach or forest. If you can't get away, try to set aside 10 minutes of every day for shared meditation practice. These and similar activities can help foster a spiritual connection that will build and reinforce your interdependence.

THE REPERCUSSIONS OF COMPETITION

In Jennifer and Kent's situation, we also can see the impact of competition on relationship dynamics and on libido. Though the two of them hadn't discussed it, or even recognized it, they engaged in rivalry on a number of levels.

Often couples are acutely aware of, but only silently acknowledge, the unique strengths that each partner brings to the relationship. Although one may have a larger income potential, the other may demonstrate greater social prowess. Similarly, though one partner may sport a tremendous sense of humor, the other shows a knack for parenting. In theory, such complementary attributes should make for an even stronger union. In reality, they often fuel debate—conscious or subconscious—over who's more valuable to the relationship.

For some couples, even extended family is fair game for competition. Partners may jockey for position over whose parents are wealthier, more supportive, or more engaged with the children.

And so it goes, until a couple reaches some sort of an impasse. Then the competition may turn more blatant and hurtful. For example, when Jennifer didn't get what she needed from Kent, she turned their professional lives into a contest. She routinely compared how hard she worked with how much effort Kent put in at the office, as well as at home. What's more, she made a point of informing Kent—and anyone else who would listen—that she was doing much more than she felt was her share.

In their personal lives, Jennifer used her chronic exhaustion as an excuse for not wanting sex. As her competitive drive became stronger, her emotional distance from Kent became greater.

Partners accommodate each other's abilities and attributes in a variety of ways. Sometimes a healthy rivalry can bring energy, playfulness, or excitement to a relationship. In addition, a partner who shows a competitive streak may seem more interesting or stimulating sexually.

The point is, competition isn't harmful in and of itself. How a couple defines competition within the context of their relationship determines its impact. If partners already are at odds over other issues, even mildly competitive behaviors can turn into explosive combat zones.

If competition between you and your partner has become unhealthy, the two of you need to talk about it. Is it a symptom of a larger problem in your relationship? If so, what is the nature of that problem?

Consider what's driving one of you to feel superior to the other. Perhaps unresolved emotions—anger, hurt, jealousy—are to blame. Or maybe one partner feels inferior, and so wants to flex his or her muscle in the relationship.

Regardless of the underlying issue, you and your partner can find more-effective options for addressing it. Think back to Jennifer, whose competitive streak was fueled by hurt over Kent's emotional distance. Her solution was to be less aggressive in relating to Kent, so he felt more comfortable being close to her. As he became more open and attentive, she felt less compelled to behave in a competitive way.

CHAPTER 20

THE MIRACLE OF MOTHERHOOD

- Pregnancy and childbirth produce a number of physical and psychological changes that have a dramatic impact on a woman's sexual desire and response.
- Because of the hormonal fluctuations that occur through pregnancy, a woman's libido may vary in each trimester.
- Most women report a decline in sexual function and satisfaction for up to 1 year after childbirth.
- Breastfeeding can diminish a woman's interest in sex, as can the sleep deprivation and vaginal dryness common during the postpartum period.
- The role of motherhood may alter a woman's perception of her sexuality.
- If low libido persists for more than a year postpartum, chances are that deeper relationship issues are at work.

Pregnancy: the ultimate outcome of sex. How ironic that it often has a profoundly negative effect on a couple's sex life!

Research shows that approximately 70 percent of new moms experience a significant decline in sex drive and sexual satisfaction for 1 year after giving birth. No doubt this contributes to another staggering statistic: As many as one in six marriages ends in divorce within 1 year of a firstborn's arrival. Despite the near universality of low libido after pregnancy, it remains a frustrating and often divisive problem for many couples.

New moms lose interest in sex for a variety of reasons—some obvious, others subtle. Not surprisingly, they may be too exhausted from caring for their babies to muster the energy for sex. Or they may continue to suffer from episiotomy pain, which makes intercourse almost unbearable.

Less evident, especially to new parents, is the complexity of accommodating another human being in their relationship. Even though they very much want their baby, the dynamic between them naturally will change. Then, too, any preexisting issues—sexual or nonsexual—between partners almost certainly will intensify with the rise in stress that accompanies their parenting responsibilities.

In this chapter, we will examine the potential effects of motherhood—from the first trimester of pregnancy through the first year after childbirth—on a woman's sexual health and identity. Of course, every woman experiences this truly miraculous life event in a unique and often unpredictable way. But many of our clients at the Sexual Wellness Center say that if they had been given even a clue about the impact of pregnancy and childbirth on their sex lives, they could have avoided much of the anger, guilt, and resentment that surfaced between them and their partners.

Our goal, therefore, is to explain the physical, emotional, and sexual changes that you could experience during the transition from mom-to-be to full-fledged motherhood. By knowing just what to expect, you and your partner might continue to foster a healthy sexual relationship even as you assume the mantle of parenthood.

What to Expect during Pregnancy

Kristen, or Kris as she insisted on being called, always was competitive. Even as a young girl, she strove to be the best at everything. And if she wasn't the best, she at least had to be the first.

As Kris blossomed into a bright and attractive young woman, her perfectionist style continued to permeate her demeanor and behavior, even sexually. Simply put, Kris loved sex. For her, orgasms were the epitome of the intensity and satisfaction that she craved for all aspects of her life. She found a willing and capable partner in her college boyfriend, Evan.

After graduating, Kris competed for and won a job that few women take: She became a trader on the floor of the New York Stock Exchange. The work was physically and intellectually demanding. But for Kris, it was exhilarating. And it in no way interfered with her sexual desire. In fact, sex offered a perfect release from the stress and tension of her daily battles on the floor of the stock exchange.

As Kris settled into her career and Evan into his, the two of them decided to marry. To their friends, they became the embodiment of the 1990s "power couple," earning promotions, wealth, and social standing.

Four years later, on a Tuesday in March, Kris did the unthinkable, the unimaginable: She slept through her alarm. When she woke up, she almost couldn't lift her head off the pillow. Then came a terrible wave of nausea. For the first time since becoming a trader, Kris called in sick.

On Wednesday and Thursday, she felt no better. On Friday, she went to the doctor. Expecting to be diagnosed with the flu, Kris was stunned by her positive pregnancy test—not that she and Evan didn't enjoy an active sex life. She had also been good about taking the Pill.

Though they hadn't planned on starting a family quite so soon, Kris and Evan nonetheless greeted the news of impending parenthood with great enthusiasm. But Kris struggled with the inevitable physical and emotional changes associated with pregnancy. During the first trimester, she barely could function during the day, even though she slept at least 12 hours a night.

Her sense of smell became so acute that she could sniff out the kimchi from the Korean restaurant down the street. Any odor caused terrible nausea.

At work, Kris's performance suffered. She would leave the floor to vomit or to urinate with an almost intolerable frequency. Her competitors—and even a few of her friends—enjoyed several hearty laughs as Kris, looking green, would run to the nearest bathroom. Back on the floor, she couldn't concentrate or handle the physical demands of her job.

Perhaps most troubling for Kris were the emotions that seemed to simmer just below the surface, always ready to make an appearance. The self-described "warrior of Wall Street" would even cry during TV commercials that showed puppies or kittens.

Not surprisingly, pregnancy took a toll on Kris's sex drive as well. Even when she didn't feel ill, Kris hated to be touched. As a result, sex with Evan—which once occurred almost daily—stopped altogether. Kris was petrified: "Will I ever feel good again? Will I ever be able to eat Chinese food without vomiting? Will I ever want sex again?"

So what is it about pregnancy that acts as kryptonite to a modern-day superwoman like Kris? How can an embryo less than an inch long and weighing less than an ounce so disrupt a woman's physical and emotional balance? In a word: hormones.

FIRST TRIMESTER: PROGESTERONE RUNS THE SHOW

By the 4th week after conception (the 6th week of pregnancy), a woman's progesterone increases to 10 times the monthly average. And it continues to rise rapidly until delivery. By then, the hormone will exceed *100 times* its normal monthly level.

As you may remember from chapter 6, progesterone is essential to a healthy pregnancy. It helps prepare and maintain the lining of the uterus to allow for implantation of the embryo. It also suppresses the immune system and relaxes the muscle fibers of the uterus, which helps prevent expulsion of the embryo. (The uterus consists of smooth muscle, a special type of muscle fiber that is not within your voluntary control. Smooth muscle also plays a role in circulating blood through the arteries and propelling food through the intestines.)

As you can imagine, a mom-to-be needs all that extra progesterone to help prevent complications, including miscarriage. Yet a high level of the hormone is not without consequences. In fact, it's responsible for many of the physical discomforts associated with pregnancy.

Probably the best known of these is pregnancy-induced nausea, or morning sickness, which affects at least two-thirds of moms-to-be. (Actually, *morning sickness* is a misnomer, because the symptoms can show up any time of day or night—not just in the morning.) It is a direct consequence of the large amount of progesterone in a mother-to-be's system, because the hormone relaxes smooth muscle not only in the uterus but all over the body, including in the intestines. As a result, any food that reaches the intestines does not get propelled onward through the digestive tract. Instead, it stays put, which causes the sensation of nausea and eventually triggers vomiting.

Nausea is not the only by-product of the high progesterone level during pregnancy. Acne, water retention, and severe fatigue all have ties to the hormone. Because the intestines aren't contracting as they usually do, many moms-to-be develop constipation as well.

As if all of these discomforts were not enough, one of the most significant consequences of a high progesterone level is low libido. As we discussed in chapter 6, progesterone is the proverbial wet blanket on sexual desire. This isn't to suggest that all expectant mothers lose interest in sex for the first trimester. Some are fortunate to maintain a strong sex drive. But they are few and far between. The good news is, a rise in estrogen—the hormonal ally for a woman's libido—is just around the corner.

SECOND TRIMESTER: ESTROGEN TAKES OVER

Just as the first trimester of pregnancy is characterized by a dramatic rise in progesterone, the second trimester might best be described as a tidal wave of estrogen. This highly profemale hormone can set in motion a cascade of physical and emotional changes during pregnancy.

What's more, the increase in estrogen affects just about every organ in the body. For example, it stimulates blood flow to the skin—the largest organ—and causes water retention. The combination gives skin a healthy, shiny appearance, which explains why moms-to-be "glow."

Estrogen also has multiple effects on the mucosa of the mouth and vagina, causing it to grow and thicken. Larger amounts of the hormone pump up blood flow to the vagina, vulva, and clitoris as well. This is why the genitalia of a woman who's pregnant may appear redder and swollen.

Together, this constellation of estrogen-induced changes can greatly improve a mom-to-be's sexual response during her second trimester. As the vagina and clitoris become more engorged with blood during sexual stimulation, sensitivity increases, as does arousal. Many women report that they experience multiple orgasms, or achieve vaginal orgasm, for the first time during their second trimesters. Between the enhanced ability to climax and the greater intensity of orgasm (thanks to stronger uterine contractions), many women have extraordinary sex during this stage of pregnancy.

The markedly elevated level of estrogen during the second trimester also influences a woman's emotions. Even the comparatively minor rise in the hormone that occurs during a normal menstrual cycle results in an increased desire for emotional contact. So naturally, the surge during the second trimester can trigger even more intense feelings and cravings. This can set the stage for positive emotional experiences that bring partners closer together in anticipation of their child's arrival. By the same token, it can magnify flaws in a relationship that is not healthy or satisfying.

THIRD TRIMESTER: YOUR BODY PREPARES FOR THE BIG EVENT

As estrogen maintains a dominating presence during the third trimester, oxytocin is on the rise as well. As you may remember from chapter 6, oxytocin stimulates the release of milk from the lactating breast. The gradual increase in this hormone serves as an indicator that the body is preparing for the postpartum period.

Normally, the combination of estrogen and oxytocin would fuel a woman's craving for physical contact as well as her interest in sex. But the physical discomforts common during the third trimester of pregnancy can take the steam out of a mom-to-be's sex drive. Symptoms such as back pain, edema (swelling and water retention), and pelvic pressure easily can override the hormonal milieu.

The Many Moods of Pending Motherhood

We should point out that many women lose interest in sex during pregnancy for reasons other than hormones. In particular, how they think and feel about being pregnant helps determine how they experience their sexuality and their sex drives.

We like to perceive pregnancy as a joyous time in a woman's life, as she eagerly awaits the arrival of her baby. But she just as easily might feel fear, anxiety, sadness, or confusion. Unfortunately, such negative emotions aren't socially acceptable for a mother-to-be. So she probably keeps them to herself, though she may question whether their presence means that she's unfit for motherhood.

What's more, many a mom-to-be is torn between her natural urge to nurture her offspring and her desire to maintain her independence. She may shift between these powerful opposing forces frequently and rather unexpectedly.

Her libido may shift just as wildly, in response to her intense emotional states. In the morning, she may feel sexy and attracted to her husband, eager to share an intimate connection with the father of her baby. Later that same day, she may be consumed with worry or dread about becoming a mother, which quashes any interest in making love. Though these emotional fluctuations may seem bizarre to her, they are a normal response to the tremendous changes occurring in her body—and her life.

Ultimately, whether and how a mom-to-be's thoughts and emotions affect her libido depends largely on how she responds to them. Some women take extraordinary pride in their bodies' remarkable ability to create and nurture another human being. They perceive making love as an opportunity to enjoy and celebrate the wondrous process they are participating in.

Other women become self-conscious and critical of their physical metamorphosis during pregnancy. Their bodies seem to take on a life of their own, behaving in ways that are beyond their control. Even the weight gain associated with pregnancy can become an issue. Sadly, the entrenched societal ideals that equate female beauty with excessive thinness can cause moms-to-be to feel ashamed of their appearance, even though their bodies are growing in ways that are perfectly healthy and normal.

For some women, the very idea of making love while pregnant is embarrassing or even repulsive. They may worry about harming the baby, or become distracted by the baby's presence. This is why they may prefer nonsexual physical contact, such as hugging or cuddling with their partners, over sex.

FATHERHOOD FEELS DIFFERENT, TOO

Women aren't alone in having to adjust to so many changes during pregnancy. The men in their lives must adjust as well.

Though dads-to-be may be spared the physical discomforts, the emotional turmoil can be just as daunting.

For men as for women, the prospect of parenthood can trigger a host of emotions, from joy to fear and anxiety. A man may feel financially unprepared to provide for his growing family. He may wonder what lies ahead for him and how his life will change after the baby is born. His complex thoughts and feelings, and the confusion they cause, may dampen his sex drive. Unfortunately, his partner may misread his lack of interest in sex as a sign of her diminished attractiveness and desirability.

Sometimes, too, men have difficulty responding to their partners in a sexual way during pregnancy. Just as your pending motherhood may remind you of the bond between you and your mother, it can prompt your partner to think about his own mother as a sexual being. The resulting confusion and anxiety can dampen his interest in sex.

For this and other reasons, a new father may require a transition period to accommodate his partner's new role of mother into her sexuality. This, too, can cause friction in an intimate relationship, as a woman personalizes her partner's response to her. In fact, it may be more related to his internal emotional conflict than to her.

On the other hand, some women find that their partners' response to them has much to do with their own interpretation of their sexuality during pregnancy. This special time can be just as uniquely stimulating and arousing for men as for women.

If you feel that your partner is nervous or uncomfortable about becoming a father, invite him to open up about his feelings. As you would in any life transition, allow time for him to adjust and gain confidence in himself in his new role. Moms-to-be can easily overlook the stress and anxiety inherent in pending fatherhood as well. Try to approach your partner with the same gentleness and understanding that you expect and appreciate from him.

MAKING ROOM FOR BABY

As each partner works through his or her own thoughts and feelings about pregnancy and parenthood, the couple as a unit must renegotiate their roles in preparation for the new family member. This is a quite complex and challenging psychological process. The expectations of both partners, for themselves as well as for each other, are changing. They have less time to devote to their couple-hood, as more of their collective energies are focused on the well-being of their baby.

Many couples find that all aspects of their relationship, both sexual and nonsexual, become less important as they await the arrival of a child. For example, rather than choosing to get away for a romantic weekend, they may be more inclined to stay home and work on the nursery. This is especially true for moms-to-be, who are usually more interested in nesting than procreating—a shift in priorities that's driven by both biology and psychology.

Naturally, all of this has a tremendous impact on a couple's sex life. In the long term, the changes brought about by pregnancy and parenthood can lead to increased intimacy between partners as their relationship evolves with the growth of their family. In the short term, however, the opposite can occur.

We should note that the adjustment process described here is typical for couples whose pregnancies are medically normal. For those with the tremendous added stress of a difficult or high-risk pregnancy, the transition can be even more challenging, both emotionally and physically.

Certainly, anything that complicates pregnancy, delivery, or the postpartum period likely will have some effect on a woman's libido. This includes traumatic experiences such as miscarriage and premature birth. We strongly encourage women in these circumstances to seek out support groups or others with whom they feel comfortable sharing their thoughts and feelings.

What to Expect Postpartum

Gretchen was almost 2 weeks past her due date when her obstetrician decided to induce labor. She was admitted to the hospital on Monday morning. By Tuesday afternoon, after 30 hours of torturous contractions brought on by Pitocin (synthetic oxytocin), her cervix was completely dilated.

By then, Gretchen felt totally exhausted. Somehow, though, she mustered the energy to start pushing. An hour later, the delivery was almost complete. Her obstetrician placed a vacuum cup on the baby's head, cut an episiotomy, and pulled.

Gretchen was overcome with emotion and exhaustion. She sobbed as she held her daughter for the first time. Never had she seen a baby so beautiful. Never had her heart been so filled with love. Never had her body hurt so much.

For Gretchen, the first 6 weeks of her baby Dana's life flew by in a sleep-deprived haze. Then the assorted aches and pains from her delivery began slowly disappearing. All except the pain from her episiotomy, which still was very apparent—though it had faded from an intense burning sensation to a dull, ever-present throb.

As Gretchen's postpartum visit with her obstetrician approached, her husband, Jim, reminded her to ask when they could start having sex again. Though Gretchen didn't tell Jim, she honestly couldn't imagine her vagina ever feeling normal enough for that.

After delivering a baby, whether vaginally or by cesarean section, a woman generally may not engage in sexual intercourse for at least several weeks. Her body needs this time to heal from the experience of giving birth. If she had an episiotomy, she may feel discomfort at the site of the scar for 3 to 4 months. In fact, some women report episiotomy pain for up to 1 year following delivery.

By 8 weeks after delivery, more than 90 percent of couples have had sexual intercourse. Most women experience some decline in their ability to climax, which can be quite distressing. Generally, though, their orgasm potential returns to a prepregnancy state within 3 to 6 months of giving birth.

CHANGES AFTER CHILDBIRTH

Still, research has shown that more than 70 percent of women report some type of sexual problem during the first year post-partum. Depending on the nature of the problem, it may affect libido. For example, if a woman developed hemorrhoids during pregnancy, certain sexual positions may be uncomfortable or even painful. Vaginal dryness also is common during the first few months following delivery—especially among nursing women, who experience a thinning of vaginal mucosa because of a decline in estrogen production. (We'll talk more about breastfeeding in just a bit.)

Vaginal dryness can contribute to a decline in sex drive for a couple of reasons. First, sex can be quite uncomfortable when a woman is not lubricated enough. Second, she may interpret her reduced lubrication as a lack of sexual arousal, when in fact it's a result of hormonal fluctuations during and after pregnancy.

Of course, probably every mother struggles with loss of sleep during the first year of a baby's life. For most new moms, the simple truth is that disrupted sleep patterns lead to diminished sex drive. The primary issue seems to be a lack of sufficient rapid eye movement (REM) sleep, otherwise known as dream sleep. It is REM sleep that women are most deprived of when they regularly awaken during the night for feedings. This is because cycling into the REM stage takes time. Normally, a woman needs hours of uninterrupted sleep to achieve this deep sleep state.

In studies, people who are deliberately deprived of REM sleep exhibit a variety of symptoms, including difficulty concentrating, irritability, and low energy. The bottom line is, humans need REM sleep to function properly. If given a choice between sleep or sex during the first year postpartum, a new mom likely will choose sleep in an effort to maintain her sanity.

The lack of REM sleep may explain why some women notice a decline in their mental sharpness during the postpartum period. But another physiological phenomenon may be at work as well. To care for her baby, a new mom draws primarily on her right brain. This is the side of the brain that promotes emotional bonding, a life-sustaining necessity for a newborn. Of course, if the right brain is doing most of the work, the left brain might get a little lazy. As a result, a woman may perceive that she isn't as mentally agile as she once was. In fact, her emotions just may be a bit more dominant than she's accustomed to.

COPING WITH POSTPARTUM BLUES

Marjory was one of the lucky ones. Her pregnancy had gone as smoothly as anyone could expect. She had loved being pregnant; truth be told, she hadn't wanted it to end. Ever since her first positive pregnancy test—she had taken three because she couldn't believe the first two—she had felt special. She embraced the magic of creating a new life.

Marjory's delivery also was easy. Just like her mother and sister, she was 8 centimeters dilated before she felt any painful contractions. She gave birth to a baby boy, David, 45 minutes later.

But within a couple of days, Marjory's mood changed dramatically. Instead of sleeping when David did, she sat in her bedroom and sobbed. She couldn't understand why. Her son was healthy, perfect; she was so blessed. Yet she felt overwhelmingly sad.

Marjory wasn't comfortable telling her mom or her husband, Rob, what was going on. She felt so guilty and ashamed. She didn't know what to do. . . .

Just as the huge surge in hormones can have a dramatic effect on a woman's emotions during her pregnancy, so can the sudden drop in hormones during the immediate postpartum period. In fact, 70 to 80 percent of new moms experience what are known as post-partum blues, or "baby blues." Beginning 2 or 3 days after delivery, they're enveloped in sadness, fear, depression, anger, and anxiety—not what they expected after giving birth. These emotions are a direct result of the huge drop in estrogen and progesterone that occurs in the first few hours after delivery.

The vast majority of women who develop postpartum blues feel better in about a week. But for some women, the negative emotions don't resolve; in fact, they get even worse. These women have what's known as postpartum depression.

Although the cause of postpartum depression is not known, the drop in estrogen and progesterone—combined with a decline in thyroid hormones—may play a significant role. In general, women who have a history of depression and who are especially sleep-deprived are at greater risk for the condition.

If you suspect that you're suffering from postpartum depression, please seek professional medical care without delay. Your doctor can prescribe an antidepressant medication that is safe even if you're nursing. She also can provide information about the many hotlines and support groups for women with postpartum depression. (To learn more about treatments for postpartum depression and other forms of clinical depression, see chapter 12.)

HOW BREASTFEEDING DAMPENS SEX DRIVE

Breastfeeding has many benefits for both mother and baby. It helps reinforce the bond between the two. It strengthens the baby's immune system and could make for a higher IQ. As for mom, she surely welcomes the metabolic boost, which can help speed post-partum weight loss. Actually, though, she isn't burning more calories. Instead, she's producing about 500 calories' worth of milk per day, which comes from her fat and calcium stores. Basically, breastfeeding is like running 4 miles a day! This is why new moms who nurse tend to shed their pregnancy pounds more quickly.

But breastfeeding can have a downside as well—all thanks to our good friends, hormones. For starters, it triggers production of the hormone oxytocin. As mentioned earlier, oxytocin causes the release of milk from the breast. It also fuels a new mom's need to be touched and caressed—not by her partner but by her infant. This is how mother and child bond. It does nothing for a woman's libido, per se.

Breastfeeding also causes a rise in the hormone prolactin, which stimulates the breast to make milk. But as we explained in chapter 6, a high level of prolactin means a low level of dopamine, a hormone that's essential for libido. If a woman doesn't have enough dopamine, she almost certainly won't have a strong sex drive.

Often breastfeeding inhibits ovulation and therefore prevents the production of estrogen. In essence, breastfeeding causes a hormonal state that might best be described as "minimenopause." This shortage of estrogen can contribute to low libido. If it persists for a prolonged period of time, the mucosa of the vagina will become thin and dry, a condition called atrophic vaginitis.

After a woman stops breastfeeding, her vagina may need up to a year to return to a normal, healthy (that is, nonatrophic) state. In the meantime, she can use lubricants such as K-Y jelly and Astroglide to relieve any discomfort associated with the condition. Still, as long as she runs low on estrogen, she may have difficulty becoming sexually aroused and reaching orgasm.

Compounding the problem, many women who are breastfeeding take a low-dose "minipill" for birth control. Though the regular Pill contains both an estrogen and a progesterone, the minipill contains only progesterone. It is preferred for lactating women, because estrogen can inhibit milk production. But as mentioned earlier, extra progesterone only depletes sex drive.

Even without the minipill, the combination of hormonal changes associated with breastfeeding really can hamper sex in the postpartum period. Evolutionary biologists believe this makes perfect sense. When a woman is lactating, she needs to focus on the health and well-being of her newborn. By limiting her sex drive and ovulation, she is less likely to become pregnant again, which would detract her attention and therefore decrease her child's chances of survival.

We certainly are not suggesting that women forgo breastfeeding. But we believe that if both partners know the facts about the hormonal changes associated with breastfeeding, it can go a long way in preventing conflict during the postpartum period. For example, a man who understands his partner's lack of sexual interest as a temporary physiological issue rather a psychological one will be reassured that it does not imply any underlying marital problem. Likewise, a woman who's breastfeeding is less likely to feel guilty about not responding to her partner's sexual advances. She knows that her sex drive should return to normal once she stops lactating.

We have a couple of recommendations for women who breastfeed. First and foremost, we are not strong supporters of the progesterone minipill. Although we recognize the importance of preventing unwanted pregnancies, other forms of contraception are as effective as the minipill but do not cause the same negative sexual side effects. Your doctor can explain your options and help you choose the best one for your particular needs.

Second, we've seen excellent clinical results from estrogen applied directly to the vagina to prevent or minimize atrophic vaginitis. Estrogen comes in three forms: cream, tablet, and an estrogen ring. Any of these will relieve the symptoms of atrophic vaginitis without hampering breast milk production. What's more, though the estrogen will not improve a woman's libido, it will enhance her arousal and lubrication and help prevent pain during sex.

Ready for Sex? Not Yet

During the postpartum period, many a new mom will struggle to integrate her roles as a nurturing mother and an exciting lover with her identity as a sexual being who has distinct needs and desires. She may feel uncomfortable reclaiming her sexuality while she's the primary caretaker of her baby. By abstaining from sex, she can avoid the anxiety associated with this internal conflict.

Then, too, new moms may worry about getting pregnant again or about leaving their babies unattended for any length of time. In fact, some women are hypervigilant about checking on their infants, which distracts them from their partners and from physical intimacy.

For women who breastfeed, the emotional landscape is even more complex, as they attempt to reconcile their perception of their breasts as both a sexual erogenous zone and a source of sustenance. They may be disturbed or alarmed if they become sexually aroused while breastfeeding. It's a quite common occurrence, because of the hormone oxytocin. But it can be disconcerting because of the context in which it occurs.

Other emotions can discourage women from becoming sexually active so soon after childbirth. Anger is a big one. A new mom may be frustrated by the amount of energy that she must expend on another human being—energy that she won't have for herself. At the same time, she may struggle to acknowledge how she's feeling, because somehow it seems wrong. So, subconsciously, she may channel her anger elsewhere—for example, toward her partner. This can interfere with their sex life, especially if the woman vents by flying into a rage or withholding sex. It's her way of saying "I just can't give any more to anyone!"

Anger also can arise from parenting issues between partners. A woman may feel that her partner does not spend enough time with their baby or that she is doing much more than her share of the caretaking. This, too, can have implications for a couple's sex life and a woman's libido.

Of course, when these sorts of emotions surface during the postpartum period, it could be a sign of even deeper conflict between partners. For example, if a man neglects his responsibilities to his child, he probably is neglecting his responsibilities to his partner as well. Often what appears to be a parenting issue is, at its roots, a relationship issue. First-time parents Celia and Rick demonstrate this dynamic.

Celia called the Sexual Wellness Center several times before actually scheduling an appointment. She obviously wasn't sure about seeing a therapist. It didn't help that her babysitter had left for college, and she couldn't seem to find a reliable replacement. She finally asked her sister to watch her 20-month-old daughter, Rachel, so that she could come to see me (Dr. Brandon).

On the phone, Celia explained that she and her husband, Rick, were having problems with their sex life. Celia had lost interest in sex during her pregnancy; almost 2 years after giving birth, she continued to spurn Rick's sexual advances. We decided that if Rick was willing, they should come together for the first session.

Celia and Rick sat stiffly in my waiting room, both holding magazines but obviously not reading them. I suspected that they may have been quarreling on the drive to my office. Seeing a therapist for the first time can be an anxiety-provoking experience, a fact not lost on either of them.

Celia and Rick took turns describing the strain and distance in their relationship, which had gotten worse over the course of several years. Celia was concerned that their daughter soon would become aware of their prob-

lems. Rachel was a needy child, demanding lots of attention during the day and sleeping in her parents' bed most nights. This infuriated Rick, who felt that any chance of intimacy with his wife was being eroded by their daughter's inevitable presence.

For almost the full hour of their session, Rick and Celia argued over parenting issues. They said little about their more personal relationship struggles. Still, I could see that Celia was protective of Rachel and uncomfortable with the prospect of changing their household or bedtime routine.

Celia and Rick had created what's known as a relationship triangle with their daughter. By definition, a relationship triangle occurs when two people bring a third person between them to discharge emotions that really belong to the two of them. In this case, Rachel had become the unintentional scapegoat for the distance between her parents.

Despite the mounting tension between Rick and Celia, Rachel was helping to maintain some equilibrium in the family system. Without her presence, Rick and Celia would have grown even further apart. I explained what was happening between them and suggested that we come up with a plan to free Rachel from their relationship triangle. This would allow them to really focus on the issues between the two of them.

When they returned the following week, Rick and Celia looked even more tense than before. The changes at home had been stressful for everyone, including Rachel. Rick and Celia were not happy with their time alone. "We just have more time to argue about Rachel," Celia said. They left with a new homework assignment: to keep arguing, only not about their daughter.

The next session, all of us laughed as Rick and Celia described several days of almost complete silence. But then they opened up, expressing and processing their anger and hurt. Both of them seemed genuinely surprised by the nature of their arguments. Issues, old and new, began to surface.

Clearly, Rick wanted sex from Celia. So I asked Rick what Celia wanted from him that he hadn't been willing to give. He was able to answer without hesitation. "Celia says I don't talk to her," he replied. "But I don't know what she wants from me. I do talk to her when I have something to say!"

Both Celia and Rick were feeling neglected—Celia emotionally, Rick sexually. To reconnect, both of them needed to make a conscious effort to give more of themselves to their relationship. This was easier said than done, as both of them already felt like they were giving more than they were getting. I asked them to consider what was more important to them—having a good marriage, or making sure not to give more than their partners. Rick and Celia opted for a good marriage, and they were able to achieve it.

RECONCILING YOUR SEXUAL AGENDAS

If you struggle with low libido during your pregnancy or your first year postpartum, don't get discouraged. The physical and emotional changes that occur during this time tend to be self-limiting. Consider it nature's way of making sure that you focus on the task at hand—that is, bringing your infant safely into toddlerhood.

From your perspective, having a baby alters just about everything in your life—your body, your daily routine, your eating habits, your sleep patterns, your social role in the world. All this causes a ton of stress. That's right: Even positive events like having a baby can trigger the stress response. Understandably, sex may be the last thing on your mind.

Your partner's perspective probably is quite different. He is aware of how the birth of your child brought about profound changes in his life and yours. But he still wants sex. This is especially true postpartum; as he watches you devote your attention to the baby, he may want more of you for himself. He expresses this through his sexual advances, just as society has taught him. For men, needing their partners emotionally is "wimpy." Needing them sexually is "masculine," and thus earns society's seal of approval.

All this adds up to two people with two very different sexual agendas—your partner wanting more sex and you wishing for a sexual time-out. To head off potential conflict, you and partner need to talk openly about your individual needs and expectations. As we've said before, ignoring these sorts of issues only breeds misunderstanding and resentment.

THE ART OF SAYING NO

If you aren't interested in sex right now, rejecting your partner in an angry or hurtful way won't help your relationship. In fact, it will increase the tension between the two of you, just when you need your partner more than ever. Why not use this time of low libido to practice saying no gracefully and lovingly?

First, let's explore how you usually respond when your partner wants sex and you aren't in the mood. More than likely, you pull away physically and emotionally—perhaps by ignoring him, pretending to be asleep, or "misreading" his sexual advances. You might mumble "Sorry, honey, I'm too tired" or "You're kidding me—again?!"

All of us have these less adaptive moments during which our finest relationship skills seem to fail us. They most often surface when we are physically exhausted or emotionally drained. But interacting with our partners in a distant or unkind manner only hurts them and us in the long run, as bad feelings build up over time. This is why we encourage you to develop strategies for turning down sex that leave you and your partner connected instead of frustrated and withdrawn.

Keep in mind that your goal is to reach out emotionally but to say no at the same time. You can accomplish this in a variety of ways. As in any disagreement, the best place to start is to acknowledge where your partner is coming from. Then he can feel heard and understood. Next, offer your truth to him. It may be that you

273

are just too tired, or you can't stand for anyone to touch your body at the moment, or you need to be alone for a while. Identify what is happening for you and why it is affecting your sexual desire and response. Share this information with your partner, and if you feel it, apologize for being unable to accommodate him.

With conversations like this, the key is to be kind. Be aware of your body and your voice. The exact same sentence can come across differently based on your tone, eye contact, and posture.

As you talk with your partner, consider a compromise. You might offer to make love at another time. Or you might suggest a creative solution for the moment. Many men are receptive to and enjoy alternatives to intercourse, such as engaging in oral sex, holding him while he masturbates, pleasuring him, reading erotica to him, or dancing sexy for him. These are just a few possibilities. Explore which options feel comfortable for you and would allow you and your partner to meet halfway.

At another time, when you and your partner are not contemplating sex, you might want to ask him how he feels when you reject his sexual advances and how you might ease the sting for him. Invite him to suggest ideas for compromise as well. If the prospect of exploring his needs bothers you, you probably are angry with him. You need to address your feelings, too. Otherwise, your saying no to sex may come across as spiteful and insincere.

When Libido Doesn't Bounce Back

In general, a woman's sexual function returns to its prepregnancy state within a year after childbirth. Even then, some couples continue to report dissatisfaction with certain aspects of their sex lives. They may choose to write off their sexual complaints as a consequence of becoming parents. This is unfortunate, because it prevents them from gaining insight into other variables that could be affecting their relationship.

The fact is, after a child's first birthday, any continued problems with low libido have little to do with pregnancy or childbirth. They're more complicated than that and are probably driven by the dynamics between partners. Still, women tend to feel more comfortable blaming a lack of interest in sex on the demands of parenthood. It's safer and less threatening than acknowledging more difficult and often painful truths about themselves and their partners.

If anything, the deeper emotional issues that may exist between partners before conception become more evident with the stress of parenthood. The addition of a child to the relationship picture acts as a sort of catalyst, driving any problems to the surface. And for most women, these problems affect their desire to make love.

Some women are less motivated to work on relationships at this time in their lives. Once they've made a commitment to raising a family, they're reluctant to acknowledge any preexisting conflicts between themselves and their partners. On some level, a woman is conscious of at least a perceived dependency on her partner for her and her baby's survival. She cannot imagine raising a child without his assistance, and she may fear further distancing him or even losing him if she attempts to address any problems between them more directly.

Though these concerns are understandable, the choice to remain silent usually perpetuates negative emotions while suppressing opportunities for resolution. If your libido remains elusive after your child's first birthday, you must consider the possibility that other factors are at work. Addressing these openly and honestly is the only way to improve the dynamics between you and your partner and to revive your interest in sex.

CHAPTER 21

NOT YOUR MOTHER'S MENOPAUSE

- Old societal notions of what it means to be menopausal are outdated and harmful to women.
- The dramatic decrease in estrogen that occurs during menopause affects the amount of blood flow to the genitals.
- The primary symptom of reduced genital blood flow is difficulty with lubrication.
- Other than difficulty lubricating, women demonstrate no increase in sexual symptoms at menopause.
- Loss of sex drive may be more related to a woman's experience of the changes in her life rather than to physiological concerns.
- To push past low libido now, creativity and flexibility are called for.

We found this chapter on sex during and after menopause to be particularly challenging to write. It's not because we have little to say. On the contrary, what we want to speak about here is of utmost importance to every woman, regardless of her age, ethnicity, or life experiences. This is so important, in fact, that we struggled to find words that will grab your attention and open your mind to our message. It isn't an easy task, as we are fighting hundreds of years of myth and misunderstanding.

What we are referring to is the universally accepted but completely unfounded belief that women become less sexual as they age. It's true that at one time in human evolution, women didn't live much beyond menopause, if they managed to survive that long. Today, however, a majority of women not only outlast "the change," they thrive in their postmenopausal years.

Like other life transitions, menopause can impact a woman's libido. But this hardly means that she's no longer capable of being sexy or enjoying her sexuality. Still, our society insists on embracing the notion that women are sexual only before menopause. This myth is so pervasive that it has remained largely unchallenged by both men and women. The reality, however, is far different.

The Physical Aspects of Perimenopause and Menopause

Let's begin with an understanding of what perimenopause and menopause really are. The World Health Organization has defined menopause as the permanent cessation of menstruation resulting from the loss of ovarian estrogen production. Perimenopause is the period of time starting with the onset of the first signs of approaching menopause (hot flashes, vaginal dryness, memory changes, mood swings, changes in the duration or interval of menstrual cycles) until 1 year after the last menstrual period.

A woman's menstrual cycle is regulated by a complex communication system between her brain and her ovaries. The brain—specifically the pituitary gland, under control of the hypothalamus—secretes what's known as follicle-stimulating hormone (FSH), which signals the ovaries to produce a mature follicle. In turn, this follicle secretes estrogen that then alerts the pituitary gland to stop producing FSH. This is called a feedback loop.

As a woman ages, her follicles become more resistant to stimulation from FSH. The pituitary secretes increasing amounts of FSH to drive the ovaries to produce a mature follicle. Eventually, they do, but because of the high levels of FSH, the follicle will "overshoot" and produce an abundance of estrogen. This creates large swings in the body's estrogen level. It is these markedly fluctuating estrogen levels that are responsible for perimenopausal symptoms. Eventually, despite ever-increasing FSH, the aging ovaries cannot respond to make a mature follicle, and the ovaries' estrogen production ceases. It is this loss of estrogen that brings on menopause and its associated symptoms.

ESTROGEN MAKES ITS CURTAIN CALL

As we explained in chapter 6, a woman's sexual response is greatly influenced by estrogen. As her estrogen levels fluctuate wildly in perimenopause, so too can her sexual response. And, as her estrogen drops to low levels after menopause, her sex drive and her sexual arousal can suffer as well. The loss of estrogen can have two effects on a woman's sex life: She may experience a decrease in libido, and even more profoundly, she may experience serious negative changes in the health of her vagina and her ability to become sexually aroused.

The labia, clitoris, and vagina all require estrogen for the maintenance of optimal sexual functioning. In addition, the blood vessels, muscles, and nerves of the urogenital tract are heavily dependent on estrogen. The overall effect of the lack of estrogen during perimenopause and menopause is decreased blood flow to the vagina and clitoris. This leads to decreased vaginal lubrication and decreased sensation during sexual arousal. Often, the strength and quantity of orgasms diminish. In addition, there is a profound thinning of the mucosa of the vagina, which, combined with decreased lubrication, can cause sex to be uncomfortable—or even severely painful.

In chapters 7 through 9, we explained how supplemental testosterone, along with other medications and herbs, can stimulate diminished sex drive. It would seem easy to treat a low sex drive that results from the estrogen loss after menopause with estrogen replacement. And, in fact, estrogen replacement has been an integral part of the health care of menopausal women for more than 60 years. Most physicians have been taught that women should have "adequate" estrogen from "puberty to the grave."

However, recent large-scale studies such as the Women's Health Initiative have called into question this long-held belief. Almost monthly, new studies report increased risks associated with estrogen replacement, including a greater likelihood of breast cancer, strokes, and heart attacks. Therefore, although we realize that estrogen replacement can help improve a waning libido, given the current uncertainty regarding the safety of this treatment, we cannot wholeheartedly endorse it at the present time.

As there are hundreds of books devoted to just this issue, we feel that addressing it is beyond the scope of our book. Therefore, we encourage you to have an in-depth conversation with your physician regarding the risks and benefits of, and alternatives to, estrogen replacement. We also suggest that you keep up-to-date on the current landscape of medical opinion by following the recommendations of respected and nonpharmaceutically affiliated medical organizations such as the North American Menopause Society (www.menopause.org) and the American College of Obstetricians and Gynecologists (www.acog.org).

A DIFFERENT APPROACH TO ESTROGEN REPLACEMENT

Although we are ambivalent about recommending oral estrogen replacement, we are convinced that localized estrogen replacement for the vulva and vagina is an important treatment for the atrophic changes that accompany menopause due to lack of estrogen. We believe that localized estrogen replacement is safe, because if used correctly, it does not raise the blood levels of estrogen and, therefore, cannot increase the risk of breast cancer, strokes, and heart attacks.

There are several different methods of estrogen replacement: creams, vaginal tablets, and estrogen rings. All three work well, but each has its individual benefits.

The estrogen creams (Estrace and Premarin) tend to be a bit messy, but they can be rubbed directly into the vulva and on the clitoris and therefore more quickly improve the health of these organs. This is especially important at the entrance to the vagina, known as the vestibule. The vestibule is especially susceptible to atrophic changes that can make penetration painful.

The vaginal estrogen tablet (Vagifem) is easy to use and not messy. It comes with a little applicator that deposits the tablet deep into the vagina. (It reminds us of a Pez dispenser.) You typically do the treatments two times weekly.

The last option is the estrogen rings (Femring and Estring). The soft, flexible ring is placed into the vagina and stays there for up to 3 months. It steadily releases a small amount of estrogen to greatly improve vaginal health. If it's positioned properly, a woman does not feel it in her vagina. The estrogen ring is good because of its ease of use. Slowly but surely, the vagina will once again become the warm, moist, inviting place that it once was.

In addition to localized estrogen replacement, we recommend vaginal lubricants until the vagina has regained its moisture and lubrication. There are dozens of products available, but we often recommend using either Slippery Stuff or Astroglide. Both are glycerin-free, water-based, odorless, tasteless, long-lasting, and latex-compatible.

The Emotional Challenge of Menopause

From an emotional perspective, we like to think of menopause as an invitation. It is your body's way of tempting you, perhaps in not such a subtle manner, to change and grow. It forces you to discard your old ways of understanding yourself, most obviously on a physical (and sexual) level. But in actuality, it also challenges you to grow spiritually, emotionally, and intellectually.

Those women who accept the invitation in all its forms seem to get more for themselves in the process. For them, menopause can be a rich adventure. The unexpected surprises and delights available at this time of life can help to balance the pain and loss that is also associated with growth. For these women, menopause can be a time of self-, and sexual, liberation.

Unfortunately, for most of us, *change* is a bad word—especially when the change is neither initiated by us nor in our control. We receive this invitation with reluctance and fear. Those who prefer to fight or ignore it will usually experience a sense of constriction in their lives. The constriction is the result of loss—losing pieces of the women they were—untempered by gain—the discovery of the women they can become. They tend to suffer more, because they struggle to hold on to what they can no longer have. Women whose lives contract in this way tend to experience their sexuality, and their libidos, as contracting right along with it.

But really, who can blame them? Our culture highlights the loss inherent in menopause. We need only look as far as our TV and movie screens to receive that message, loud and clear, on a daily basis. The career trajectories of Hollywood's most popular movie stars provide poignant examples.

Those actors who epitomize masculine sexuality bring us back to the box office repeatedly over the years. Even as they show signs of aging, such as graying hair or changing muscle tone, they become only more enticing and distinguished. Our masculine idols seem to actually gain power and status as they mature.

For their female counterparts, however, a completely different scenario unfolds. Our love for them is much more fickle. A sexy actress can hold our attention until her youth begins to fade. Then we lose interest—and she is cast aside for a younger, more physically perfect specimen.

Although this may be the "truth" our culture perpetuates, we suggest opting for a different reality. It's time for us to open our minds to a healthier, more realistic appraisal of what makes a woman valuable, and what sexuality during menopause and beyond can be. Losing the capacity to create new life is not synonymous with losing the capacity for rewarding sexual experience and a healthy sex drive. Louise was a casualty of just such caustic thinking patterns.

Louise was a vibrant, intelligent 70-year-old widow. She lost her husband to colon cancer 6 years before calling me (Dr. Brandon) to schedule an appointment. On the phone, she told me she was lonely, in spite of her many friends and busy calendar. She loved her work as the manager of an expanding medical practice. But, she explained, something just wasn't feeling right.

Louise adapted quickly to the rhythm of therapy. She thoroughly enjoyed the self-exploration and growing connection between us. After several months in treatment, she arrived in my office looking grave and determined. "I have something very important to discuss," she announced. "You might think I'm crazy, but I need to say it."

My heart went out to Louise; she looked scared and uncomfortable. I listened quietly, though my mind was racing. What could she possibly be preparing to tell me?

Louise spoke with tears in her eyes. "I miss having a man in my life. But it's more than that," she confided. "I miss having sex." Silence. The word sex *loomed large in the air between us. Could it be the source of Louise's shame and discomfort?*

The answer to this question, I am so sorry to say, is yes. This lovely woman felt like a freak because she missed sex and wanted it back in her life. Louise believed that a widowed septuagenarian shouldn't be thinking about such things, let alone desiring them for herself.

Myth versus Reality

If it is a myth that women lose their sexuality with age, then what's the reality? Research repeatedly demonstrates the same conclusion: Women's sexual concerns do not increase as they transition through menopause and beyond. In fact, many women report a decline in sexual difficulties during this time. Though this research is relatively new on the sexual scene, and primarily based on surveys rather than physiological facts, it is nonetheless exciting.

The exception appears to be lubrication—women *do* report difficulty lubricating with increasing age. As we already discussed, this age-related sexual symptom is fairly easy to treat.

We believe that this is a pivotal message because, as we've discussed before, your expectations can have a huge impact on the reality you embrace. So, if you expect to lose your libido as you age, to find sex uncomfortable, and to view yourself as asexual, your chances of living that out increase substantially. Why not create a different, sexually satisfied, existence?

Interestingly, it is men who experience sexual struggles at midlife and beyond. They are more likely to suffer significant age-related sexual dysfunction than women are. To give you a few examples, men need more time and stimulation to become erect as they get older. Their erections are not as rigid. They need more time between erections than their younger counterparts. And potential health problems such as heart disease and diabetes can have more-intrusive effects on a man's sexual performance than on a woman's. So here's the real irony: Despite our culture's perceptions, men's sexual prowess can be said to suffer more with age. The apparent decreases in a woman's libido are more likely to be related to a decline in her partner's health or his reduced interest rather than her own. Likewise, her partner's sexual function is an important indicator of her level of sexual satisfaction.

Sneaky Thieves of Sex Drive

So what about those women who report a diminished level of desire during or after menopause?

First, many of them have been struggling with low desire since before their perimenopausal transition. So low libido isn't necessarily a new concern for them. In fact, it seems that some women speak about it at this time in their lives because they finally feel justified in doing so. Menopause may offer a more socially acceptable understanding of their decreased sexual interest, so they may feel less shame and self-criticism about it.

Second, menopause is a time of great emotional change. New self-definitions are created as outdated ones are left behind. We call it a menopausal transition because, from an emotional perspective, it involves a process of self-discovery that is usually several years in the making.

During this time, a woman is challenged to relearn herself in pivotal ways. For a while, she really doesn't know who she is becoming. Her body is changing and in many ways unfamiliar. She hasn't "lost control" of her body since pregnancy, and that was almost 2 decades ago. Sudden hot flashes, night sweats, and urinary urgency feel unwelcome and intrusive. Her family is changing, too. Her children are probably moving out of the house, and with them, her major life role as mother and caretaker.

For all of these reasons, the experience of making love can be particularly difficult. That's because a woman must essentially find a way to share herself intimately without even knowing who she is yet. This can be frightening, and it can cause a woman to lose interest in sex.

Some women seem particularly traumatized by the changes going on in their bodies. As we discussed, the decline in estrogen can have profound effects on a woman's sexual organs. Accepting the changes that result from decreased blood flow to the genitals isn't easy. She may feel particularly demoralized by it, and it has a direct impact on her desire to make love. Sex simply reminds her of these changes. If she can't accept her new body, she will have a difficult time sharing herself intimately and sexually.

Menopause as Sexual Liberation

If you are searching for your lost libido during menopause, the first step in reclaiming your desire is to shift your perspective and understanding of what's happening to your body. Rather than focusing on the aspects of menopause that are sexually constricting, we invite you to see the other side of the coin.

Menopause *does* involve loss and forced change. And you are losing something that's valuable and worth grieving for. We urge you not to ignore the grieving process—take the time your soul needs to say goodbye to that part of yourself. Letting go is a real milestone in the process. Respect yourself and your body enough to do it consciously. However, with all loss there is gain. Your sexuality is no exception to this rule. We extend to you the invitation to explore how menopause really can be a sexually liberating transition for you.

Let's start with the most obvious facts. First, you are free from worrying about pregnancy. No longer do you have to concern yourself with birth control when making love, or anxiously wonder why your period is late. Your sexuality really can be all about pleasure now.

Second, remember that you are not alone. Think of the women you've known and loved who have moved through menopause while maintaining their sensuality. If you can't identify any, then consider Lauren Hutton, Raquel Welsh, and Sophia Loren.

Remember, too, that your partner is experiencing unwelcome sexual changes. He's probably feeling self-conscious about his aging body. Together, the two of you can create a new, shared sexuality.

Use this transition to let go of outdated societal notions about what it means to be a woman. You are moving into a wiser, richer time of life. Let go of perfectionist standards of what makes a woman valuable in Western society. Is it really her thin thighs? Her ability to conceive babies? We think not.

Also use this transition to make your own rules. It's not about society telling you what makes you worthwhile. Now is the time for you to decide this for yourself. Women who are post-menopausal make up about a third of the female population. Use the strength in your numbers to redefine what it means to be sexy. Allow your more assertive, more "masculine" energies to find their true voice. Discover what you want to do, rather than what you "should" do.

This work facilitates knowing yourself on a much deeper level than you may have in the past. You learn more about who you really are, under all the layers of your socially acceptable exterior. And your sexuality can be freed up along with you. This is where your deepest passion lies. If you go there, you are in for a sexual treat.

There is another gift for you embedded in this change. The loss of the physical allows you to spend more time and energy on what is really you, what is really important to and about you. Rather than giving birth, you can now focus on your own rebirth. Your sexual experience can reflect this. As your sexuality becomes less physically based, you make room for the emotional. Many women find this leads to much more meaningful and satisfying sexual relationships.

We'd like to note that some women simply need time to reclaim their sexual desire at menopause. Time allows them space to get to know themselves. Many women find this necessary before they are comfortable sharing themselves with someone else in as intimate a forum as making love.

Freeing Up Sexually

If you are struggling with low libido during menopause, we encourage you to turn your focus to what many call the most powerful sex organ: your brain. Give yourself permission to rediscover your sexuality, just as you are discovering other aspects of yourself as well. Usually, this entails exploring new ways of being sexual alone with yourself, as well as with your partner.

Start by setting the conscious intention to relearn your sensuality and enjoy it in new ways. Focus on creating and receiving pleasure through your five senses, rather than your sex organs. After all, the root of the word *sensual* is "sense," implying that your senses are necessary to the experience of sensuality.

There are always different ways for you to explore your sexuality through your senses. It really doesn't matter what your past experience has been. Stop thinking of sex as having to involve orgasm and intercourse. We've discussed previously how sex can involve masturbation, mutual masturbation, oral sex, and vibrators. We now invite you to expand your sexual repertoire even more.

In approaching sensuality from the perspective of your senses, don't think about sex as you may be accustomed to defining it. Your focus is on finding sensuality in sounds, smells, tastes, textures, and sights of typically nonsexual matter. For example, the sounds of waves can be a sensual experience for many, as can the "sound" of perfect silence early in the morning. Spend time at a record store searching for sensual music. Some people find classical music or opera stimulating; others like drumming or exotic, foreign selections. Many music stores now have ways for you to listen before you buy; so do Web sites that sell CDs. Take advantage of the opportunity to develop your sexuality in this creative fashion.

What about touch? Believe it or not, sensual touch doesn't have to involve a human body. In fact, nature provides us with many alternatives on a daily basis. Running your fingers over fur, for example, can be a sensual experience. Or experiencing the tingling sensation of cool water on your inner elbows as you stand at the kitchen sink. Try it for yourself. Feel the sand against your body as you keep your grandchild company in her sandbox. Lie in lush, green grass and meditate on the experience of allowing sunshine to penetrate your skin. Feel it entering your body from your feet, the crown of your head, and all the places in between. Feel a breeze as a full-body sensation, rather than just on your face. Offer yourself tactile delights such as these in your efforts to find the new sexual you.

Find sensual delights for your eyes as well. Stare into a candle flame. Hold a piece of glass to the light and watch it sparkle. Stand under a tall tree and look toward the sky. Check in with your body to feel an even deeper experience of these visual sensations.

You probably already know what a sensual experience certain tastes can be. Chocolate, fruit, wine, and olives are good places to start. Let your taste buds lead you to new sensual delights.

And don't leave out your nose—your sense of smell can trigger all kinds of sensual responses. Roses are an obvious erotic pleasure, as are perfumes and home-baked bread or cookies. These aromas fill our senses and envelop us. Notice this powerful effect the next time you smell something wonderful. Take a moment to scan your body, and you will find that your entire body reacts to a fragrance—not simply your nose.

As you can see, creativity and flexibility are key as you redis-cover your sensuality. You can take these same qualities to your lover as well. Try out new patterns together—for example, vary the time of day that you typically make love. Again, be sure to focus on plea-surable interchanges rather than orgasm and intercourse. Spend time massaging each other's hands and feet. Savor a piece of choco-late cake together. A decreased focus on physical activity can free up space for deeper, more emotionally powerful connections. Pat and Clarence certainly found this to be true.

Pat came to my (Dr. Brandon's) office about 1 year after experiencing her first hot flash. She had never been to therapy before; she was trying it in an effort to avoid starting an antidepressant. Pat had mixed feelings about therapy. Although she didn't necessarily want to take another medication every day, she didn't think simply talking to someone would make much dif-ference in her mood and quality of life.

When asked about her depression, Pat hesitantly spoke about feeling lonely in her life and in her marriage. In the previous few years, Pat's hus-band, Clarence, rarely expressed any direct sexual interest in Pat. This was fine with her, she assured me, as she didn't feel much like being sexual any longer. She had apparently been rejecting his advances for a while. "I've had my children," she said. "No need for that any more." I asked why not.

To begin with, Pat wasn't happy with the changes going on in her body, sexually and otherwise. Her hair—including her pubic hair—was thinning. Her skin was less elastic and more translucent than in the past. Her vagina didn't feel as tight as it used to. She believed that her genitals had developed an odor. The last few times she and Clarence had made love, she noticed that she hadn't lubricated as much. She was painfully aware of having more cellulite and less muscle than when she was younger. Sometimes when she coughed or sneezed, she was afraid she'd lose control of her bladder. It all added up to Pat wanting a break from sex.

We talked about how bound to her body Pat's perceptions of her sexuality were. Not only that, she held on to an image of what her body used to look and feel like as her sexual ideal. If she kept this up, sex probably would never be rewarding for her again. But there was an alternative. Would her sexuality become more interesting to her if she expanded her understanding of her sensuality? It seemed like a way to help Pat rediscover her sexuality while simultaneously working on her depression by engaging her more fully in her world.

I started Pat on homework of exploring sensual pleasure through her senses. She found painting with vibrant colors to be a particularly erotic experience. When focusing on the paint, Pat found herself transported by the vivid splashes of light across her canvas. Pat then learned to focus on the ways that pleasure manifested itself in her body—she described it as a "tingling, alive" sensation in her torso. Pat used her awareness of these sensations to facilitate similar reactions in her body at other times, such as in the bathtub or when walking in the sun. Before she knew it, she felt more alive and engaged with her surroundings and their impact on her body than ever in her life. She began to get interested in branching out and including Clarence in her rediscovery.

Pat built up the courage talk with Clarence about her discomforts with her changing body. She learned that he, too, disliked the way his body was changing. When Pat talked with her friends about how they were changing sexually, it became clear to her that she was not alone. Setting her own standards for her sensuality began to make more and more sense to her. Pat's increased interest in bodily pleasures was met with much enthusiasm by Clarence. They found a new softness when relating together, even outside of the bedroom. Pat's courage in breaking the mold of what it meant for her to be sexual was paying off.

CHAPTER 22

SURVIVING AND THRIVING AFTER DIVORCE

- As with any major life change, divorce throws a woman out of balance, and as a result, her libido may suffer.
- Women whose partners end the relationship may be at a higher risk for losing their sex drives.
- To rebalance, reacquaint yourself with the aspects of your personality you disowned and expressed via your partner.
- Spending quiet time in nature and practicing breathwork can help you ground yourself again.
- When dating, be prepared to discuss health and condoms before having sex.

The process of recovering from divorce or the ending of any intimate relationship can be an emotional, spiritual, and sexual roller coaster. For most women, it is a time of crisis, characterized by intense feelings, uncertainty, and change. Divorce can affect libido in several ways. Some divorced women feel that their libidos die with the demise of their relationships. Others experience divorce as a wake-up call for their libidos, an opportunity for revitalized sexual energy.

Many women find that for their libidos to thrive after divorce, some effort is required. That is, libido usually doesn't just return naturally. This is because divorce is a long, emotionally and spiritually draining process. A woman's body must mobilize for this process over many months. After a while, her body remains in a constant state of tension—always ready to protect her from assault. The longer she remains in this state, the further away her sex drive becomes.

Among other things, safety and calm are required ingredients for a thriving, healthy libido. These elements are generally in short supply after a divorce. As a result, recovering your emotional and spiritual balance is a necessary step in reclaiming your desire.

The Choice Is Yours

Here's the good news: If you decide to rise to the challenge, your time of crisis can evolve into a personal and sexual renaissance. You can use the aftermath of divorce to explore and enhance your sexuality independent of your partner. Seize this opportunity to enjoy the power and pleasure of your own sexuality for yourself. Even horrible relationships can provide tremendous opportunities for growth. We've seen this happen time and time again. Our most profound growth never occurs out of the blue or when things are going smoothly in our lives. It is always—and we do mean always—the result of struggling. It is while searching our dark places that we find new light.

Not all women want their libidos back after their relationships end. For some, it is a part of their lives they'd rather leave behind. If you want to find your lost libido, set the intention to use this transition as a healing process. You must be determined to get something good for yourself now, because it will not always be an easy passage. Your mind must be set clearly on your goal—to experience yourself wanting and enjoying sex again, whether it be alone with yourself or with a partner.

How It Ends

The way a relationship ends has a lot to do with a woman's recovery from it. In general, women who were not in control of the divorce decision have a more difficult time finding their lost libidos. Even if they believe that the divorce was necessary, the simple fact that the decision was not theirs makes all aspects of recovery more difficult. Sexuality is no exception to that rule.

Most divorced women, however, experience some of the same challenges. No matter how a relationship ends, the simple fact that it is over reminds us that all relationships are impermanent. This truth is a difficult one to digest under any circumstances. Divorce makes it impossible to ignore. Thus, many women find themselves in an existential crisis at this time—seeking meaning for their lives, their purpose on this earth, and reasons for the pain they endure. If you find yourself struggling with these questions, we urge you to explore the suggestions later in this chapter under "Reclaiming Desire through Balance." Such questions can affect libido. It can be difficult to open up emotionally and sexually when you are conscious of the ultimate impermanence of your union.

In addition to the big-picture issues, most divorced women experience sexual challenges as well. As we've discussed, sexuality is sensitive and reactive—and a life change as drastic as divorce seldom leaves a woman's sexuality unaffected. Many women need time to assimilate the changes before libido returns. For the moment, more-immediate concerns must take precedence. Go slowly and be gentle with yourself. Tackle your libido after you get your more pressing needs in order.

WHEN IT'S YOUR DECISION

If the decision to divorce was in your control, you may be aware of feeling sexually free, just as you are probably feeling emotionally free. You may also find yourself hesitant to fall in love again.

As a result, your libido may suffer. You may find it safer to "turn off" that part of yourself rather than risk getting intimately involved again. Though this approach works for some, we suggest you consider focusing on pleasing yourself sexually rather than shutting down your desire. Once you make the decision (consciously or subconsciously) to turn off your sexuality, it's harder to jump-start again. How about masturbation as an alternative? To explore your options, we encourage you to review the section "Welcoming Back Your Libido" at the end of this chapter.

WHEN IT'S HIS DECISION

If the choice to end the relationship was your partner's, your life probably seems out of control at the moment. You are overwhelmed by your feelings—but do your best to let them out rather than shut them down. Although your instinct may tell you to ignore them, this "solution" will only block your energy and make your libido less accessible. Inhibited emotions of any kind usually result in an inhibited libido as well. As we've previously discussed, this is because you can't selectively choose which emotions to disconnect from. It's an all-or-nothing proposition: Shutting down an uncomfortable feeling means that you shut down joy, happiness, desire, and all the positive feelings along with it. And right now, you need all the good feelings that you can access.

If you tune in to yourself, you will find a variety of emotions lurking around your psyche. Anger, rejection, and fear will require your attention. If left unresolved, each of these will constrict you sexually and sabotage your libido. Unresolved feelings can live in your subconscious mind. They may make brief forays into consciousness, but if their primary address remains your subconscious, they will present a problem for you. As we've discussed, feelings in your subconscious exert control over your behavior. Everyone but you can see them. Feelings that live in your conscious mind do not have that ability. You have much more control over them—how you express them and how they impact your behavior. So, in finding your lost libido, start by letting those difficult feelings flow.

So what are you experiencing? You are angry—angry that your husband left you, angry that you married him in the first place, angry that your entire life must now change in so many ways. You may need to tighten your budget, and you may need to move. For this, and more, you rage.

Anger can be easier to access than other emotions because it feels powerful to express. You will find softer, more vulnerable emotions hiding underneath your anger. Rejection, abandonment, and betrayal are here. So is the grief you feel in losing the future you had expected, and in losing not only your husband but also members of his family and usually some mutual friends. This sadness is real and painful.

You may become mistrustful of men and of starting another relationship. You may doubt that you're strong enough to deal with further rejection. You may feel sexually inadequate as well—fearful of how you'd even go about starting a new romantic relationship, let alone allowing one to develop without getting anxious about your future.

These emotions are typical of women recovering from divorce. Each woman also has her own unique circumstances and emotions that she must contend with. Give yourself the time and space you need to work thorough all of the pain. You don't necessarily have to do anything with the emotions. Just let them flow so that they don't stay in your body and psyche, blocking your sex drive. Finding your emotional footing again is necessary for your libido to return.

Revisiting Past Pain

As if all these new emotions weren't powerful enough, unresolved ones from the past are probably coming up as well. That's what unprocessed feelings do—they hang out in your subconscious until something brings them to the surface. Old anger feeds into new anger; old grief into new grief. This is why you overreact to things—your response is the result of unresolved feelings reviving in the present. Your emotions can quickly become intense and confusing.

The bad news is that you can't resolve them in this way. That is, you cannot channel old anger through new anger. Old anger will make itself known at any point, but unless you connect it to where it originally belonged, you won't get relief. This means you must sort through the anger you are experiencing—how much of it belongs to your ex-husband and your present situation, and how much belongs to your past? What pieces of the rejection you are feeling were actually prompted by other important people in your life? Now is the time to figure this out, in order to free your libido. It may be easier and cleaner to blame all your current emotions on your ex, but that usually isn't the reality. You will only hurt yourself by holding on to that notion, because you effectively prevent yourself from healing old hurt, so your libido will stay locked up behind it.

This holding-on process is largely responsible for the subjective sense of losing libido over time. It's not that your libido fades, it's that more and more unresolved feelings get stuffed in front of it. As a result, your libido becomes more elusive as the years go by. And difficult life events, such as divorce, result in an even more rapid accumulation of feelings, if you opt not to express them. The way out of all this is to delve into your emotions. You must go through them, not around them, to heal. Your body will thank you with gifts of libido and freed-up life energy.

Change or Stagnation

When an important relationship ends, you inevitably reach a turning point. You must choose between personal growth or stagnation. There really is no other option. This can be terrifying because neither choice is pain-free. Not changing is the "safest" route, in that you don't need to grow. You maintain your current understanding of yourself, and your behavior remains consistent. This allows you to place much of the blame on your former spouse, because you don't need to examine the roles you played in your marriage. (We are not implying that the blame is yours; rather, the reality lies somewhere in between.) This is the least threatening option, although it is a ticket to stagnation. Over time, it yields more emotional pain. Think of stagnant water. From the outside, it looks calmer than a flowing stream, but it houses lots of bacteria under the surface.

Women who choose the status quo find themselves repeating the same mistakes in new relationships. You need only look around at divorced acquaintances for proof of this dynamic. Behavior patterns repeat themselves unless you mindfully and intentionally approach your psyche with a desire to learn more about who you are.

But self-exploration can be a pretty threatening option. It involves accessing your subconscious mind to discover more about what went wrong in your relationship. And who wants to go in there? You initially stored stuff in your subconscious because of the simple fact that you didn't want to look at it. Now we are proposing that you actively pull it out again. Yuck. Remember, though, it is this work in your subconscious mind that will help you recapture emotional balance—that same emotional balance that is necessary for your libido to thrive.

Reclaiming Desire through Balance

Throughout this book, we have explored the theme of balance in your life and its relationship to a healthy libido. Maintaining balance is a lifetime commitment. Perhaps at no time is the need for balance more obvious than following the breakup of a marriage. Divorce has the impact of a hurricane on the landscape of your life. Nothing in its path is left unaffected. Both your mind and your body have been thrown into the turmoil; thus, a return to equilibrium involves efforts aimed at both emotional and physical healing.

Finding your emotional balance after divorce begins with the identification and expression of previously disowned parts of your personality. Throughout our lifetimes, we allow certain traits to fully express themselves. Any that we assess as undesirable could get relegated to our subconscious mind. This pattern of denying parts of our personalities can become exaggerated when we marry. In a sense, we can get lazy by attempting to use our partners to complete us. In uniting with them, we seek to make use of their assets as our own. In other words, we are at risk of ignoring in ourselves whatever traits—savory and unsavory—our partners exhibit freely. In this way, we lose touch with ourselves and all of who we are. It is a process that kills libido, because it results in emotional imbalance.

When a couple splits, this imbalance becomes even more apparent. Your partner leaves and seems to take with him part of who you are. Many women in this situation literally have the sensation of not knowing themselves any longer. Finding your emotional balance involves reclaiming all of your personality—the good and bad—some of which your spouse was quite agreeably expressing for you (as you were doing for him).

This process may become clearer if you think in terms of dichotomies. Taoists refer to balancing yet opposing energies as yin and yang; Jungian therapists call them anima and animus. These are essentially fancy ways of labeling feminine and masculine traits. Most marriages develop their own balance of energies—some of them expressed by the woman, others by the man. When a couple splits, real growth involves each partner finding wholeness. For many, it presents the first opportunity in their lives for such growth. It is a golden opportunity to discover yourself and live a life more true for you.

The priceless benefit of reclaiming your whole self is that you won't need to find a man to complete you. Translated, this means that when you fall in love in the future, it will be about love first and need second. This is the recipe for a loving long-term relationship. We can almost guarantee that old relationship patterns won't repeat themselves if you do this work. It is also essential for reclaiming your desire.

MOTHERING YOURSELF

The process of discovering your whole self will require some good mothering. In essence, you are experiencing a growth spurt, perhaps your most significant one since adolescence. Such changes will involve growing pains. In order to tolerate the pain, you will need some good, solid nurturing. And because you are now an adult, the appropriate person to provide that nurturing is you. You need to become your own loving mother.

Just what will that entail? The basic ingredients of good mothering are honest guidance and feedback, coupled with huge amounts of warmth and love. This is your task—being honest with your self-appraisal and being generous with your noncritical self-acceptance. This is no easy process, because it's about seeing your human weaknesses for what they are but loving yourself anyway.

Just one element without the other will only get you into trouble. For example, loving yourself without honest self-examination will result in narcissism. The alternative, identifying your faults without loving yourself, leads to low self-esteem at best, and outright masochism at worst. Either choice kills opportunities for healthy relationships. And either choice can negatively affect your sex life.

REALISTIC SELF-APPRAISAL

In the spirit of mothering yourself well, it's time to take a realistic assessment of who you are and who you were in your relationship. What aspects of your personality did you allow your partner to express for you that you need to claim as your own? Was he the initiator and you the follower, such that you never had to take charge? If so, it's time for you to start feeling your power instead of always acquiescing. Did you find him emotionally withholding? How do you experience your own withholding? As you reclaim your whole personality, you create the balance necessary for your libido to resurface.

Doreen came to therapy as she and her second husband, Daniel, were ending their marriage. She showed every symptom of depression, including low libido. But Doreen wasn't concerned about wanting sex at that point. "I don't trust myself with men at the moment," she said. "I'm better off without a sex drive for a while." She wanted to stop the pattern of marrying men who weren't good for her.

Doreen described the similarities in both of her marriages. Both began as fantastic love affairs. Both men appeared kind and gentle. It all seemed so right in the beginning. But as Doreen described the evolution of her relationships, the darker dynamics became clear. Doreen was an overfunctioner—always on top of her game and taking care of business; nothing slid when she was around. She managed everything from paper towels and dog food to chlorine for the pool. But because people tend to polarize in marriages, as Doreen functioned more, her husbands functioned less. In this way, her marriages maintained a balance—unhealthy as it was.

Doreen's overfunctioning was extremely apparent to her and everyone around her. It was easy to respect that trait in her and pinpoint Daniel as the problem. Was he just plain lazy? Doreen recalled that he didn't seem so when they first met.

Doreen used her therapy to understand what her overfunctioning was all about and to determine which traits in Daniel she was disowning in herself. These were the keys in preventing the same pattern from developing a third time in her life.

Doreen learned that Daniel's underfunctioning was actually in re-

sponse to her subconscious cues guiding him to do so. In essence, he was doing what she wanted him to do, which was let her take over. Doreen felt safe when she was in charge—if she was needed by those around her, they wouldn't leave her. This safety was how she felt loved, until it reached an extreme point and turned into something negative. This is the danger when a marriage polarizes: Polarizing maintains balance for a while, but eventually neither of the partners likes functioning at extremes. That's because it's not who they really are. All of us carry aspects of every trait within us. And our souls really want to express all of them.

I (Dr. Brandon) asked Doreen to explore her unexpressed, underfunctioning side. At first, she denied its existence. But she was able to identify brief moments, like when she really wanted to stay in bed on a Saturday morning, or her secret desire to quit her public relations job and work at a pet shop. Why didn't she gratify any of these needs? Guilt was the conclusion she came to. Doreen felt guilty when she nurtured herself. And just as she refused to meet her underfunctioning needs for herself, she subconsciously discouraged anyone else from gratifying them as well. Projecting all her underfunctioning needs onto Daniel, she could disdain him rather than herself.

I encouraged Doreen to give her underfunctioning side some attention. If she continued to ignore it, she'd have to use her next partner to hold that balance for her. Forcing nurturing on herself was not easy, but with time she learned to even enjoy it. As she recognized this previously disowned part of herself, her sex drive returned naturally. She was pleasantly surprised by its arrival, and she took it as a sign that she was ready to be in a romantic relationship again. With her newfound balance, she wouldn't need to find a man to perform that function for her.

FIND YOUR CENTER

There are a variety of things you can do to help find your center. Emotional balance can be supported through experiences that serve to return you to yourself. For many people, nature has a grounding effect. Thus, as you engage in self-appraisal, we suggest that you simultaneously spend quiet time outdoors. Nature can function as a limitless energy source for the spirit. Imagine how you'd feel looking up at a magnificent snow-capped mountain, or watching waves crash onto a shoreline. It is no mistake that so many people vacation in nature; they innately know that these experiences enhance their spirit and vitality. Nature has a way of centering you—helping you sort through the static that keeps you from knowing yourself. But you don't have to relegate these experiences to vacations only. Try long walks alone in the park on weekends. Spending mindful time in natural surroundings will facilitate your self-appraisal.

Likewise, breathwork offers several key benefits to facilitate the centering process. First and most obviously, mindful breathing is relaxing. And relaxation is imperative for your self-appraisal. No one has access to their subconscious if they can't slow down enough to listen. Mindful breathing allows for stillness of both mind and body.

Second, breathing is an everyday activity. You breathe whether or not you are aware of it. Breathing mindfully allows subconscious material to flow into your conscious mind. This is one reason that some people find meditation difficult. Mindful breathing can give them access to feelings and thoughts they might rather ignore. In your self-appraisal process, use this entrée into your core to your advantage. Despite its simplicity, mindful breathing is a powerful tool for self-discovery.

Third, with mindful breathing, you learn to slow your body. This skill will come in handy when you resume a sexual relationship. Slowed movements increase intensity and lead to powerful sexual experiences.

To breathe mindfully, all that is required is a focus on your breath. The beauty of this technique is that it is free and available anytime you can be alone in a quiet location. Simply make yourself comfortable while maintaining a relatively straight spine. Sitting on the edge of a chair or cross-legged on a mat works well. Some people practice mindful breathing lying down, but that makes it exceptionally easy to fall asleep.

Bring your attention to one aspect of your breath, such as the sensation in your nostrils or the expansion of your belly as you inhale. Set the intention to focus on your breathing, maintaining a rhythm that is slow, steady, and deep. Observation of your breath is all that is required.

Studies show that breathwork practiced on a regular basis supports energy, sleep, digestion, and an overall sense of peacefulness. Breathwork seems to ground your psyche and your body. Many folks find that it raises spiritual awareness as well. Most of these benefits can also have an indirect positive impact on your sex drive. So what have you got to lose? Try mindful breathing once or twice a day for a few weeks. It is the repetition over time that assists your body in making beneficial adaptations and counteracting stress.

Welcoming Back Your Libido

As you work to create emotional balance after divorce, you can simultaneously reawaken your libido in more-direct ways. In doing so, we encourage you to focus primarily on the lighter aspects of your sexual self. Your body probably needs to play for a while. Heavy relationship sex is probably not where you're at, so your libido is unlikely to respond to that.

Being playful sexually means different things to different women. Some enjoy the sexual energy of silly but sexy movies or books. Others enjoy wearing novelty panties and bras, or maybe skipping panties altogether for an evening. You might prefer shower play, or closing your drapes and watching TV naked. Light and easy sensual fun can coax your libido out of hiding and remind you that sex doesn't have to be serious business. Think of it as waking your libido with a slow morning stretch as opposed to a strong cup of coffee.

Masturbation is another way to coax your libido out of hiding in a playful way. Try to masturbate with the intention of spending pleasurable time with yourself as opposed to achieving orgasm. This will help keep the experience light rather than driven by a specific goal. Use regular masturbation both as a way to reclaim your desire and as a way to reduce stress while promoting relaxation. Let go of the notion that you should masturbate only when you are feeling turned on. Instead, consider it another way to spend quality time with yourself during the process of self-discovery.

Welcome back your libido with kindness. Find things to appreciate about your sexuality. It might be reluctant to return if the atmosphere is harsh and judgmental. How can you support your sex drive? Acknowledge those aspects of your sensuality and your body that you like. Are the shape and color of your nipples particularly striking since you gave birth? Do your toes look stunning with rich red nail polish? Close your eyes and run your hands over the soft curving shape of your hips. Admire your voice as you sing a love song. Make friends with your sexuality so that your libido feels welcome.

In keeping with a soft, gentle approach, acknowledge any sexual worries or frustrations that have developed through your divorce. The trauma of divorce can also exacerbate sexual fears that you've carried over the years. Take some time to sit with these discomforts so that you can help yourself heal. For example, if you always were sensitive about how long it takes you to climax during sex, this may become a greater concern as you prepare to involve a new man in your life. Maybe you are afraid of not being able to let go enough to climax at all. Or you are worried that your vagina may not lubricate as it once did.

The point is, most women harbor sexual fears. They tend to be so personal that they aren't shared even with partners. Don't let a divorce destroy your sexual self-esteem. Acknowledging and accepting your sexual fears can go a long way toward keeping them in perspective as you develop new romantic connections.

Returning to the Dating Scene

Preparing to date again is usually a nerve-racking experience for divorced women. Obviously, the longer you've been out of that scene, the more difficult the reentry process can be. Times have changed, and so have the rules for relating sexually.

The good news is that you are wiser this time around. Dating is no longer about behaving so that the boy will like you. It's not about peer pressure or having sex because everyone else is doing it. You've learned the hard way that what matters is how you feel about your partner. So relax; dating is no longer about selling yourself. Enjoying yourself is the new name of the game.

If you find someone you'd like to have a physical relationship with, talking about sex before doing it is expected and generally appreciated. Condoms are the rule, not the exception. Carry some yourself so you're not stuck without one. Make sure to check the expiration dates on the condoms you keep. If you want to start a conversation about sex, sexually transmitted diseases, and condoms, you don't have to do it with a tremendous amount of finesse. You can state that it's a difficult conversation, but that you need to know that the person doesn't have anything you could catch. If you get a shocked reaction, think twice about whom you are choosing to sleep with.

The first time you make love again, it is likely to be an emotional experience. Tell your partner beforehand that you may be extra sensitive under the circumstances. If feelings bubble to the surface, try not to resist them. Relax and let them happen. It may be your body remembering, and grieving, just as you have grieved. Alternatively, your tears may be tears of gratitude that you can feel loved again in such an intimate way.

EPILOGUE

We hope that you approach the process of reclaiming your sexual desire as an adventure of body, mind, and spirit. We applaud you for wanting more for yourself sexually. You should applaud yourself for embarking on this journey of self-exploration and discovery.

Ultimately, reclaiming your sexual desire is about finding the balance that is necessary for your life energy—your essence—to flow freely. Sometimes a blockage stems from a physical problem, like a hormonal imbalance in the body or a neurochemical imbalance in the brain. It might evolve from an emotional problem, such as depression or low self-esteem. A lack of intellectual stimulation or spiritual fulfillment can dampen sex drive, too.

Regardless of where a blockage originates, it can feed into other imbalances over time. Identifying the true source of trouble becomes more challenging. Attention to all the elements that drive your life energy—physical, emotional, intellectual, and spiritual— is necessary for sexual desire to return.

As we've seen, it doesn't take a major life change to trigger the cascade of events that eventually stifles your sex drive. The simple act of living can cause your life energy, and your libido, to stagnate. It happens to every woman at some point in her life.

Likewise, every woman is entitled to a robust sex drive. It's an important part of being female and a vital source of pleasure in life. Maintaining this desire, and the life energy that supports it, requires mindfulness and effort. That's true for everyone, even when libido is healthy. You need to decide for yourself whether the time and commitment is worth the eventual payoff.

Rest assured, you don't need to achieve absolute balance among the physical, emotional, intellectual, and spiritual components of your sexuality and your self in order to reclaim your desire. You can want sex again without resolving all the underlying issues that may be affecting your libido. For most women, the simple act of consciously and fastidiously attending to the need for balance is enough to bring about change.

The fact is, some of the issues that affect your libido may not be solvable. That's the reality for us. Even so, if you acknowledge them and make the best of them, the odds are good that you'll want sex again.

Of course, reclaiming your sexual desire won't happen overnight. During this time, it's easy to isolate yourself from the rest of the world and to succumb to feelings of helplessness and hopelessness. Rather than sinking into self-criticism and blame—as women often do when exploring their sexual selves—use your low libido as a tool for personal understanding and growth. You'll learn more about yourself, your relationships, and your place in the grand scheme of things.

We've provided the necessary information to start you on the path to reclaiming your sexual desire. The rest is up to you. Fear of the unknown is your most formidable adversary now. We routinely work with clients who—when faced with the prospect of discovering their deepest, most intimate selves—tearfully ask, "What if I don't like the woman I find?" Although this may be a possibility, neither of us has ever seen it. What we have seen is women achieving a heightened sense of self in their pursuit of a healthy, satisfying sex drive. We wish the same for you.

FOR MORE INFORMATION

A though we've made every effort to present a comprehensive exploration of low libido, we easily could have filled another book on the subject. We also recognize the uniqueness and complexity of each woman's situation. If you have a specific question that we did not address here, or if you wish to talk further about anything that we covered, you can contact us through our practice.

The Sexual Wellness Center
2002 Medical Parkway, Suite 215
Annapolis, MD 21401
(410) 897-8477
www.sexualwellnesscenter.com

You also might wish to look into the following resources, which we routinely recommend to our clients. The information, products, and services available through them can support your efforts to reclaim your desire.

Recommended Reading

Anand, Margo. *The Art of Sexual Ecstasy: The Path of Sacred Sexuality for Western Lovers.* New York: Penguin Putnam, 1989.

Barbach, Lonnie. *For Yourself: The Fulfillment of Female Sexuality.* New York: Penguin Putnam, 2000.

Bass, Ellen, and Laura Davis. *The Courage to Heal: A Guide for Women Survivors of Child Sexual Abuse.* New York: Harper & Row, 1988.

Berman, Jennifer, and Laura Berman. *For Women Only: A Revolutionary Guide to Overcoming Sexual Dysfunction and Reclaiming Your Sex Life.* New York: Henry Holt & Company, 2001.

Butler, Robert, and Myrna Lewis. *Love and Sex After 60* (large-print edition). Boston: G.K. Hall & Co., 1996.

Delaney, Gayle. *Living Your Dreams*. San Francisco: Harper, 1996.

Friday, Nancy. *My Secret Garden*. New York: Simon & Schuster, 1973.

Goddard, Jamie, and Kurt Brungardt. *Lesbian Sex Secrets for Men: What Every Man Wants to Know about Making Love to a Woman and Never Asks*. New York: Penguin Books, 2000.

Haines, Staci. *The Survivor's Guide to Sex: How to Have an Empowered Sex Life after Child Sexual Abuse*. San Francisco: Cleis Press, 1999.

Hebert, Lauren Andrew. *Sex and Back Pain: Advice on Restoring Comfortable Sex Lost to Back Pain*. Greenville, Maine: IMPACC USA, 1997.

Heiman, Julia, and Joseph LoPiccolo. *Becoming Orgasmic: A Sexual and Personal Growth Program for Women*. New York: Simon & Schuster, 1988.

Kabat-Zinn, Jon. *Wherever You Go, There You Are: Mindfulness Meditation in Everyday Life*. New York: Hyperion, 1994.

Kaufman, Miriam, M.D., Cory Silverberg, and Fran Odette. *The Ultimate Guide to Sex and Disability: For All of Us Who Live with Disabilities, Chronic Pain, and Illness*. San Francisco: Cleis Press, 2004.

Keesling, Barbara. *Getting Close: A Lover's Guide to Embracing Fantasy and Heightening Sexual Connection*. New York: HarperCollins, 1999.

Kievman, Beverly, and Susie Blackman. *For Better or Worse: A Couple's Guide to Dealing with Chronic Illness*. Chicago: Contemporary Books, 1990.

Lazarus, Judith. *Stress Relief and Relaxation Techniques*. Lincolnwood, Ill.: Keats Publishing, 2000.

Matsakis, Aphrodite. *I Can't Get Over It: A Handbook for Trauma Survivors* (second edition). Oakland, Calif.: New Harbinger Publications, 1996.

Moseley, Douglas and Naomi. *Dancing in the Dark: The Shadow Side of Intimate Relationships*. Georgetown, Mass.: North Star Publications, 1994.

Paget, Lou. *How to Be a Great Lover: Girlfriend-to-Girlfriend Totally Explicit Techniques That Will Blow His Mind*. New York: Broadway Books, 1999.

Schover, Leslie. *Sexuality and Cancer*. New York: The American Cancer Society, 1988.

Siegel, Daniel J. *The Developing Mind: Toward a Neurobiology of Interpersonal Experience*. New York: The Guilford Press, 1999.

Siegel, Daniel J., and Mary Hartzell. *Parenting from the Inside Out: How a Deeper Self-Understanding Can Help You Raise Children Who Thrive*. New York: Putnam, 2003.

Stewart, Elizabeth. *The V Book: A Doctor's Guide to Complete Vulvo-vaginal Health*. New York: Bantam Books, 2002.

Wolf, Naomi. *The Beauty Myth*. New York: Anchor Books, 1991.

Female Gynecologic and Sexual Health

The following Web sites cover the latest news and advances relevant to female sexual disorders, including low libido. They also are excellent resources for general gynecologic information.

www.hisandherhealth.com

www.newshe.com

www.ourgyn.com

www.sexualhealth.com

Compounding Pharmacies

For compounded hormone preparations, like the testosterone gel or ointment in chapter 7, we suggest the following resources.

International Academy of Compounding Pharmacists
PO Box 1365
Sugar Land, TX 77487
(800) 927-4227
www.iacprx.org

The Web site features a search tool that allows you to find a compounding pharmacist in your area.

Cape Apothecary
1384 Cape Saint Claire Road
Annapolis, MD 21401
(800) 248-5978
www.capedrugs.com

Clients of the Sexual Wellness Center often use this pharmacy, which offers compounding services.

Sexual Aids

These companies sell a range of erotic merchandise, including toys, books, and videos. If you visit their respective Web sites, you'll find solid educational information for both women and men.

A Woman's Touch Sexuality
  Resource Center
(888) 621-8880
www.touchofawoman.com

Good Vibrations
www.goodvibes.com
(800) BUY-VIBE

Xandria Collection
www.xandria.com
(800) 242-2823

Sexual Pain Disorders

If you've been diagnosed with one of the sexual pain disorders presented in chapter 2, the following organizations are among your most important resources for managing the condition and minimizing its impact on your libido.

Center for Vulvovaginal
  Disorders
908 New Hampshire Avenue
  NW, #200
Washington, DC 20037
(202) 887-0568

The International Society for
  the Study of Vulvovaginal
  Disease
8814 Peppergrass Lane
Waxhaw, NC 28173
(704) 814-9493
www.issvd.org

National Vulvodynia Association
PO Box 4491
Silver Spring, MD 20914-4491
(301) 299-0775
www.nva.org

New York Center for
  Vulvovaginal Pain
340 East 63rd Street, #1A
New York, NY 10021
(212) 832-0477
www.vulvodynia.com

INDEX